Henry E. Huntington
and the Creation
of Southern
California

Historical Perspectives on
Business Enterprise Series
Mansel G. Blackford and K. Austin Kerr, Editors

Making Iron and Steel:
Independent Mills in Pittsburgh, 1820–1920
John N. Ingham

Daniel Willard and Progressive Management
on the Baltimore & Ohio Railroad
David M. Vrooman

Eagle-Picher Industries:
Strategies for Survival in the Industrial Marketplace, 1840–1980
Douglas Knerr

Henry E. Huntington and the Creation of Southern California

WILLIAM B. FRIEDRICKS

Ohio State University Press

COLUMBUS

Parts of chapters 1, 5, and 8 first appeared in article form. The author would like to thank the original publishers for permission to reprint material from the following: "Capital and Labor in Los Angeles: Henry E. Huntington vs. Organized Labor, 1900–1920," *Pacific Historical Review* 59 (August 1990); "Henry E. Huntington and Real Estate Development in Southern California, 1898–1917," *Southern California Quarterly* 71 (Winter 1989); and "A Metropolitan Entrepreneur Par Excellence: Henry E. Huntington and the Growth of Southern Caliornia, 1898–1927," *Business History Review* 63 (Summer 1989).

Library of Congress Cataloging-in-Publication Data

Friedricks, William B., 1958–
    Henry E. Huntington and the creation of southern California /
William B. Friedricks.
        p.   cm.—(Historical perspectives on business enterprise series)
    Includes bibliographical references and index.
    ISBN 0–8142–0553–4
    ISBN 0–8142–0556–9 (pbk.)
    1. Huntington, Henry Edwards, 1850–1927.   2. Businessmen—
California. Southern—Biography.   3. Entrepreneurship—California,
Southern—History—20th century.   I. Title.   II. Series.
HC102.5.H87F75   1991
338'.04'092—dc20
[B]   91-21542
                                                                CIP

Text and jacket design by Bruce Gore.
Type set in Baskerville by Tseng Information Systems, Durham, NC.
Printed by Braun-Brumfield, Ann Arbor, MI.

The paper in this book meets the guidelines for permanence and durability
of the Committee on Production Guidelines for Book Longevity
of the Council on Library Resources. ∞

Printed in the U.S.A.

9 8 7 6 5 4 3 2 1

To my parents
Burt and Ginny Friedricks

Contents

1

Introduction: Metropolitan Entrepreneurship and the Los Angeles Basin

The sprawling Los Angeles basin, today the nation's second-largest population center and a leader in agriculture, commerce, and industry, attained its modern configuration during the first two decades of the twentieth century. Greater Los Angeles is, in fact, one of the best examples of areas where urban entrepreneurs have played a primary role in creating and expanding a metropolis. Of this group, Henry Huntington stands out among the rest. His southern California business empire was based on a triad of interrelated businesses critical for regional development. It consisted of a vast trolley network, electric power generation and distribution, and real estate development. Because Huntington operated this group of companies in an era when city and county planning commissions held little regulatory power, he became, in effect, the region's metropolitan planner. Early in his southern California career, he expressed his vision of the Los Angeles basin's future: "I am a foresighted man and I believe Los Angeles is destined to become the most important city in this country. It can extend in any direction as far as you like. . . . We will join this whole region into one big family." [1] Huntington did this by building interurban lines where and when he wanted, and in so doing, he determined the spatial layout of the area. Then, as a large-scale subdivider, he also decided the socioeconomic mix of many suburbs. Besides operating his triad of companies, Huntington, a builder by nature and the possessor of immense energy, worked in many other ways to develop southern California. The huge scale and scope of Huntington's ventures, combined with the lasting imprint he left on the Los

1

Angeles basin, put him in a category by himself: the metropolitan entrepreneur.

Although urban entrepreneurs remain an important topic of study, the focus has shifted away from the elites' role in urban development and instead usually concerns the social dynamics and composition of a regional urban elite. Fewer works offer analyses of individual city-builders and their contributions to urban economics. An especially important book that returns the focus to the entrepreneurs' role in establishing prosperous cities is Burt W. Folsom, Jr., *Urban Capitalists* (1981).[2] Similarly, although scholarship on Los Angeles is growing, recent works have concentrated on the post-1920 period.[3] With this in mind, what follows is a study exploring Huntington's primary role in the development of metropolitan Los Angeles.

Originally a Spanish pueblo founded in 1781, Los Angeles, a town 15 miles from the coast and 120 miles from a natural harbor at San Diego, did not appear to have any great economic prospects in the early nineteenth century. The severe droughts of the early 1860s brought about the collapse of great *ranchos* and the cattle industry as well as the region's land values.

In 1868, the Southern Pacific began construction of a rail extension from California's central valley southward. Thinking that the railroad would eventually reach Los Angeles and knowing that such a link would stimulate the area's economy, adventuresome businessmen began investing in southern California. Yet when the rail connection was completed in 1876, it set off only a minor real estate boom, and by 1880 Los Angeles remained a small town of 11,200 inhabitants.

The stage was set for the town's first major boom in 1885, when a competing transcontinental line, the Santa Fe, reached southern California. A rate war ensued between the rival railroads until, by early 1887, a passenger could travel from Kansas City to Los Angeles for only one dollar. Lured by low ticket prices and enticing advertising, large numbers of Midwesterners came to purchase land and settle in Los Angeles. Although the boom collapsed toward the end of the decade, Los Angeles's population reached 50,400 by 1890. From this point on, until about 1920, real estate speculation became the main dynamic for growth in southern California. Local banker H. S. McKee explained in 1915: "The most conspicuous fact about Los Angeles lies in its being a residential and not industrial community. The half million people who reside here did not come here in any considerable numbers to engage in business, they came to reside."[4] To accommodate the swelling population, commerce and services dominated the Los Angeles economy until after World War I, when the movie industry and oil production rapidly expanded and became the region's leading sectors.[5]

In the 1880s Los Angeles entrepreneurs arrived at the formula that would be repeated over and over and would ultimately be successful in developing the area. To overcome the region's major natural handicaps—lack of transportation, fuel (oil had not yet been discovered), and water—they combined heavy capital investment with slick advertising and promotion to attract settlers and encourage growth.[6] Carey McWilliams, a keen observer of the southland, has written:

> Without lumber and minerals, with only one natural harbor [San Diego], lacking water and fuels, and surrounded by mountains, desert, and ocean, there was seemingly never a region so unlikely to become a vast metropolitan area as Southern California. It is an artificial region, a product of forced growth and rapid change. . . . Like the entire region, Los Angeles, its heart and center, has developed in spite of its location rather than because of it. Southern California is a man-made, gigantic improvisation.[7]

Prior to Huntington's arrival, many local entrepreneurs had been active in establishing the infrastructural industries of southern California. In the 1880s, James Crank and banker Isaias W. Hellman operated a local horse-drawn and cable car system; they were supplanted in the 1890s by electric trolley barons Moses H. Sherman and his brother-in-law, Eli P. Clark. The real estate market for individual home lots was concentrated in the hands of several prominent land speculators, including Benjamin Wilson; his son-in-law, J. de Barth Shorb; John D. Bicknell; Andrew Chaffey; and Jonathan S. Slauson. Still in its infancy, the hydroelectric power business in the 1890s was headed by such entrepreneurs as William G. Kerckhoff and Allan C. Balch. Thus, by 1898, when Huntington initially invested in southern California, the established urban elites of the business community had already laid much of the groundwork for the southland's future growth.[8]

Although Los Angeles was one of the most visible and spectacular successes of urban entrepreneurs, these businessmen operated in other West Coast areas from the mid-nineteenth to the early twentieth centuries. As population grew and transportation improved with the spread of the railroads, thousands of new communities were created. Many of the new settlements were established along railroad routes that acted as the cities' economic lifelines to the rest of the country. Entrepreneurs recognized the importance of the transportation industry to the expansion of new cities, and they generally worked to secure rail lines for their regions of interest. Similarly, these urban businessmen were frequently involved in the primary infrastructural industries necessary for the growth of a city—real estate development, construction, public utilities, and banking.

Thomas Burke (1849–1925), a successful lawyer and judge, became involved in the expansion of Seattle, Washington, through real estate speculation and investments in area banks and mines. He realized the importance of railroad connections and organized a company to build and operate a railway from Seattle to Walla Walla. But Burke's major contribution to the city's growth was his work with James J. Hill to make Seattle the western terminus for the Great Northern Railroad.[9]

Several entrepreneurs played key roles in the development of San Francisco: two of the most important were William C. Ralston and James Phelan. Ralston (1826–75) came to San Francisco in 1854 as a partner in the steamship company of Garrison and Morgan. During his career in the city, he organized several banking firms, among them the Bank of California, which soon became the leading bank of the region. Along with banking, Ralston expanded into other areas with such companies as Mission Woolen Mills, Kimball Carriage Factory, and Pacific Insurance. In addition, his activities in real estate development took him into the hotel business, and he built the grandest hostelry in the city, the Palace Hotel. Like Burke, Ralston knew the importance of a railroad connection and loaned the Central Pacific $3 million to complete its line.[10]

James Phelan (1824–92) came to San Francisco following news of the discovery of gold and became a successful merchant. In 1870 he entered banking by incorporating the First National Gold Bank (it would later become Crocker First National Bank) and then served as its president. He also invested heavily in San Francisco real estate, and in 1881–82 he constructed the $500,000 Phelan Building.[11]

Across the bay, Francis Marion ("Borax") Smith (1846–1931) began making huge investments in Oakland in the 1890s. With a fortune made in the borax business, Smith and several partners formed the Realty Syndicate and purchased thousands of acres in and around Oakland. Then Smith merged the streetcar lines of Alameda and Contra Costa counties, and when this network was combined with his ferry service between Oakland and San

Francisco, it became the Key Route System. Not designed to make money on their own, the Key Route trolleys were used to promote and sell lots in Smith's many real estate subdivisions.[12]

In many respects, Huntington resembled such West Coast entrepreneurs. Like other city-builders, Huntington was audacious, future-oriented, and willing to gamble on the growth of his area of choice—the Los Angeles basin. In addition, with his supreme optimism and self-confidence, Huntington seemed to personify the avid boosterism that pervaded the southland's business community.[13] Finally, he was interested in a number of different businesses and concentrated on the infrastructural industries of transportation, power generation and distribution, and real estate development, which encouraged expansion. With these three basic businesses, Huntington tied his financial success to metropolitan growth. If the expected expansion took place, Huntington, with his multifarious enterprises, was destined to benefit handsomely from the urban economic boom he had helped create.

But Huntington also differed from other entrepreneurs. His operations were spread over an entire metropolitan area, and his investments were huge and in several sectors basic to urban growth. He possessed several attributes that set him apart from the majority of city-builders; these characteristics enabled him to lay out metropolitan Los Angeles and prompt its development over a period of twenty years. Most urban entrepreneurs conducted business on a small scale and were almost always seeking additional capital to expand their operations. Many went into banking in attempts to locate needed financing. Unlike others, Huntington began his career employed as a manager for several large-scale railroads. His move through various administrative posts culminated in 1900 in the position of vice-president of the Southern Pacific (SP), of which his uncle, Collis P. Huntington, was president. Because of a close link to Collis, Huntington inherited a fortune estimated at $15 million, which gave him the ability to finance many large projects simultaneously. With the necessary capital and a railroad management background, he envisioned development on a massive scale.

Predictably enough, Huntington undertook his first business venture in southern California in an industry in which he had previous experience—street railroads. His partners included men with whom he had been associated in San Francisco's trolley company, the Market Street Railway. Together, Huntington and his fellow investors—Isaias W. Hellman, Antoine Borel, and Christian DeGuigne—purchased the downtown-oriented Los Angeles Railway in 1898. By the end of that year, Huntington and his syndicate had acquired most of the city's smaller urban railroads. They soon dominated the market. Three years later, when it became clear that he would not succeed his deceased Uncle Collis as president of the SP, Huntington moved quickly to increase his investments in greater Los Angeles.

The majority of the wealth that Henry Huntington infused into Los Angeles was inherited from his uncle's estate, the lion's share of which was divided by Huntington and Collis's widow—later Henry's second wife—Arabella Huntington. When Collis died, Henry received one-third of his uncle's Southern Pacific stock, valued at $4.35 million, and another $4.9 million worth of stocks, bonds, and real estate. Arabella Huntington received the largest share of the estate; she was granted two-thirds of her deceased husband's SP stock, valued at $8.7 million, and another $6.3 million worth of stock, bonds, and real estate. The value of the SP stock was based on its market value; at the time of Collis's death in August 1900—$33.5 per share. When Henry and Arabella sold their 432,700 shares of SP stock to E. H. Harriman in February 1901, they received $51.5 per share, or $22.3 million.[14]

The inability to emulate his uncle and mentor by following him as head of the SP had a profound effect on Huntington. Unable to match Collis's achievements, Huntington apparently sought to build a business empire that would rival or even surpass that of his famous relative.[15] To carry out this vision, he had to maintain a free hand and avoid future situations where his plans might be thwarted. Therefore, his southern California enterprises were usually set up as small syndicates that Huntington dominated by holding a controlling share of stock. His penchant for working with a few partners, or completely alone, also reflected the faith he had in his own judgment, and it was only on rare occasions that he allied himself with other members of the business community.

Huntington continued to concentrate on the transit sector of the southland metropolis. With his experience in railroads, he understood the relationship between the location of rail lines and corresponding land values; property served by rail was more desirable and hence much more valuable than land remote from convenient transportation.

Adding to the largely downtown Los Angeles Railway, Huntington, his syndicate partners, and several other local investors incorporated the interurban Pacific Electric Railway (PE) in 1901. The PE was intended to connect many of the basin's small peripheral communities, located at distances ranging from ten to ninety miles away, to the downtown core of Los Angeles. Yet unlike the commuter-carrying Los Angeles Railway, the interurban PE's primary purpose was not the passenger business but rather the promotion of residential real estate. Other entrepreneurs also understood the promotional power of the streetcars but lacked the capital to build trolley lines wherever they wished. Prior to Huntington's arrival in the southland, trolley lines were usually paid for by landowners along the proposed routes who thought their property would appreciate once the railways were completed. Moses Sherman, a Los Angeles interurban builder, described how this worked: "We might build five, or six, or even seven miles of road, and we might build less, according to the amount of money they [the landowners] raise, but the understanding is that the Railway Company does not put in anything." [16]

Huntington, however, did not face such constraints. With access to vast capital, he was free to select routes for his electric railway lines and then build them. Huntington explained his rail expansion strategy in 1904: "It would never do for an electric line to wait until the demand for it came. It must anticipate the growth of communities and be there when the builders arrive—or they may very likely never arrive at all, but go to some other section already provided with arteries of traffic." [17] Many of his interurban lines were planned in exactly this manner. When people later decided to move into these areas, Huntington was among the developers ready to sell them real estate.

In order to take full advantage of the developmental power of the trolleys, Huntington formed two companies to operate closely with the interurban. He incorporated several land companies to purchase, subdivide, and sell real estate. Of these, Huntington's first and foremost was his solely owned Huntington Land and Improvement Company, established in 1902. Also in 1902, Huntington and several other investors incorporated the Pacific Light and Power Company (PL&P). Its purpose was first to generate and supply electricity to the rapidly growing trolley network and second to distribute excess power to various parts of Los Angeles County.

The trolley, the key to Huntington's southern California development scheme, was so successful in blanketing the region with rail lines that E. H. Harriman and the Southern Pacific were pushed to acquire a half-interest in the PE to protect their regional steam transportation network from electric railway competition. Once the SP became his trolley partner in 1903, Huntington was not always able to build interurban routes to sites he had selected for future residential subdivision. Although the SP encouraged expansion of the interurban if the extension benefited its own regional transit system, it blocked construction of some proposed lines if they might be detrimental to the SP. For example, the SP scotched Huntington's equally grand development project for San Diego County, which involved thousands of acres of subdivisions, the construction of hydroelectric power stations, and an electric railway from Los Angeles to San Diego. The rationale was that a PE line to San Diego would compete with the Atchison, Topeka, and Santa Fe's existing track and upset the harmonious relationship that Harriman had recently established between the SP and the AT&SF.[18]

The expansion of southern California during the first two decades of the twentieth century was spectacular. From 1900 to 1920, the population of the city of Los Angeles increased from 102,479 to 576,673, and Los Angeles County grew nearly sixfold, from 170,298 to 936,455. During the same period, bank clearings in the city of Los Angeles rose from a mere $123 million in 1900 to $4 billion in 1920. From 1899 to 1920, the value of products manufactured in Los Angeles jumped from $15 million to $790 million, and the value of the city's building permits increased from about $2 million to $60 million.[19]

Local observers explained the rapid growth of the Los Angeles basin in a variety of ways. Writer and booster Charles Fletcher Lummis believed the area's success was directly related to its mild climate. Yet many contemporaries attributed the expansion and development of the Los Angeles basin to bold entrepreneurs whose broad vision, large capital investments, and innovative promotion turned an area lacking in natural resources into a bustling southern California metropolis. Among this group of entrepreneurs, Huntington was clearly the most important. In 1905, William M. Garland, one-time president of the local realty board who sometimes acted as Huntington's land agent, placed a full-page advertisement in Los Angeles newspapers extolling the trolley magnate's importance to the region: "Mr. Huntington's advent into Los Angeles placed our city ten years ahead of its natural growth."[20] Twelve years later, Southern California Edison president John B. Miller expressed similar sentiments. He thought Huntington's "faith in Southern California has been the dominating factor in its return from the depression of the latter eighties and its new and wonderful growth, substantiality and prosperity."[21]

Huntington's impact was far reaching. Rapidly pouring his

financial resources into the southland, he increased his investment in the Los Angeles basin from approximately $200,000 in 1901 to more than $45 million in 1917. The majority of his capital investments went into the three legs of his southern California business operations that, functioning together, shaped the region and spurred its urban boom.[22]

With the exception of Sherman and Clark's 180-mile Los Angeles Pacific Railway, which dominated the western section of Los Angeles County, particularly along the coast, Huntington at one point held a virtual monopoly in the Los Angeles basin's public intracity and intercity transit. From 1901 to 1904, Huntington owned a controlling interest in both a money-making transit system, the city-oriented Los Angeles Railway, and the sprawling interurban PE. From 1904 to 1910, he acquired the Los Angeles and Redondo Railway, remained the majority stockholder of the Los Angeles Railway, and shared equal ownership of the PE with the Southern Pacific. By 1910, the Huntington trolley systems stretched over approximately 1,300 miles of southern California.[23]

This streetcar network serviced downtown Los Angeles and sent lines north and east to the foothill communities of Glendale, Pasadena, Sierra Madre, and Glendora; east through Whittier and La Habra; southeast to Anaheim, Santa Ana, and Orange; south to the coastal villages of Long Beach and San Pedro, Newport, and Balboa; and southwest to Redondo Beach. With the exception of the PE connection to the San Fernando Valley and the Los Angeles Pacific, the 1910 Huntington system was "a detailed sketch for the whole Los Angeles that exists today."[24] While it would be left to the automobile—which encouraged development between and beyond the trolley lines—to fill in and extend this outline, the basic spatial design of downtown Los Angeles and the surrounding suburbs was created by Huntington's streetcars.[25]

Many of the transit corridors Huntington laid out for his interurbans remain important to present-day Los Angeles commuters— several of the region's major freeways closely follow rights-of-way of the PE system.[26] But Huntington's transportation legacy in southern California runs even deeper. Angelenos, who once gave up the electric railway in favor of the automobile, have decided to build another rapid transit rail system and are presently constructing a $3.4 billion subway, the Metro Rail, as well as three light-rail lines running to various parts of the county. As Neal Peterson, executive director of the Los Angeles Transportation Commission, explained in July 1989: "What we are trying to do is re-rail Los Angeles. Basically, we are trying to re-create the old Red Car [Pacific Electric] system."[27]

In 1927, historian Robert G. Cleland noted the enormous effect of the PE on the expansion of the Los Angeles basin. The interurban system "has . . . knit the surrounding cities into a compact community with the larger city, made possible the upbuilding of hundreds of square miles of rural territory, and furnished easy access to the beaches and mountains for the city's population." He added that the extensive trolley system had enabled "the wage earner to own his own home in one of the many subdivisions which have sprung up along the company's various lines."[28]

The immense value of trolley lines was well recognized by contemporary real estate developers. Promoters advertising subdivisions in local newspapers almost always emphasized the developments' proximity to trolley lines and their accessibility to Los Angeles. In 1903, for example, the Carlson Investment Company stressed that three Huntington lines reached its Pasadena Villa tract; thus, homeowners were only minutes away from downtown Los Angeles.[29] Historian Mark S. Foster noted that up to 1920 almost all real estate promotions tried to attract buyers by emphasizing the locations of the trolley connections. Because residents generally relied on such transportation, few advertisements offered homes with garages.[30]

Furthermore, just as local governments and business groups in the latter decades of the nineteenth century had viewed steam railroads as engines of progress and struggled to obtain railway connections for their towns and communities, in the early decades of the twentieth century, urban leaders tried to cajole street railway companies to build to their respective communities. A trolley linking a suburb with the downtown core was considered not only synonymous with but necessary for growth and prosperity. This belief in the connection between interurban access and progress was captured by the *Santa Ana Blade*, quoting a resident of Tustin— an Orange County community northwest of Santa Ana—in 1906: "We've just got to have it [a trolley], and that's all there is to it."[31]

Besides being a major factor in the growth of outlying communities, Huntington trolleys also shaped the retail districts of many suburbs. Established where passenger traffic was heaviest, suburban retail centers often were formed adjacent to major PE lines running through the various satellite cities. The main retail and business district in Glendale, for example, rose on either side of the PE line on Brand Boulevard. Similar concentrations of merchants and retailers occurred along the PE arteries on Pine Avenue in Long Beach, Colorado Street in Pasadena, Second Street in Pomona, Third Street in San Bernardino, and Fourth Street in Santa Ana.[32]

Wherever Huntington's electric railway lines were extended, undeveloped land was subdivided and brought on to the real estate market. From 1904 to 1913, for example, approximately five hundred new subdivisions were opened every year, and almost all were within a block or two of a streetcar line.[33] Because Huntington decided the direction trolley lines were built and because trolley access was crucial to successful real estate development, he in effect determined how, when, and where the region would grow.

With the increasing population being dispersed by the trolleys to the many burgeoning suburbs, Huntington's land companies and power firm also played significant roles in the region's expansion. The southland's market for new residential land was dominated by its wealthy elite. According to historian Frederic C. Jaher, between 1885 and 1915 the region's elite—comprised of business, civic, professional, and political figures—numbered about four hundred. Jaher categorized the group according to primary occupation, and he found that twenty-two men were primarily interested in real estate. Others whose primary occupations were not in real estate owned substantial amounts of undeveloped property. A more accurate number of elites actively involved in southern California real estate may be obtained by including men in closely related occupations. Businessmen in professions that usually crossed over into real estate development included six in transportation, five in agriculture, fifty-two in finance, and four whom Jaher termed general capitalists. Thus, approximately ninety men were paramount in real estate in the Los Angeles basin, and the leaders were Harrison Gray Otis, Harry Chandler, Sherman, Clark, and Huntington.[34]

Such subdividers wielded tremendous power in the pre-1920 southland. Although the state of California, and more specifically the city and county of Los Angeles, led the country in regulating the real estate industry and passing regional land-use zoning laws, the major impact of these statutes was not felt until the 1920s.[35] In the absence of all but minimal government regulation over urban planning, "subdividers who engaged in fullscale community development . . . performed the function of being private planners for American cities and towns."[36]

Huntington, one of the largest landholders in southern California, transformed vast stretches of rural undeveloped land along his interurban lines into many suburban residential districts.[37] Aware that there were several distinct classes of people seeking home-sites in the Los Angeles basin, Huntington designed subdivisions to appeal to various markets. His developments differed, for example, according to street arrangement, lot size and price, and various deed restrictions such as minimum value of construction required. These controls determined the clientele each subdivision would attract.[38]

Sometimes, Huntington supplied his residential developments with utilities. His Pacific Light and Power Company, one of the three major power firms in the Los Angeles basin and the largest developer of hydroelectric power, often provided electricity and sometimes natural gas to these new communities. Through his San Gabriel Valley Water Company, Huntington provided water to most of Alhambra and San Marino and parts of San Gabriel, South Pasadena, and Pasadena.

Thus, Huntington's major interests in southern California—the three legs of his business triad—were entrenched in critical sectors for regional growth. Operated together, these enterprises not only shaped the southern California landscape but also stimulated the area's economic boom, and they, in turn, benefited from such expansion.

Besides directing these companies, Huntington acted in many other ways to nurture and encourage the growth and development of the metropolis. Huntington wore many hats: he was at once a farmer, a city booster, an industrialist, a hotelier, a philanthropist, a member and promoter of exclusive social clubs, and a collector extraordinaire of rare books and fine art.

As in many of his ventures, Huntington's involvement in agriculture was actually a spin-off from another business interest. While purchasing immense tracts of southern California property for subdivision, Huntington obtained many acres of ranch land planted in fruit trees and other salable crops. Such incidental acquisitions led him into agriculture and created the possibility of making money from land otherwise idle until it was subdivided for residential development. Besides producing oranges, the almost mythical citrus fruit that brought fame and fortune to the southland, Huntington's ranches also yielded lemons, grapefruit, peaches, walnuts, hay, barley, alfalfa, and flowers.

In addition to growing produce, Huntington, in association with several other ranchers in the area, formed the San Marino Growers' Packing Association to prepare, box, and market the citrus fruit.

Always the entrepreneur, he was also interested in developing new crops for the area. In July 1911, Huntington signed an agreement with the U.S. Department of Agriculture to experiment with the feasibility of growing avocados in southern California.

Through his acreage devoted to citrus crops, Huntington helped further the romantic image of southern California as a Mediterranean garden and a lush land of sunshine. He understood that highlighting the area's fertility and mild climate as well as its Spanish past would attract visitors, some of whom might become permanent residents.

In order to exploit and even exaggerate the region's colorful past, Huntington financed the transformation of Frank Miller's Glenwood Tavern, a roadside inn located in Riverside, a rich agricultural community east of Los Angeles, into a grand hotel modeled after the Spanish mission design. Known for its meticulous service, the inn attracted wealthy clientele from both the local area and the East Coast. Yet the Mission Inn turned out to be much more luxurious and ostentatious than anything out of the region's past. Writer Kevin Starr described the hotel as "a Spanish Revival Oz: a neo-Franciscan fantasy of courts, patios, halls, archways, and domes, which he [Miller, the proprietor] furnished with statuary, stained glass windows, and religious artifacts of Spain, Italy, and Mexico, gathered on pilgrimages abroad."[39]

Huntington played a more direct role of regional booster. Hoping to bring new industry to southern California, he believed if he set up a successful manufacturing business in the area, others might be encouraged to follow.[40] Informed that the region had all the prerequisites for felt manufacture—sunshine, wool, and water, available from wells in parts of the San Gabriel Valley—he decided in 1903 to set up a felt factory. Created to produce piano hammers and shoes, the felt company was named after Alfred Dolge, the expert Huntington brought from New York to manage the operation. Unfortunately the felt enterprise was not a money maker. Even though it went through reorganization, the venture proved to be a constant financial drain on the primary stockholder, the Huntington Land and Improvement Company.

Huntington's failure to create a prosperous felt industry in southern California did not deter him from entering new businesses that might spur the area's development. Like his entrance into agriculture, Huntington had gone into the hotel industry because of his real estate investments. In 1906, in association with other developers, he opened the prestigious Oak Knoll subdivision in Pasadena. Several acres of the property had been reserved for the construction of a luxury hotel. The partially completed Hotel Wentworth opened its doors in February 1907. It soon encountered financial troubles, and less than six months later the hotel was closed.

After being entangled for over three years in complicated bankruptcy court proceedings, the Hotel Wentworth was put up for sale in 1911. The following year it was purchased by Huntington, who intended to fulfill the original plans of establishing a first-class hotel. Huntington added two stories to the hotel and directed his personal botanist and gardener, William Hertrich, to lay out the gardens. Renamed the Huntington Hotel, the beautiful structure opened for business in January 1914. A pamphlet advertising the new hotel used florid language to paint a romantic portrait that emphasized the sumptuous Spanish design of the building and surrounding grounds: "What you read about of palaces in Spain—what you have dreamed of Moorish architecture—graceful arches pillared on fragile columns—vine trailed balconies—low broad windows that make for daylight everywhere—tree embowered patios where fountains tinkle—trickling streams that wend through wondrous gardens, all these are 'come true' here."[41] In three years the bankrupt property was turned around into a popular guest house for the wealthy, and Huntington sold it in 1917.

Like many urban entrepreneurs, Huntington was also a philanthropist. He donated land to cities for parks and schools and provided money to youth organizations such as the Boy Scouts and the YMCA. Huntington also wanted to enrich the intellectual and cultural life of the area, and he gave generous support to such regional institutions of higher education as Occidental College, the California Institute of Technology, and the University of Southern California. While his largess was designed to benefit strictly the local area, Huntington understood the ramifications of providing such gifts. Private monies and property granted for civic improvements made the region more alluring to outsiders. They encouraged migration to southern California and accelerated the growth of the metropolis.

To establish further the southland's civility and to provide places where well-to-do businessmen could meet others of their ilk, Huntington was active in promoting several of the area's most prestigious social clubs. He reasoned that these organizations brought together many elite entrepreneurs who had the necessary capital and shared the desire to build a major urban center in southern

California. Belonging to the same "correct" clubs, the area's urban entrepreneurs met socially, and out of these meetings, business deals were often forged. These conservative, all-white organizations tended to cement the region's elite into a cohesive unit.

Affiliated with most of the southland's prominent country clubs, Huntington was also a member of the exclusive Bolsa Chica Gun Club, the California Club, and the University Club. His most intimate involvement was with the Jonathan Club. Besides serving as this organization's president, Huntington set aside the top two floors of his nine-story Pacific Electric Building at the corner of Sixth and Main streets in downtown Los Angeles for the club's facilities.

Huntington's major cultural contribution to the area was the now famous Huntington Library, Art Collections, and Botanical Gardens in San Marino, a wealthy residential community lying east of Los Angeles and on the southeast side of Pasadena. Always interested in book collecting, he began to take the hobby more seriously after 1900. Ten years later, Huntington started to disengage himself from his various business concerns and devote more time to collecting rare books and paintings. By 1916, Huntington's library consisted of approximately sixty thousand volumes, and it held one of the largest collections of early English literature in the world. His collection soon rivaled the library assembled by another great private collector, J. P. Morgan, but Huntington's method of acquisition and the ultimate purpose of his library drastically differed from those of the famous financier. Rather than purchase individual rare works or manuscripts, as Morgan generally did, Huntington often bought entire libraries. In addition, although both men intended their collections to be open to the public, Huntington designed his institution to include facilities for scholarly research and to provide exhibitions for tourists. The Morgan Library, on the other hand, emphasized the museum aspect, offering changing exhibits for the public view and underplaying the library's research component.

In 1919, Huntington endowed a trust creating an institution that established the Huntington Library, Art Collections, and Botanical Gardens. They stand on part of the original San Marino Ranch that he purchased in 1903. Because he also wished to expand the area's research facilities, Huntington called for bringing world-renowned scholars to study at the library and make use of his many fine rare books and manuscripts.

When the deed of the trust was recorded, construction began on a library building about two hundred feet northeast of Huntington's San Marino home. Although not completed until 1923, the structure was occupied in September 1920, when Huntington's library headquarters were transferred from New York to San Marino. Thus, Huntington gave southern California a major library and helped create an atmosphere conducive to intellectual and scholarly activity in the area.

Of all his achievements, Huntington was apparently proudest of the library. When asked if he wanted a biography of himself written, Huntington replied: "I have been approached regarding a biography, but I do not want that. This library will tell the story. It represents the reward of all the work I have ever done and the realization of much happiness."[42]

Whether justifiably most satisfied with the library he established for the public or overly modest about his major achievements in southern California, Huntington, from his first investment in the area in 1898 to his death in 1927, was involved in such a wide array of projects that his name became ubiquitous throughout the region. In 1914, writer Isaac F. Marcosson stressed Huntington's tremendous involvement in the area by relating the story of a mother taking her inquisitive young daughter on a trolley excursion to the beach. Early in the journey, the little girl asked a string of questions:

> "Whose streetcar are we riding in?"
> "Mr. Huntington's," was the reply. Passing a park, the little one asked:
> "What place is that?"
> "Huntington Park."
> "Where are we going, mother?" continued the girl.
> "To Huntington Beach." Arriving at the sea, the child, impressed by the sameness of all the replies, ventured one more query:
> "Mother, does Mr. Huntington own the ocean or does that still belong to God?"[43]

Although it is unlikely that a single man combining Huntington's wealth and management background could have replaced him or could have rapidly established such a widespread business empire, various individuals or business syndicates might have operated a similar array of firms as separate and independent entities. However, because southern California entrepreneurs were short of capital, financing was often a problem. Without Huntington and his vast wealth, which was quickly poured into essential sectors in the economy, the Los Angeles basin would have developed much more slowly and possibly differently.

Rather than being rapidly built or constructed ahead of demand, the streetcar system would have been laid out by interurban builders such as Sherman, but because it would be financed by landowners along the route, it would have spread much more slowly and only through areas where property owners were willing to capitalize lines. Furthermore, because of this slow growth, the Southern Pacific, not feeling a threat to its steam railway system in the Los Angeles basin, might not have become involved in the region's interurban network or continued to expand it.

Although the power business would have been dominated by Kerckhoff and Balch's San Gabriel Electric, John Miller's SoCal Edison, and C. O. G. Miller's Los Angeles Gas and Electric, the demand for electricity would not have been as high because of the trolley network's slow expansion. This being the case, massive hydroelectric projects that Huntington built would not have been needed for years.

Finally, without Huntington the southern California real estate market would still have been dominated by a small group of entrepreneurs. However, with the interurban system being built piecemeal and financed by landowners along the route, the Los Angeles basin would have been subdivided much more slowly. This sluggish suburban expansion could have led to a city much more dominated by a downtown core, and vast metropolitan sprawl would have awaited the advent of the automobile. Later suburban development, generated by the automobile rather than established by the trolleys, as well as a more concentrated downtown area, could have altered Los Angeles's metropolitan layout.

The Los Angeles basin lacked many of the obvious natural resources for becoming a large population center. But creative and energetic businessmen took advantage of the region's chief asset—its mild climate—to promote the southland and lay the necessary foundations for metropolitan civilization. During the first two decades of the twentieth century, once people had been lured out to southern California, Huntington trolleys, powered by his PL&P, carried them to newly opened subdivisions—many times, Huntington developments—and there they were frequently provided with utilities by Huntington companies. These enterprises made Huntington the foremost city-builder who transformed the rural southern California landscape into a major urban center. On 5 August 1927, the remaining directors of the Huntington Land and Improvement Company recorded their beliefs about their recently deceased associate, Henry Huntington, in the firm's minutes: "No single individual has done so much to promote the phenomenal growth of southern California."[44]

Huntington's broad strategy resembled other smaller-scale Los

Angeles entrepreneurs, but he operated on a much grander level. Like others, he became involved in urban infrastructural industries. Unlike others, he had experience with mammoth ventures and had the capital and vision to carry out such large undertakings. These advantages, combined with Huntington's tenacious drive and indefatigable energy, led him to dominate the area's streetcar industry, electric power generation, and the real estate business. The very size and scope of Huntington's enterprises—spanning metropolitan Los Angeles—set him apart from other urban developers. Operating his three businesses together, Huntington developed, and dictated where others would develop, Los Angeles. He became, in essence, the region's metropolitan planner, determining transit corridors, establishing a mix of subdivisions along the interurban routes, and frequently providing utilities to the new communities.

The epitome of the successful metropolitan entrepreneur, Huntington was a shrewd developer of key industries in the area and a prime example of an individual who caused economic change and thereby benefited from it. The success of his numerous ventures produced a snowball effect. His activities generated opportunities for other businessmen to invest in the future of southern California. Huntington had used his wealth as well as managerial and organizational talents to shape greater Los Angeles and accelerate even more the growth of a metropolitan area that was destined to become the nation's leader in manufacturing and entertainment services by the last quarter of the twentieth century.

2

Business Beginnings

Once the teenaged Henry Huntington entered the business world, his uncle, Collis Huntington, soon became the most important figure in the young man's life. When the lure of greater opportunities brought Henry to New York City, the friendship between the two men grew. Sensing a competence in his nephew, Collis provided Henry with a management position in a sawmill and several years later brought him into the railroad business. But Collis was much more than an employer; he became Henry's teacher and guide as well as his close friend and role model. Under his tutelage, Henry developed into a highly skilled and knowledgeable administrator.

Early in his life, Henry exhibited a drive and determination to succeed. At twelve years old, he struggled with his English lesson one day and afterward wrote his sister: "I intend to go through my grammer [sic] tomorrow and then commence it again the next day for I intend to go through it again and again for I want to learn to talk correctly as I have not learnt yet."[1] This trait carried over from the schoolhouse into the business world.

The fourth of seven children, Henry, usually called Ed or Edwards by his family, was born on 27 February 1850 in the village of Oneonta, New York. His father, Solon Huntington, had migrated from Connecticut to Oneonta—a town of approximately two thousand residents—in 1840 in search of new opportunities. The following year he opened a general store.[2] Henry's mother, Harriet Huntington, was the daughter of a physician from Burnt Hills, New York. The Huntingtons, an old-stock, middle-class merchant family, traced their English ancestors' arrival in America

19

back to 1633.[3] Besides his mercantile activities, Solon was a part-time farmer and land speculator. Conservative by nature, he did not have the entrepreneurship needed for great financial success.[4] Solon's younger brother, Collis, on the other hand, did. It was Collis, a forceful and astute businessman, who had the greatest influence on Henry's early business career.

Collis P. Huntington was a partner with Solon in the general store in Oneonta in 1845. The business prospered, but Collis, lured by the discovery of gold in California, headed west in 1849. In Sacramento, Collis set up a branch store of the Oneonta partnership, which Solon kept stocked with goods. Soon, however, Collis dissolved this partnership and joined Mark Hopkins, "the firmest friend Collis would ever have," in the hardware business.[5]

In 1860, Collis Huntington and Mark Hopkins heard Theodore Judah describe his plans for building a transcontinental railroad. Charles Crocker, another successful Sacramento merchant, and Leland Stanford were also present. In June 1861, the Central Pacific Railroad of California was incorporated, and its capital stock was fixed at $8.5 million, or 85,000 shares at $100 each. The company initially sold only 1,580 shares, on which only 10 percent had been paid. Of the initial subscribers, Huntington, Hopkins, Crocker, and Stanford each held 150 shares. Stanford was named president, Huntington was vice-president, and Hopkins became secretary.[6]

The following year, Congress passed the Pacific Railroad Act, which gave federal aid to create the country's first transcontinental railroads. The Central Pacific was to build east from Sacramento and the Union Pacific from the Missouri River west. Promontory, Utah, was the eventual meeting place. The federal government's aid to the railroads took the form of massive land grants and huge loans. Money, in the form of thirty-year, 6 percent bonds, was advanced to the railroads for each mile of track completed, with the amount varying from $16,000 to $48,000 per mile depending on the terrain.[7] The loan, however, did not become available until forty miles of track had been laid.

Sanguine about the future of their railroad, the men of the Central Pacific held ceremonies on 8 January 1863 to mark the beginning of construction. Stanford, now the governor of California, assured onlookers there would be no delay in connecting the West to the East by rail.[8]

But the Central Pacific officers failed to raise enough capital through sales of stocks and bonds on the West Coast to finance construction of the first forty miles of track, the minimum required to receive the loan from Washington, D.C. In December 1862, Collis was dispatched to New York City to seek additional financing as well as purchase materials. Political trips to Washington, D.C., to lobby the railroad's cause were also frequent during his years in New York. His stay in the East was originally considered temporary, but Collis's success in raising money and in encouraging Congress to pass a more liberal railroad act in 1864 made his presence invaluable, and he made New York his permanent home.[9]

From his arrival in New York until mid-1869, Collis was occupied with his job as financier and purchasing agent of the Central Pacific. But as the transcontinental railroad neared completion, Collis's work load decreased and he was free to consider other ventures. Following the joining of the Central Pacific to the Union Pacific on 10 May 1869, Collis was visited by Harvey Fisk and Alfrederick Hatch, partners in a brokerage house. Fisk and Hatch had assisted Collis in the sale of millions of dollars of Central Pacific and federal government bonds. These men had also supported the bond price by purchasing the securities on the open market when it appeared their value might fall. For these services the Central Pacific owed this banking house over a million dollars. Under such circumstances, Fisk and Hatch called on Collis and presented a recommendation. Collis, fully aware of their previous aid, was a willing listener.[10]

The partners introduced Collis to a representative of the financially troubled Chesapeake and Ohio Railroad (C&O) who hoped to entice Collis to rescue the floundering railroad. Unable to assist the C&O alone, Collis formed a syndicate and presented his proposal to General William C. Wickham, head of the C&O. The general accepted the offer in November 1869; Collis was named president, and Wickham became vice-president and general superintendent.[11]

It was to this man, the shrewd and dynamic Collis Huntington, rather than his father, Solon, that Henry Huntington looked for inspiration. Childless, Collis became in effect a surrogate father after Henry moved to New York City in 1870. Thus began a close mentor-student relationship that lasted until the death of Collis in 1900. Under the guidance of his uncle, Henry received some of the best practical management training of his day—working for several of Collis Huntington's railroads.

In obtaining a job from Collis, Henry was not exceptional. Over the years Collis employed many young relatives in various capacities. Only Henry rose to a position of great responsibility, however.[12] Undoubtedly one key to Henry's rise was this connection with a powerful relative, combined with initiative, hard work, self-confidence, and a fierce determination to succeed. The years Henry spent working under his uncle provided him with an important apprenticeship where he took to heart many maxims that he followed throughout his career.

Henry's first business experience was a part-time job in an Oneonta hardware store. At seventeen, he went to work there full time. He stayed with this firm for two years, leaving in 1869 to take a position in his brother-in-law's hardware store in the small town of Cohoes, New York. Unhappy in Cohoes, Henry left in February 1870 to look for a job in New York City. By May, he was employed at Sargent & Co., hardware manufacturers and manufacturing agents, as a porter. He wrote home explaining that he had taken the job for lack of other opportunities: "I wanted to get into someplace soon as it was getting lonesome here doing nothing, and I proposed to Uncle [Collis] that I should go there till I could do better."[13]

Henry's letters home during this period reveal his close relationship with his mother. He sent her notes frequently, often describing commonplace matters and usually making reference to his religious beliefs or church activity. After discussing his new position, he wrote, for example: "I thank you mother for the interest that you take in me and you may rest assured that love is returned. I think that if I ever amount to anything, I owe it all to my parents and my God."[14]

While employed at Sargent & Co., Henry spent much time with Uncle Collis. Henry's work day was 8:00 a.m. to 6:00 p.m., but he often passed his one-hour lunch break at his uncle's office. Many weekends were spent with his Uncle Collis and Aunt Elizabeth. These frequent visits gave rise to a special bond between nephew and uncle. Henry often sought his uncle's advice and believed Collis would watch out for him. "I asked him what he thought about me staying at Sargent & Co., and he said that I had better stay awhile yet, for it would be worth more to me to work for nothing here than for twelve dollars per week out in the country. He said he was thinking what he should do for me and told me not to be in any hurry. I think Uncle will do what is right with me if I try to help myself."[15]

The wage for beginners at Sargent & Co. was usually three dollars per week, but Henry anticipated that "they will pay me more on account of knowing the good will of Uncle Collis." It was wishful thinking. He received the standard salary, which consistently fell short of covering his living expenses. The difference between his $3.00 weekly earnings and his seven dollar per week room and board was made up by his meager savings, some help from his parents, and money from Collis. Fiercely independent, however, Henry was uncomfortable in this situation. "I got twenty dollars from Uncle Collis yesterday, yet I do not like to get money from him and it seems like begging, yet I do not think that he would like it if I were to leave here he seems so willing to help me all the time. Yet I am getting to the age that I do not like to feel dependent on anyone." Nonetheless, Henry remained dependent on monetary support from his benevolent uncle for the remainder of his stay in New York City. He decided in July that the only way he could accept more money was in the form of a loan, which he promised to repay.[16]

Although Henry felt underpaid, he stayed at Sargent & Co. because of his uncle's advice. Then, as he had hoped, Collis rescued him from the hardware business. Collis Huntington, almost always a good judge of people, discerned an adroitness for business in Henry. In April 1871, Collis took his nephew on an inspection tour of his expanding eastern railroad system.[17] The Chesapeake and Ohio Railroad was the heart of this network. After Collis obtained charge of this railroad in November 1869, he set out to execute the previously planned C&O construction—a rail line from Virginia west to the Ohio River. This was the first of many extensions that, combined with purchases of bankrupt railroads, was designed to create a continuous line north through Memphis, Paducah, Louisville, and Cincinnati; it then would run through St. Albans, Covington, and Richmond to its Atlantic Coast terminus at Newport News.

While surveying his burgeoning transportation empire, Collis noticed a small sawmill located on the Coal River just outside the railroad connection at St. Albans, West Virginia. An abundance of timber was available nearby, and Collis thought that if this mill were expanded it could guarantee a supply of railroad ties and trestle supports for his growing eastern railways. He promptly purchased the mill and the surrounding land and offered his nephew a promised opportunity.[18] Eager to work for his uncle, Henry, now twenty-one, accepted a job as manager of the St. Albans sawmill. So began Henry's almost continuous thirty-year association with Collis Huntington's enterprises.

In May 1871, Henry moved to Coalsmouth, West Virginia. Initially he concentrated on increasing the production of railroad ties. He hoped to cut three hundred logs per day; to accomplish this goal, he decided to run the mill both day and night.[19] Henry immersed himself in the new job and worked long hours. Skeptical at first, the thirty or so mill employees became impressed with their young chief's hard work. Henry, in fact, lowered the cost of production, and the St. Albans mill soon produced ties more cheaply than surrounding plants.[20]

All seemed to be going well for Henry. In January 1872, he returned to Oneonta and New York City for a visit. In the city, he became engaged to Mary Alice Prentice, the sister of an adopted daughter of Collis Huntington.[21] The engagement and subsequent marriage on 17 November 1873 further cemented the relationship between uncle and nephew.

Henry's hard work at the mill continued to impress his uncle. Early in 1872, Henry expressed his single-minded devotion to business in explaining to his mother why his visit to New York had to be cut short: "For you know mother that anyone attending to business must be punctual if they [*sic*] succeed." Several months later, his actions illustrated his dedication. On 20 May 1872, a flood washed away thousands of dollars' worth of timber from lumber mills along the river. Henry managed to save all his lumber, however. Resourcefully, he beat nature by tying the logs into fifty rafts and securing them to shore. He recorded the incident in a letter to his mother:

> There have been great losses here, some parties have lost three or four thousand dollars worth. Everyone has said that it was impossible for me to save a stick of my timber but I showed them different. Before I got through I got but nine hours sleep from Sunday morning to Thursday night. But I did save all my timber and the inhabitants said that it was something that had never been done before.[22]

After a successful beginning at the mill, Henry formed a partnership with S. P. Franchot—the son of Richard Franchot, a friend of the family and chief Washington lobbyist for the Central Pacific Railroad—and together they purchased the lumber mill from Collis. Henry's investment was financed by Collis, who allowed his nephew to pay the purchase price at a later date. Collis had high hopes for his nephew: "I am glad to hear that your prospects for business are so good, but I did not expect anything else."[23]

The partnership, however, did not fare so well. Henry's independence and his desire to operate the mill on his own created problems between the two young partners. These strains were compounded by the Panic of 1873 and the subsequent economic downturn, which hurt the firm of Huntington and Franchot. By June 1874, each man was blaming the other for the mill's failure to prosper, and each wished to dissolve the partnership.[24] But Collis, thinking that business conditions would soon improve, persuaded the partners to stay together. Collis's hopes for an economic rebound were overly optimistic, the firm's debts mounted, and he was eventually forced to take the mill back at a loss in 1875. Free of ownership, Henry returned to his former position as manager.[25]

Regardless of these difficulties, Henry remained self-confident. Not satisfied with serving as the mill manager, he wrote Collis: "I am anxious to be doing something better than I am doing now and think I could do well merchandising." Henry asked his uncle for a loan to start up a new business, but Collis was unable to spare the money. Henry then sought another position from his uncle where "I would be useful to you and you could help me."[26]

When nothing materialized for Henry, he left the mill in 1876 for Oneonta to aid his ailing father in his business affairs. This hiatus from Collis and his companies was brief; the business relationship between nephew and uncle resumed in 1881.

Although the sawmill episode was one of Henry's few business failures, it illuminates two key traits already surfacing in the young entrepreneur. First, Henry's independence and desire to run business affairs his own way made it difficult for him to work for, or even with, anyone else. Second, there appeared to be one exception to this rule: Henry could work well for, and with, his uncle, Collis Huntington.

Henry's first business experience with Collis was not, however, a total failure. Learning the importance of self-reliance, cost cutting, and efficiency, he had shown signs of promise. This potential opened the door for a railroad career in his uncle's empire. In July 1881, Collis decided to give his favorite nephew another opportunity. Collis was expanding his eastern railroad system east to Newport News and south to New Orleans. Once completed, he planned to link this network with the Southern Pacific under construction from California to create his own transcontinental railroad.[27] But the Chesapeake and Ohio remained financially troubled, and the company went through a reorganization in 1878. Collis remained in control, and the new C&O owned tracks running from Richmond, Virginia, to Huntington, West Virginia. From 1878 to 1880, Collis built tracks between Richmond and Newport News and finished laying rails from Huntington, on the Ohio River, through Lexington to Elizabethtown, Kentucky. Then, to hasten the growth of this system, Collis purchased the Kentucky Central and a number of other regional railroads then in receivership. The bankrupt roads were merged into the Chesapeake, Ohio and Southwestern, and the new company owned a line between Elizabethtown, Louisville, Paducah, and Memphis. Additional construction was needed to connect these various properties and form a through line. Henry was appointed superintendent of construction for this stretch of road.[28]

The new superintendent set up an office at Trimble, Tennessee, and although he had no formal engineering experience, Henry completed the task of laying fifty-four miles of track in July 1882. While overseeing this work, he frequently received warnings from Collis to avoid unnecessary costs or extravagant spending. Henry reassured his uncle: "I think I have received one hundred cents worth of labor and material for every dollar paid out."[29] But this was not all that pleased Collis. Deft at handling new situations, Henry finished the job nearly two months ahead of schedule by noting inefficient work practices and correcting them. After seeing a large number of men unloading railroad ties, Henry reasoned that by decreasing the size of the work crew and increasing the space between the workers, the job could be done more quickly.[30] Years later, one of Huntington's assistants paid tribute to Henry in his first railroad job:

> I wish to express my best wishes for the good health and happiness of my dear friend and boss, Mr. Huntington, for whom I worked twenty-three years since as his Principal Asst. Engineer of Construction. . . . He is the one you should be *proud of*. I am proud to be able to say I worked for him three years without *being fired*. But I did not work half as hard as did Mr. Huntington. He never *stopped* working.[31]

Henry thought his labor was bearing fruit. He wrote to his mother in October 1882: "I received an encouraging letter from Uncle Collis about my work here, which was very gratifying to me. I have never worked harder than I have on this work and have more to continue with and I cannot tell you how gratified I am to know that he appreciates [me], and I feel fully repaid for my labor."[32]

Henry followed his triumph on the Louisville to Memphis line with more construction work. In Kentucky, Henry laid rails from Paris to Livingston, thus opening a rail connection from Livingston to Richmond. Then working as the construction engineer for the

Kentucky Central Railroad, Henry supervised the completion of the 143 miles of track between Ashland and Covington.[33] In March 1885, Collis looked to Henry to revitalize the struggling Kentucky Central (KC); the nephew accepted the position of superintendent on the condition that he be allowed to run the railroad his own way. When the KC passed into receivership several months later, Henry was appointed receiver of the railway and then promoted to vice-president and general manager.[34]

In his new post, Henry learned two more lessons: first, make use of the latest technology; second, reinvest earnings back into the firm. When he took over the railroad, the number of operable freight and passenger cars was declining and many of the usable cars were antiquated. Much of the roadbed was in disrepair. These elements, plus tough competition from the Louisville and Nashville and the Illinois Central, cut into the KC's earnings.[35]

In order to remedy the situation, Henry purchased new, updated cars and renewed the roadbed. To regain the losses in the valuable freight-carrying business, the vice-president lowered shipping rates and rapidly expanded his freight car fleet. Sometimes, Henry employed shrewd and even devious methods to fight the competition and obtain additional traffic. In later years, he often recounted one episode of which he was especially proud. Henry suggested that a heavy shipper who used a competing railway line have a switch line built connecting his warehouses to the railroad. The merchant agreed but said he would continue transporting his goods over the other railway. Henry said that was fine; he built the switch and promised to transfer the merchant's cars to the competitor's line. When the switch was completed, Henry prepared to transfer several of the merchant's cars but informed him the charge would be $100 per car. However, if the cars were carried on the Kentucky Central, there would be no switching fee. The merchant, not wishing to pay the fee, began sending his freight over the KC.[36]

While Henry increased revenues by enlarging the KC's amount of freight traffic, he also decreased operating costs by economizing. Then, refusing to pay dividends, he poured all the profits back into the company to upgrade the railroad. His Spartan reorganization succeeded, and Henry led the KC out of receivership.[37]

After his nephew had turned the KC around, Collis sold it at a profit to the Louisville and Nashville in 1890. This transaction followed Collis's sale of his stock in the Chesapeake and Ohio in 1889 to a Drexel Morgan–led group of investors. Thus began Collis's eastern railroad retrenchment. None of his eastern lines showed any steady earning power, and Collis soon sold the Louisville, New Orleans and Texas Railroad, the line connecting New Orleans to Memphis, to the Illinois Central.

Following his work on the KC, Henry took charge of the Elizabethtown, Lexington and Big Sandy Railroad. He supervised this company until Collis leased it to the Chesapeake and Ohio in February 1892. Twenty-one months later, in November 1893, the last link of Collis's eastern railway, the Chesapeake, Ohio and Southwestern, was sold under foreclosure.[38] Now divested of railroads east of the Mississippi, Collis concentrated on the Southern Pacific.

The Southern Pacific Company (SP) was a holding company incorporated in Kentucky in 1884. The joint western interests of Stanford, Crocker, Collis Huntington, and the Hopkins estate were placed under one management. In 1885 the various railroads owned by these four associates were leased for a period of ninety-nine years to the SP; they included the Central Pacific, the SP of California, the SP of Arizona, and the SP of New Mexico, as well as a few smaller lines in Texas and Louisiana. Stanford was named the company's president, Huntington was first vice-president, Crocker was second vice-president, and Timothy Hopkins, the foster son of the late Mark Hopkins, became treasurer.[39]

Although these railroad associates remained together through the years, strains in the relationship later developed. The major feud was between Collis Huntington and Leland Stanford. Collis believed Stanford was not devoting enough time and energy to their railroads, and he feared that, as a result, the business suffered. Stanford did have a variety of other interests besides the railroad. In the 1870s he began spending more time and money on horses, stables, wineries, and traveling. By the 1880s Stanford had taken on even larger and more diverting projects. He founded a university in memory of his deceased son, Leland Stanford, Jr., and he was elected to the U.S. Senate. Spending less and less time contemplating SP affairs, Stanford was little more than a figurehead president. The situation rankled Collis; if Stanford failed to use his post for the maximum good of the railroad, he needed to be replaced by a more forceful leader. Collis believed he was that person.[40]

By 1890 Collis was taking a much more active interest in the Southern Pacific, and took steps to remove Stanford from the SP helm. Previous disputes between Huntington and Stanford had been masterfully settled by Charles Crocker. But Crocker had died in 1888, and his eldest son, Charles Frederick Crocker, had taken over his SP position. Although Fred Crocker traveled to New York and tried to mediate the Huntington / Stanford differences, he lacked his father's flair for peacemaking, and the rift between the two widened.[41]

Collis's first step to dethrone Stanford was to court Edward T. Searles, a young interior decorator who had married one of his elderly, widowed clients, Mrs. Mark Hopkins. When Collis was assured that the Hopkins / Searles stock in the SP Company would be voted the way he wished, he was ready to blackmail Stanford about the so-called Sargent Affair, which was related to the senatorial election in California in 1885.[42] The ploy succeeded. Huntington, Stanford, and those representing the Hopkins / Searles interests met in New York on 28 February 1890. Collis announced that he wanted to be elected president of the Southern Pacific at the next annual meeting in April; in exchange, Huntington would either destroy the papers relating to the Sargent Affair or turn them over to Stanford. On 9 April 1890, in accordance with the agreement, Collis Huntington was installed as president of the SP Company. Soon changes were made on the board of directors that strengthened Collis's position. Ariel Lathrop, Stanford's brother-in-law, lost his place on the directorate to Thomas E. Hubbard, one of Mrs. Searles's attorneys.[43]

Collis was now firmly entrenched in the SP presidency, but internecine battles brewed beneath the surface. The Crockers and Stanfords, all in California, remained bitter over the ousting of Stanford; they were not going to accept the new president's authority or policies without a struggle. Since Collis remained in New York, he needed someone to watch over these factions and represent him in the Southern Pacific's San Francisco office. In April 1892, Collis appointed as his personal assistant his nephew Henry, now a proven railroad manager, and sent him to northern California.

By the time Henry—or H. E., as he had become known in business circles—arrived in San Francisco, the first phase of his apprenticeship was over. His tremendous energy and drive to succeed had been harnessed by Collis. During the long and close association with his uncle, Henry had become a skilled, resourceful businessman in his own right, well versed in all aspects of steam railroads. But it was the eight years Henry was to spend with the SP in California that provided the ultimate educational experience and prepared him for his later career in the Los Angeles area.

3

Apprenticeship Years in San Francisco, 1892–1901

Henry's successes on his uncle's eastern railroads, coupled with Collis's trust and affection for his nephew, landed the younger Huntington a position with the Southern Pacific in San Francisco. Henry's years there proved to be ones of continuity and change. Although he remained in the railroad business and applied precepts learned earlier, he faced new challenges. In northern California, Henry was introduced to the streetcar industry and observed its connection to real estate development; learned the importance of retaining skilled, loyal managers; and, because of the Pullman Strike, was instructed on labor relations and unions. His work with railroads also took on a new dimension as Henry was forced to deal with stiff competition from the Santa Fe in the southland. Equally significant, Henry's many trips to southern California during this period led to his first investment in that region. Yet the biggest changes for Henry involved his uncle. Collis had maneuvered himself into the position of SP president by 1899, and Henry, as vice-president, looked to be the heir apparent. The following year, however, Collis died unexpectedly, and when majority stockholders barred Henry from succeeding his uncle as head of the SP, he turned his attention southward to the Los Angeles basin.

Placed in San Francisco to ensure that the presidential policies of his uncle were carried out, Henry also was employed to counter the influence of the family's rivals. The leading figure in this opposing camp was Fred Crocker, who not only inherited his father's position as second vice-president of the SP Company, but also succeeded Charles Crocker as president of the SP Railroad of California, a subsidiary of the parent SP. From the time of

30

his arrival, however, Henry's presence aroused suspicion and created animosity among the longtime employees at Southern Pacific headquarters. Bitterly divided, the major SP shareholders, or their representatives, could not agree on corporate policy. Henry was thrown into this situation to act as his uncle's alter ego, and Collis readily acknowledged his nephew's role. He wrote Southern Pacific official Joseph Willcutt: "I wish you would consult with Henry E. Huntington in reference to this matter [street railroads] as when I am not there he—as you may say—stands in my shoes. . . ." [1]

Henry quickly discovered that although his position carried the authority of president in his uncle's absence, it was unclear exactly where he fit in the established hierarchy. After two months on the job, he was unsure of his role but eager to get involved. In a June 1892 letter to Collis, he wrote: "As yet I do not find my time very fully occupied, but presume that I shall soon get into the harness." [2] Shortly thereafter, Henry found a niche, an area over which he could exert some control: the Southern Pacific–owned street railway system in San Francisco.

Initially, Central Pacific interests—namely, Leland Stanford, Charles Crocker, and Mark Hopkins—had become intrigued with the possibility of urban streetcar transportation. The first San Francisco cable car line (the first in the world, in fact) was built on Clay Street between Kearny and Leavenworth streets in 1873. The technical as well as financial success of the line led Stanford and his associates to ask the city's board of supervisors for a franchise, which they received in 1876. The investors then built a cable road down California Street from Kearny to Fillmore Street. [3] Although they all sold their holdings in the California Street Cable Railroad by 1884, this early interest in the streetcar business led to a major SP involvement in the industry.

In November 1878 Fred Crocker and another group of capitalists entered the streetcar field with the Geary Street Park and Ocean Railroad. Beginning as a horse car line, it was operated down Geary Street between Market Street and Presidio Avenue. Converted to cable and opened for business in 1880, the line was later extended to Golden Gate Park. From the outset, this cable system, the fourth to be built in San Francisco, was successful. [4] But the largest of the cable railway systems, and the one most often associated with the Southern Pacific, was the Market Street Cable Railway.

Originally incorporated as the San Francisco Market Street Railroad Company in 1857, the firm began with horse car lines. It took over the first street franchise granted in San Francisco and built a line on Market Street between California Street and Mission Dolores. By 1863, the line was extended to the waterfront and to Twenty-fifth and Valencia streets. In 1868, the railroad obtained additional franchises to build on McAllister from Market to Laguna Street, on Hayes Street to Divisadero Street, and on Market between Valencia and Castro streets. These franchises, combined with the original grants, covered almost all the lines operated by the later Market Street Cable Railroad. By 1870, even without rail routes on the streets acquired by the new franchises, the Market Street cable system was one of the largest of the eight street railway companies in the city.[5]

In 1875, the Central Pacific transferred its ferry landings from Vallejo and Davis streets to the foot of Market Street. This move shifted the city's major business thoroughfare from Broadway to Market Street and sent streetcar companies scrambling to obtain franchise rights on Market Street. Because the main lines of the Market Street Railroad already ran down this commercial artery, the company soon emerged as the city's most important street railroad.[6]

Seven years later, in 1882, Leland Stanford, Fred Crocker, and other investors incorporated the Market Street Cable Railway Company. Capitalized at $5 million, the company took over all lines of the Market Street Railroad and began converting the horse and steam lines to cable. Construction of the roadbed was considered to be excellent, and the company's rolling stock was viewed as first class. Edgar M. Kahn noted that "the line was in competition with eight other streetcar companies, and it immediately became the favorite with the riding public owing to the convenience and comfort of the cars, the speed with which they traveled, and their frequency."[7]

Extension of the railway from Market down Valencia Street in 1883 stimulated real estate development south of Market and in the Valencia district. In the 1880s the population began to migrate slowly from the highly concentrated northeastern corner of the city. By 1910, people were more widely dispersed, moving southeast and west of the inner city along transportation lines. Shortly after the Valencia Street line was completed, the McAllister and Haight Street cable lines were opened from Market Street to Golden Gate Park. Between these two streets, and paralleling their lines, an extension was built on Hayes Street. Then in 1887, another cable route was constructed south from Market down Castro Street to Twenty-sixth.[8]

Popularly known as the SP line, the Market Street Cable Railway served the major commercial and shopping areas and then radiated out into residential districts.[9] When Henry arrived in San Francisco in 1892, Market Street was the city's largest cable railway. It operated a main line composed of fourteen miles of double track and twelve miles of single track; its property included eighty-four horses and two hundred thirty-two cable cars. Leland Stanford was president, Fred Crocker was vice-president, and Joseph L. Willcutt was secretary.[10] However, Stanford was preoccupied with his philanthropies or with Stanford University, and Crocker had the larger interests of the SP to look after as well as the Geary Street cable line. Thus, with the support of his uncle, Henry stepped in to fill the void on the Market Street line.

Henry busied himself with all aspects of the Market Street Cable Railway. He conceived several innovative ideas; some were successful, and others were gently but firmly scotched by his uncle. For example, Henry called for moving the major Southern Pacific offices, which included the headquarters of the Market Street Railway, from the location at Fourth and Townsend streets. He reasoned that because the city's commercial center had shifted, it made sense to have offices near the merchants on Market Street.[11] The move took place, and the SP offices were relocated on Market and Montgomery streets in September 1894. Another of Henry's ideas was to run larger streetcars on some new lines, particularly down Mission Street, which the company was electrifying. This new motive power was capable of propelling bigger, heavier cars, and Henry correctly estimated that larger cars could be kept filled, increasing profits.[12]

Sometimes Henry's exuberance overcame his better judgment. In an attempt to attract more patrons, he suggested introducing two-story cars. His uncle, however, quashed the plan: "Maybe doubledeck cars are not the best idea—San Francisco is a windy city."[13] Collis felt that even if two-tiered cars were safe, the cool breezes would keep riders off the second level. Henry concurred: "I think probably we had better use the regular cable cars i.e. single deck on Mission Street line, and we can decide afterwards whether we should try one or two double deck cars as an experiment."[14]

Although Henry's early association with the Market Street Cable Railway familiarized him with all facets of street railway operations, the experience provided limited preparation for later challenges in southern California. Fortunately, Henry's arrival in San Francisco coincided with discussions about a consolidation of many of the city's streetcar lines. Henry's role in the merger and his administration of the resulting company filled in the remaining gaps of his business education.

On 13 January 1893 Willcutt, secretary and general manager of the Market Street operations, sent Fred Crocker a plan to consolidate several of the city's street railway companies. He suggested combining Market Street with the Market Street and Fairmount Railway, City Railroad, Potrero and Bay View Railroad, and the Southern Heights and Visitacion Railway.[15] Of these five companies, the first four were already controlled by the Southern Pacific, and the merger was proposed largely to rationalize streetcar operations. Collis and Henry backed this idea but hoped to bring more of the other large street railway lines into the consolidation. One of the larger firms, the Omnibus Cable Company, established in 1861, had inaugurated an expansion program in the late 1880s designed to build a system rivaling the Market Street Cable Railway. However, because Market Street already held franchises on the business district's major thoroughfares, most of the Omnibus lines were built on secondary rather than primary streets. George W. Hilton noted: "The company's main line on Howard Street was two blocks in the wrong direction (south) from Market Street where it was unable to attract a large part of the traffic to the south and west." Ridership was light on these less important business streets, and the company was never very profitable. Nevertheless, the Omnibus Cable Company was viewed as an aggravation by the Market Street management, who considered it an intruder that cut into their territory and profits.[16]

The major value of the larger companies not mentioned in the proposed merger—Omnibus Cable Company, Ferries and Cliff House, or North Beach and Mission Railway—lay not so much in their existing track or rolling stock but in their street franchises. These exclusive contracts granted one company the right to build a railway line on a particular street. Collis's awareness of the importance of franchise rights was a major reason he wished to acquire the Powell Street line, a cable road operated by Ferries and Cliff House and the Omnibus Cable Company.

Henry sought to obtain the Ferries and Cliff House Railway and the Omnibus Cable Company, believing that both lines were valuable properties. He noted the expanding business of the former but agreed with Collis that the cost of acquisition through outright purchase was too high.[17] The takeover was eventually accomplished through an exchange of stock. Talks commenced between the Market Street and Omnibus people, and Henry was optimistic about the movement toward consolidation. But the self-confident Henry, rather than wishing to rely on Fred Crocker, believed he could drive a harder bargain. "Fred is talking with the Omnibus people. I think I could probably do a better job than he could as I do not think he is much of a trader."[18]

Henry ultimately did most of the negotiating because Crocker was heavily involved in other aspects of the SP, and Collis had supreme faith in his nephew. Collis wrote Henry regarding the merger: "I told him [Thomas Hubbard] you were at home in such kinds of trades—I should expect nothing but a good trade from you."[19]

After several months of talks, Henry engineered a deal with the Omnibus Company. The Omnibus owners were granted 20 percent of the stock in the new company; Market Street shareholders received 80 percent. These percentages were shaved down somewhat to provide the smaller companies entering into the merger a share of stock in the new firm. Besides Market Street and Omnibus, the new Market Street Railway was a consolidation of the Market Street and Fairmount Railway, City Railroad, Potrero and Bay View Railroad, Southern Heights and Visitacion Railroad, Park and Ocean Railroad, Ocean Beach Railway, Central Railroad, North Beach and Mission Railway, and the Ferries and Cliff House Railway.[20] Collis wished to make Henry president of the company, but the Crocker and Stanford faction demanded that Fred Crocker be named instead, and the Hopkins / Searles interests cast the deciding vote in favor of Crocker. Crocker became president; Henry became vice-president.[21] Henry took a more active role in the company's affairs than Crocker, however.

The new Market Street Railway Company was organized on 13 October 1893. It comprised 158.5 miles of track, of which 56 miles were horse lines, 68.5 were cable lines, 18.3 were steam lines, and 15.7 miles were electric lines. Six San Francisco street railroad companies remained outside the merger, but none compared in size to the new Market Street.[22] Besides owning the largest share of San Francisco's transit mileage, Market Street rail lines dominated the city's business district, running from the commercial center out into both established and growing residential areas.

In order to manage the enlarged Market Street Railway, Henry applied the same principles that had proven so successful in his earlier railroad career. He aggressively economized, paring away extravagance and waste. Unnecessary positions were eliminated, departments trimmed down, and the operating efficiency of the

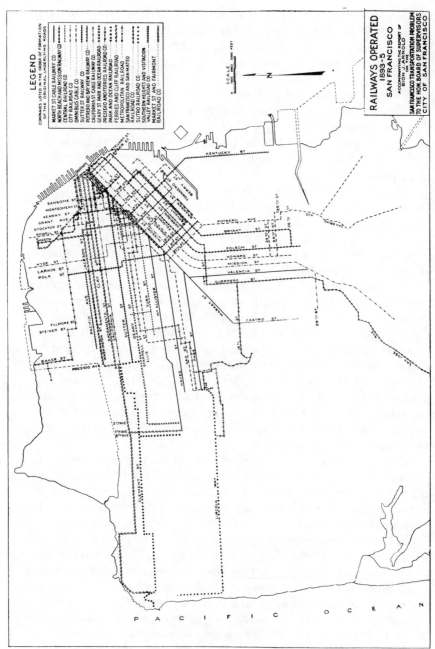

Street railways in San Francisco, 1893–95. Source: Bion J. Arnold, *Report on the Improvement and Development of the Transportation Facilities of San Francisco* (San Francisco: The Hicks-Judd Co., 1913), 419

street railway was increased. Henry then updated the system by using the latest technology; vigorously pushing the introduction of electricity as motive power and phasing out many of the horse and cable lines. He also tried two new strategies. He planned and then pursued the continued expansion of the streetcar lines, and he filled administrative vacancies with skilled managers with whom he had previously worked.

Lowering expenses and increasing efficiency meant higher net earnings. The sooner the street railway increased its earnings, the sooner it could pay dividends to stockholders. Collis wrote Henry: "The amount of dividends declared upon the shares is what influences the people more than the interest on the bonds. That is, the bonds are a contract and of course must be paid, but the net that the road earns currently goes to the shareholders."[23] When the Market Street Railway started paying dividends, the current stockholders, largely SP people, would directly benefit, and the stock, looking more attractive to prospective investors, would likely increase in value.

Henry cut excesses wherever he thought necessary. He first looked to the mechanical and repair shops, where he shortened the work day to eight hours and then decreased the work week to four days. Little street railway construction was under way, and he discharged the street railway construction office staff. Henry even contemplated laying off Lewis Clement, the engineer in charge of the street railway construction. Collis, however, stopped his ambitious nephew; although he felt discharging people was a move in the right direction, he believed that Clement was too valuable to be laid off.[24]

His desire for efficiency led Henry to champion the use of electricity to power the railway's cars. When the Market Street combine was formed, less than 10 percent of the 158.5 miles of track was serviced by electric cars. In addition to providing faster service, electric trolley cars were cheaper to operate and maintain than the cable or horse car lines. On Mission Street, for example, Henry noted: "We are losing money on the cars everyday we run them as a horse car line and would make money when we run the cars by electricity."[25]

Although city officials initially opposed the electric cars because their use required poles considered unsightly and because it was feared that a network of electric wires strung overhead would be dangerous, Market Street proceeded to convert all its lines to electric power. The first line changed over to electricity was Mission

Street, completed on 15 September 1894. By the end of the year, Market Street had increased its electric track to 53.4 miles. During the same period, Henry oversaw the decrease in cable mileage from 68.5 to 65.9 and the diminution of horse lines from 55.9 to 32.7 miles. The company's annual report of 1894 stated:

> As was anticipated by your Directors, the conversion of horse car lines into the electric system has not only developed much new business but has enabled the company to make a large saving in all branches of the animal service, and it will gratify you to learn that since the electric lines have been in operation their net earnings to the present time are shown to have been upwards of $60,000 while there was a loss of $30,000 in the operation of the last year.[26]

The use of electricity to propel streetcars was much more efficient than any other motive power, but Henry wished to ensure that his motormen made the best use of this power and did not waste energy. Having read about a new device that measured the amount of power wasted by trolley operators, Henry instructed E. P. Vining, the line's general manager, to investigate this invention. The firm obtained several of these "currency recorders" on a trial basis. After running tests, the general manager reported that the device functioned properly on level roadbeds but not on hills. Vining, however, did not give up hope; he informed Henry that General Electric offered a similar appliance, and his staff would test it.[27]

While promoting efficiency in his staff, Henry also tried to learn all about running a street railway. Whenever Collis offered advice on managing the trolley system, Henry eagerly accepted it. While Market Street was rapidly electrifying its lines, Collis wrote his nephew concerning the use of electricity in urban transit and the significance of procuring water rights for future hydroelectric power generation:

> Electricity is coming into use fast as a motive power. Just how far it can be transmitted is as yet unascertained, but I am inclined to think that they will succeed in utilizing it for long distances where it would be generated, and in this connection I think it would be well for us to secure water power in a number of localities in anticipation of the time when we shall want it and when it will be very valuable.[28]

The younger Huntington agreed with his uncle but was unable to convince others on Market Street's board of directors of the importance of securing a source of power. Henry later put his uncle's proposals into practice; his Pacific Light and Power Company's hydroelectric facilities provided power for his southern California projects.

The conflict over obtaining water rights was a minor quarrel within the Market Street ranks. A greater dispute occurred over the issue of expansion and pitted Henry against Fred Crocker. Just as Henry had rapidly pursued the conversion of horse and cable lines to electricity, he also sought the swift expansion of the Market Street Railway system. Henry wanted to extend the railroad to streets that ran from the city's center toward the growing regions west and south and to lay track down Ellis Street to the west and Folsom Street to the south. On some lines, especially the one on Mission Street, Henry hoped to build as far as the city line, even though the track would extend beyond the present urban population. He reasoned that the population had been moving in that direction, and people would soon follow the transportation lines out from the central district of the city.

Although there is no evidence that Henry combined real estate development with the Market Street Railway, it is clear that in San Francisco he observed the relationship between streetcars, population movement, and real estate. By the late nineteenth century, in fact, it was widely held that trolleys promoted residential real estate. A Milwaukee newspaper, for example, called for expanding the franchises of its street railways because "Milwaukee is in the business of growing."[29] Although Henry was rarely explicit about his business strategies and never mentioned how or when he decided to combine streetcars with land development, he must have conceived the idea during these years in San Francisco. It would not be put to use, however, until he moved to southern California.

Although Henry's proposed expansions to the Market Street system made sense to Collis, financing was a problem.[30] A panic on Wall Street in 1893 and the subsequent depression made loans difficult to obtain and the sale of stocks and bonds uninviting. Yet the tight money market did not deter Henry from carrying out planned extensions. Rather than acquiring the necessary funds from the immediate sale of bonds, he procured money to start the project from the SP via its construction arm, the Pacific Improvement Company, and by withholding dividends and reinvesting profits back into the line.[31] With the financing worked out in 1894, Henry began the building program. His rationale for expansion was simple—new lines would increase traffic, and dividends would be increased many times over at a later date because of higher ridership revenues and the lower cost of operating the new electric railways.

Once money was found, Collis encouraged his nephew's plans of expansion. By September 1895, however, no bonds had been sold, and Fred Crocker, long opposed to further construction until a large bond sale could be arranged, put his foot down. As president of Market Street Railway, Crocker would not approve any additions until a minimum of $2 million of the authorized $17.5 million in bonds was sold. Also, Crocker and his family, large shareholders of Market Street stock, were no longer willing to see potential dividends reinvested in a building program. In October, banker Isaias W. Hellman, who later worked with Henry in several southern California projects, contracted to take a large number of Market Street bonds. This deal provided money for expansion and made profits available for dividends. Crocker was appeased, and he approved further development of the transit network.[32]

Under Henry's guidance, the Market Street expansion proceeded, and the growing company proved very successful. The number of tracks in operation rose from 169.3 miles in 1895 to 183.2 miles in 1900. More telling was the vast increase in electric line mileage, which jumped during the same period from 53.3 miles to 103.9 miles. While revenues rose from $3.4 million in 1897 to $3.9 million by 1900, operating expenses steadily declined. In a letter to Collis, Henry boasted that Market Street Railway's operating expenses, as a percentage of gross earnings, had steadily dropped from 67 percent in 1894 to 58.7 percent by 1898, a total reduction of more than 8 percent.[33]

Henry's emphasis on expansion and cost cutting carried over to the larger steam railroad system as well. When he arrived in San Francisco in 1892, the SP no longer held a monopoly of California's railroads. The fiercest competition came from the Santa Fe and took place in southern California. Once the Santa Fe broke into this area with a through line to San Diego in 1885, the company moved quickly to lay its own tracks to Los Angeles. Reaching this destination in 1887, the Santa Fe merged its lines with several local roads it had purchased. The rapid expansion of the Santa Fe in southern California cut into the SP's near monopoly of the area's transportation system. By the early 1890s, the Santa Fe had surpassed the SP in the percentage of traffic carried in southern California.[34]

The rapid expansion of the Santa Fe into the southland was only one example of a new strategy being employed by most of the nation's leading railroads. When attempts to lessen growing post–Civil War competition between railroads through voluntary agreements and alliances failed in the 1880s, corporate leaders adopted a new policy. Rather than try to eliminate competition through cooperation, they sought to build huge, self-contained rail systems that, by controlling connections with major traffic sources, guaranteed a constant flow of freight and passengers over their lines.[35]

Trained in a corporate culture that stressed system building, Henry expanded SP routes either by purchase or construction to protect and even increase the company's share of southern California traffic. He countered the Santa Fe by extending SP lines into the fertile agricultural areas of San Bernardino and Riverside and the growing residential regions of the San Gabriel Valley. In 1893 the SP acquired the San Gabriel Valley Rapid Transit Railroad, which ran from Los Angeles through Boyle Heights and Alhambra to Monrovia. In January 1896 a branch line from Alhambra to Pasadena was completed, and the Monrovia line was extended to Duarte. Henry also encouraged the building of tracks southeast of Los Angeles to reach the rich citrus-growing areas. Southern Pacific rails reached San Dimas on 7 March 1895 and were extended to Pomona by 22 August 1895. The following July the SP obtained the Southern California Motor Road, which operated between San Bernardino, Colton, and Riverside. Reconstruction of the tracks was necessary, but by 11 May 1898, SP trains arrived in Riverside.[36] Proud of these achievements, Henry wrote Collis:

> Every foot of track built at my instigation in southern California has been through a densely populated and highly fertile territory, which yields most bountifully its share of traffic that we would otherwise not get, thereby helping to sustain the many miles of barren, desert lines that produce nothing, of which you know we have more than our share. The expense for operation of these branch lines has not increased in proportion to the mileage, as the men have been required to go in and out on them within the day's time, in addition to the ocean runs, I hardly believe any of our people today question the wisdom of reaching out and building these branches which enable us to get about 53% of the southern California traffic, when we formerly did not get 40%.[37]

While directing SP's expansion, Henry also sought to curtail the cost of running the railroad. Although road building continued in the 1890s, the SP did not expand nearly as rapidly as it had in the 1880s. With less construction, fewer land and right-of-way agents were required, so Henry cut back on staff. He also reduced the number of seasonal and trip passes issued. In 1897 Henry told his uncle: "This list today is drawn so closely to our actual business requirements and we are not giving passes excepting for value received, so the list is not one third what it was [in 1892]."[38]

Henry's policy of saving nickels and dimes and still maintaining a standard of efficiency was as successful on the SP as it had been on the Market Street Railway. He wrote Collis in 1895:

> Upon my advent here, as you know, I made it my business to produce every possible economy that did not interfere with the maintenance of the highest efficiency of the property, and you can well imagine that this was not a popular thing to do. . . . By analysis, you will see that we have operated 9% more miles of road, carried over the Pacific System lines 4% more revenue trains, 7% more revenue cars, and 15% more freight and passenger mileage *for 3%* less actual operating expense than it cost us in the previous period with which the comparison was made.[39]

The *Los Angeles Evening Express* of 6 November 1897 praised Henry's management of the Southern Pacific, crediting him with introducing discipline to the railroad's employees and running the trains on schedule: "He has shown himself to be considerable of a railroad man, and if his life is spared it is on the cards for him to go still further."[40]

Henry was not, of course, solely responsible for the success of the Market Street Railway or the improvement of the Southern Pacific. Throughout his tenure with the railroad, Henry had many knowledgeable, skilled men working with and for him. Surrounding himself with capable lieutenants was one of the major reasons for his achievements in San Francisco and later in Los Angeles. Much like his uncle, Henry displayed an almost uncanny ability to select talented, qualified professionals and place them in positions of authority.

When the SP positions became available, Henry quietly brought in former associates and assistants who had previously worked for him on railroads in the East. A prime example was Epes Randolph, who at one time had worked for Henry in Kentucky and was then general superintendent and chief engineer in Louisville for the Newport News, Mississippi Valley, and Ohio Railway. Both Collis and Henry wished to bring Randolph to San Francisco to manage the Market Street Company. But for reasons of health, Randolph required a drier climate, and he was placed in charge of the SP line from Yuma to El Paso. Men previously associated with Henry who later filled SP positions in California included S. F. Morse, J. S. Frasier, and W. S. Millspaugh.[41]

If Henry could not fill a vacancy with past associates, he looked elsewhere for proven administrators. Vining was such a man. Lured from the Union Pacific by a salary of $1,000 per month, Vining took the job Randolph could not, as general manager of the Market Street Railway. Vining cut costs, expanded the system, made no concessions to organized labor, and carried out the instructions of his boss.[42]

Henry expected the same loyalty from his labor force. He had come to believe that if workers were treated fairly, they would respond by working faithfully. In these early years, one event occurred that taught Henry not to compromise with labor. While managing the Kentucky Central, Henry found it necessary to cut wages by 10 percent, including his own. The yard crew went on strike and rather than negotiate, Henry and the office staff ran the yards; the strikers returned to work the following day.[43] The failure of a strike in the face of a management that stood firm and refused to make concessions must have lodged in Henry's mind; henceforth, he used this method in dealing with labor agitation.

In May 1894 the Pullman Strike erupted. Initially, it was a labor dispute over wage cuts, and in protest, the Pullman Palace Car Company employees walked off their jobs. On 26 June the strike spread beyond Chicago and became a national concern when Eugene V. Debs and his American Railway Union (ARU) supported strikers by refusing to haul trains hauling Pullman cars. This action soon immobilized the SP.[44]

At the strike's outset, Henry wrote to his uncle: "I think we should make a fight to the finish and there is no doubt in my mind but that we shall succeed." He added: "This is the first strike we have ever had here and as we are making history [I] think we ought not to take a step backward and make such concessions that we will hereafter regret. As we are into it I think we had better stay . . . and win our fight."[45]

By 28 June, trains within California had stopped moving. With their cars immobilized, SP officials estimated their losses at $200,000 per day.[46] Henry believed that negotiating with the union would be tantamount to turning the running of the road over to the ARU. He expressed these sentiments later in 1903: "When questions shall arise as to what, or how many, men shall be employed or how business shall be managed, labor must stop right there as before a stone wall to step over which means to trespass on another man's domain."[47] The Southern Pacific, therefore, stood firm and refused to negotiate with the union. In order to protect private property and bring an end to the strike, the state government in Sacramento sent militiamen to aid the SP. The federal government, under the pretext of ensuring the transport of the mail, sent national guard troops to guarantee the movement of SP trains. With such assistance, the strike, as Henry had predicted, was broken. On 22 July, after a more than three-week disruption of service, the ARU admitted defeat in California.

Determined not to repeat the experience, Henry and Collis decided that the railroad would no longer employ ARU members. A month after the conflict was settled, Henry assured Collis: "We have not taken an American Railway man back without his first resigning and severing his connection with that organization."[48]

Henry thought the strike's failure taught laborers a lesson: they could not dictate policy to the SP, and the company would do everything in its power to thwart such an attempt. Henry stressed discipline within the ranks of labor. "Amongst such a large body of men as we employ [the Southern Pacific] we must have pretty strict discipline, if we do not we might as well throw up the sponge."[49] Such action, however, did not go far enough. Although Henry was not antilabor, he became, largely because of the Pullman affair, violently anti-union. After this experience, Henry's policy was to avoid employing union members. With these views on labor relations, Henry, when blocked from succeeding Collis as Southern Pacific president, established himself in a region in which he had already invested and that was known for its anti-union, open shop tradition.

Henry's contact with southern California had begun in 1892 when, on his way to San Francisco, he was entertained by J. de Barth Shorb on the San Marino estate, the property Henry would later purchase. Impressed with the region, Henry traveled to the southland from the Bay Area many times during the next eight years. He was struck by the mild climate, the rapidly expanding citrus cultivation, and the potential for future growth. Believing that profitable ventures could be launched, Henry, along with a syndicate made up of I. W. Hellman, Antoine Borel, and Christian DeGuigne, purchased the Los Angeles Railway in September 1898. By the end of that year, this group owned all the city's street railways except the Los Angeles Traction Company.[50]

But Henry's primary interests remained in northern California. On the rare occasions when he was not occupied with affairs of the Southern Pacific or the Market Street Railway, he spent most of his free time in San Francisco with family members. However, because he worked long hours and was frequently away on business trips,

Henry's wife, Mary, often took one or two of their four children away on extended vacations. In 1897, for example, Henry's wife and daughter, Clara, traveled to Europe for five months. Since his immediate family was rarely together, Henry saw a lot of his favorite sister, Caroline, and her husband, Edmund Burke Holladay, who also resided in San Francisco. When Collis and Arabella were in California, the five were often together, and they sometimes passed time playing card games of cinch or whist.[51]

Some of Henry's time away from the SP office was spent tending to his uncle's personal affairs. For example, he oversaw the home improvements being made on Collis's San Francisco mansion and even rehung the paintings himself. On another occasion, Henry prepared Collis and Arabella's surprise gift for Caroline and Burke Holladay, a fully furnished home.[52]

When not in San Francisco or southern California, Henry traveled to New York. In New York City, he talked over SP business with Collis and enjoyed socializing with both his uncle and Arabella. From there, he usually headed upstate to Oneonta to see his mother and then escort her to the West Coast for her annual extended stay of several months.[53]

Henry, in fact, seemed very fond of Oneonta, and his continued interest in his hometown was manifested in several ways. Although there is no indication that religion remained very important to the middle-aged railroad man, he was still a member of the Presbyterian church and made several donations to the Oneonta Presbyterian Church, including a thousand-dollar gift toward a new organ.[54] In addition, much later in life, Henry gave his boyhood home to the city of Oneonta to be used as a library and park.[55] Once he settled in southern California, Henry named one of his subdivisions (located in South Pasadena) Oneonta Park.

Despite Henry's many trips, some of which were for pleasure, most of his time was devoted to business. By 1898 he was president of Market Street Railway, and he continued as assistant to the president of the Southern Pacific. The following year, however, Collis, to appease and gain support of the Crocker interests, abolished the position of assistant to the president. With Henry out of the SP hierarchy, George Crocker, Southern Pacific's second vice-president, became the undisputed voice of management on the West Coast. Henry stayed on as the head of the street railway, and a few months later, he was back with the SP as second vice-president. Toward the end of 1899, Collis worked out an agreement with the investment firm of Speyer and Company to jointly purchase both the Hopkins / Searles and the Crocker shares in the Southern Pacific.[56] As a result, Collis, because of his forceful personality and the bankers' confidence in his abilities to administer the railroad, gained absolute authority over the Southern Pacific. George Crocker resigned as second vice-president, and on 1 March 1900, Henry replaced him. In June, Henry was promoted to first vice-president and looked to be the heir apparent.[57]

Then, in August 1900, Collis died suddenly of a heart attack at his lodge on the shores of Raquette Lake in the Adirondack Mountains. Devastated by the loss of his friend, advisor, mentor, and business associate of the last thirty years, Henry eulogized: "I am simply broken up over it and business of every kind seems to me secondary, and in a way of no importance while I am trying to pull myself together. . . . His character always seemed to me unique in very many respects and among all men I have known, he came nearer to rounding the circle than anyone else."[58]

Henry's responses to letters of sympathy reflected his feelings about Collis's death. For example, he wrote William Crocker: "My uncle was all in all to me . . . and when I received the news of his sudden death it seemed as if nearly everything had gone out of life for me."[59] Rather than mourning the death for too long, however, Henry was soon back at work pushing to continue his uncle's policies. Three weeks after the funeral, he wrote that he was "determined as far as my power lies to carry out his [Collis's] wishes and policy with respect to the Southern Pacific Company."[60] To do this, he required the same authority his uncle had possessed; he needed to become the SP president. With this power, Henry hoped to continue Collis's practice of putting a large percentage of profits back into the company. But Speyer and Company held the balance of power on the board of directors, and the bankers had other ideas. They wanted the SP to pay large dividends, thereby enhancing its stock on the market.[61] Henry and his aides, backed by Arabella Duval Huntington, Collis's widow, worked behind the scenes to make Henry president of the SP. But in October 1900 Charles M. Hays of the Canadian Grand Trunk Line was selected for the post. The dream of following in his uncle's footsteps was shattered, and, as vice-president, Henry was not in a position to dictate SP policy. Unable to keep the SP under Huntington family control, Henry and Arabella sold their large holdings to New York financier E. H. Harriman in February 1901. Nine months later in November, Henry closed a deal selling the Market Street Railway to a Baltimore syndicate.[62]

In 1902, divested of major interests in San Francisco, Henry decided to leave the Bay Area and settle in southern California. With the millions of dollars he received from the sale of the SP stock he had inherited from Collis, the fifty-two-year-old businessman could have retired to a life of luxury. But Henry the entrepreneur was a builder, and unable to continue his uncle's expansion plans for the SP, he sought other challenges.

Yet there seemed to be another force pushing Henry to pursue a second career in southern California. Although he had a pious regard for his uncle, and once noted that "his memory will be the most sacred thing in my whole life,"[63] Henry also appears to have used Collis as a yardstick against which to measure his own achievement. If he could not follow in his uncle's footsteps, Henry would compete with his mentor by building a rival business empire in the Los Angeles basin.

For such an endeavor, Henry brought with him experience culled from his days at the sawmill and on Collis's eastern railroads, which provided him with a solid business foundation. In San Francisco, he had mastered the technique of running profitably a large streetcar system. In addition, by thinking strategically and moving to expand the SP system in southern California, he had successfully dealt with competition from rival railroad lines.

Henry Huntington's apprenticeship ended with the death of his uncle. He no longer had the special friendship and guidance of the man who introduced him to the world of big business and nurtured his development. When the SP presidency position, for which he had been groomed, was snatched away from him, Henry sold his stock in the company and set off on his own. His new vision was of an electric railroad kingdom in southern California.

4

Trolleys, Real Estate, and Electric Power, 1898–1903

By 1898, Henry Huntington had proven himself a capable manager of both a large streetcar company, San Francisco's Market Street Railway, and a transit giant, the Southern Pacific. After numerous trips to southern California, Huntington decided to launch his own venture in the Los Angeles area. The region was tailor-made for him: its Mediterranean climate encouraged a large tourist industry, which introduced visitors to the area and frequently led to their settling there, and its citrus cultivation brought the region national attention and provided a steady demand for a freight-carrying business. Meanwhile, the region's streetcar system was in its infancy.

The undeveloped nature of the local transportation system appealed to the builder in Huntington. Here, he believed, was the opportunity to lay out and operate his own trolley network. Early in his Los Angeles career, the usually reticent entrepreneur told a young reporter about his expansive plans "to build an interurban system that will cover Southern California."[1] With his railway experience and proper financial backing, Huntington thought he could run a profitable streetcar property. He convinced a group of associates who held an interest in the Market Street Railway to join him in the Los Angeles trolley business.

Thus, Huntington's initial investment in southern California was in railroading, with his syndicate's purchase of the Los Angeles Railway in 1898. Still preoccupied with his interests in San Francisco, he did not make a major commitment to greater Los Angeles until November 1901 when the new Pacific Electric Railway was incorporated. Once he focused on the southland, Huntington started building a streetcar empire by applying many techniques that had been successful in his career.

Because Huntington was a quiet, retiring man who did not speak of or write much about his personal life, it is difficult to determine the reasons for his endeavors in the Los Angeles basin. Whether they were due to his entrepreneurial character or an attempt to get out from under the shadow of his uncle by outdoing him in the business world, Henry Huntington was clearly a man driven to create an empire. To turn his vision of a great southern California metropolis into reality and to prevent his plans from being blocked, the independent Huntington remained unwilling to share decision making. He maintained all his business options in his many ventures by holding a controlling share of their stock. To ensure that his wishes were carried out, Huntington depended on several trusted and highly qualified managers to oversee his growing enterprises. His tendency to operate freely and without constraint made Huntington somewhat of a loner within the Los Angeles business community, and during his first years in southern California, he avoided working with men outside his various syndicates.

Often referred to locally as the "trolley man," Huntington spent his first few years in southern California setting up the infrastructure for an enormous electric railway system. Steeped in the tradition of system building and the importance of controlling traffic access, he began piecing together his streetcar network by purchasing and consolidating five existing Los Angeles lines. After acquiring this nucleus, he expanded the existing trolley system through a large-scale building program.

Like many other streetcar magnates, Huntington simultaneously entered two industries he intended to operate in conjunction with the trolleys: real estate development and electric power generation and distribution.[2] Already aware of the direct relationship between the location of a rail route and the rising value of the land it served, he purchased thousands of acres with the idea of providing trolley transportation to the undeveloped land and then subdividing the property. He became involved in the electric business to guarantee a constant source of power for his railway; however, Huntington's generation and distribution of electricity became a money-maker on its own, selling electric current to the city's growing population.

Because the southland was so vast and its population so dispersed, Huntington built and operated two distinct trolley companies, the Los Angeles Railway and the Pacific Electric (PE). Each was based on a different model, built for a different purpose, and managed as an individual enterprise. Resembling the Market Street network, the Los Angeles Railway was constructed and run as an intraurban company to transport people; the goal was to generate profits from streetcar operations alone. The Pacific Electric, on the other hand, was in many ways modeled after the SP and was designed as an interurban to carry both passengers and freight. Although Huntington's hopes that the PE would be profitable were not realized, when operated with his various land companies, the trolleys were indispensable in the promotion and sale of lots in his newly created suburbs.

Six major streetcar companies operated in various parts of the city the year before the Huntington syndicate's purchase of the Los Angeles Railway. Although not nearly as dramatic as the expansion and electrification of the Market Street system, the Los Angeles lines followed a similar, albeit more modest, program in the mid-1890s. The largest company, the Los Angeles Railway, held 73.7 miles of track.[3] In 1895, led by general manager Fred W. Wood, an expert in street railroads, the Los Angeles Railway electrified all its lines. Like most other streetcar systems of the time, this company retained the narrow-gauge, three-foot six-inch track inherited from the cable car days.[4]

The tracks of the Los Angeles Railway covered the central downtown business district around Main, Spring, and Commercial streets. From this core, its lines extended to the city limits in all but the northern direction, reaching Boyle Heights to the east, Vernon and Inglewood to the south, and Pico Heights to the west.[5] The other city lines included the Los Angeles Traction Company, operating fifteen miles of track; the Main Street and Agricultural Park Railroad, owning ten miles; and the small Temple Street Cable Railway, holding four and a half miles. In addition to these city lines, there were two interurban trolley companies—the Pasadena and Los Angeles Electric Railway, which maintained forty-four miles of track, and the Pasadena and Pacific, which held sixty-five miles.[6]

The investors Huntington assembled to purchase the Los Angeles Railway included men familiar with the streetcar business and with southern California. Isaias W. Hellman, a prominent banker in Los Angeles and San Francisco, had been involved in trolley companies in both cities for many years. Both Antoine Borel and Christian DeGuigne had previous experience with streetcar systems. A fifth man in the syndicate, although he played no real role in the acquisition or subsequent managing of the railway, was Collis Huntington. Unaware of his involvement until he read about it in a newspaper, the surprised Collis asked Henry for information: "I would like to know, just what, if any, interest I have in that Los Angeles Street Railway. As you know, I would do almost anything to please you or help you make money, but I am not altogether sure about the success of that road and that doubt is based on the fact that I do not know enough about it to have an opinion."[7] Henry brought Collis into the syndicate either because he needed more money for his share of the railway or because he felt it was a good investment for his uncle.

The Los Angeles Railway was established in 1895 to take over all the property and franchises of the Los Angeles Consolidated Electric Railway, the bankrupt line of southern California's inter-urban pioneers, Moses H. Sherman and Eli P. Clark. Although the new company quickly modernized its lines, net earnings fell in 1896, and the bondholders wanted to sell the firm. Henry Butters of San Francisco represented a South African syndicate that was interested in purchasing the fledging streetcar line. But when the deal fell through, Henry Huntington and his partners stepped in and acquired the company.[8]

On 1 September 1898, Huntington and Lovell White, the chair of the bondholder committee of the Los Angeles Railway, agreed to terms transferring ownership of the company to the Huntington group. The new company was a consolidation of the former Los Angeles Railway, the Main Street and Agricultural Park Railroad (already leased to the Los Angeles Railway), and the San Pedro Street Railway. The new Los Angeles Railway (LARY) was to issue $5 million in capital stock and had a bonded indebtedness of $5 million. Then, to purchase the road, the Huntington syndicate issued $3.5 million worth of the new bonds and paid $365,000 in cash to the bondholders of the former company. Huntington and his fellow investors paid an additional $38,000 in cash for the Main and Fifth Street Railroad.[9]

Huntington was named president, Borel became vice-president, and Hellman was treasurer of the LARY. The new owners planned some major changes, including laying heavier T-rails on paved streets, increasing the frequency of service, building a better style of car, and expanding the system.[10] Huntington's 55 percent ownership gave him control of the LARY. Self-confident as ever, the new owner wished to check on the recent purchase himself and

The Los Angeles Railway in 1898. Courtesy of the Huntington Library

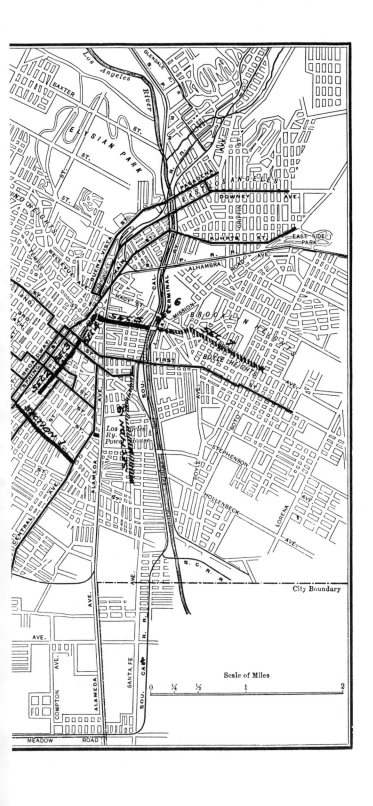

spent several days traveling over and inspecting the lines of the
Los Angeles Railway. Afterwards, he ordered the first of many improvements. Work crews removed the light rails on East First Street
and replaced them with the longer-wearing, heavier T-rails. At the
same time, Huntington called for several new additions. One line
was built from First Street down Los Angeles Street to Evergreen;
the other line was constructed on East Ninth Street from Main to
Santa Fe Avenue.[11]

As with the Market Street Railway, Huntington had grandiose
plans for the Los Angeles streetcar company. Besides improving
the existing system, he sought to dominate urban transit in Los
Angeles and vicinity. This goal was to be accomplished by purchasing and consolidating the lines that were outside his control.
In October, Huntington acquired the Mateo Street and Santa Fe
Avenue line, and in December he purchased his first interurban
line, the thirty-three-mile Los Angeles and Pasadena Electric Railway (formerly the Pasadena and Los Angeles). Initially, the latter
was run independently of the Los Angeles Railway.[12]

Improvements and expansion of the LARY were concurrent
with scheduling reforms and new service offerings. Commenting
on the railway in January 1900, the *Los Angeles Times* said: "A new
feature has been introduced during the past year for the conve-
nience of visitors who wish to see the city at a small expense. Twice
a day a car is run from the business center through the most attractive residence sections of the city, the trip lasting several hours,
at a cost of twenty-five cents."[13]

Based in San Francisco, Huntington continued to rely on men
in Los Angeles to manage the growing company. Fred Wood, who
oversaw the electrification of the former Los Angeles Railway's
cable and horse lines, was retained as the general manager of the
new firm. C. W. Smith, affiliated with the Los Angeles and Pasadena prior to its purchase by Huntington, was named president
and manager of the interurban company. Huntington was content
to allow these managers, both thoroughly familiar with the city and
their respective streetcar lines, to make the day-to-day operational
decisions. But in 1899, when Huntington was temporarily ousted
from the Southern Pacific, he took a more active interest in his
southern California ventures. During this brief hiatus from the SP,
he and his Los Angeles attorney, John D. Bicknell (earlier retained
by the SP and a member of the board of directors of the former
Los Angeles Railway), incorporated the Pacific Electric Railway of
Arizona. Although established as an interurban company, the PE

held only one short local line, the Main and Fifth Street Railway. Huntington's interest in this new firm was short-lived; when Collis regained control of the SP, he returned his nephew to its hierarchy in 1900.[14]

However, after the death of his uncle, Huntington sold his San Francisco interests and headed for Los Angeles. Just two days after he agreed to sell the Market Street Railway, Huntington announced the incorporation of the Pacific Electric of California, on 10 November 1901. This short period in the fall of 1901 marked the end of one phase of Huntington's life and the beginning of another.

Prior to the formation of the PE of California, Huntington had been setting the stage for new and larger projects in southern California. He brought previous associates to manage his growing interests, surveyed property for possible rail routes, and procured financial backing. Aware of these activities, the *Los Angeles Express* predicted that "a syndicate, of which H.E.H. and some of his associates in the ownership of the Los Angeles Railway Company are to be the controlling spirits, is at present figuring upon a complete gridironing of the country tributary to L.A. with electric lines."[15]

In July 1901, Epes Randolph, the engineer Huntington and his uncle had asked to manage the Market Street Railway, was recruited from the SP's Yuma and El Paso division and appointed general manager of Huntington's street railroads in Los Angeles. Randolph replaced Fred Wood, who had died, and C. W. Smith, who was acting as interim manager of the Los Angeles Railway. The *San Francisco Bulletin* considered Randolph an excellent appointment, noting: "HEH has secured for his electric line construction one of the cleverest of railroad managers, and it is his expressed intention to thoroughly gridiron the south with electric lines."[16]

Randolph was an essential figure in Huntington's management team during these early years in Los Angeles. A friend of the Huntington family, he had years of experience serving as superintendent and chief engineer on several eastern railroads and was highly regarded in the steam railway business. An in-house publication of the PE noted that "while H.E. Huntington is the father of the Pacific Electric . . . Epes Randolph can truly be designated as the architect of the PE system." Although Randolph's tenure with the PE lasted only three years—stricken with tuberculosis, he returned to the drier climate of Arizona in 1904—he was responsible for laying out many of the network's most important lines.[17]

For Huntington to concentrate on his Los Angeles investments, he needed a loyal and knowledgeable associate to supervise his eastern concerns. He had become interested in some major U.S. firms as a result of his adept investing in the 1880s and 1890s, but most of his eastern holdings were inherited from his uncle. In addition to granting his nephew one-third of his SP holdings, Collis, through his will, divided much of the estate between his widow and Henry. Interests shared by the two Huntingtons included the Newport News Shipbuilding and Dry Dock Company, real estate holdings, and stocks and bonds in various eastern railroads.[18] Huntington selected Charles E. Graham, long associated with the Pacific Improvement Company and later Huntington's private secretary with the Southern Pacific, as his confidential agent and sent him to New York.[19]

Another key man in Huntington's business operations was John A. Muir. Like Randolph and Graham, Muir was lured away from the SP management. Superintendent of the SP's Los Angeles Division, Muir knew southern California well. When the PE was incorporated, the directors decided that the job of managing both the Los Angeles Railway and the PE was too much for one man. In February 1902, Muir resigned from the SP to accept the appointment of general manager of the LARY, and Randolph moved from heading both companies to running only the PE.[20]

Even with these carefully selected managers, Huntington remained the dynamic force behind the growing street railway system. Before the PE's incorporation, there were indications of an interurban expansion program. One newspaper noted that Huntington had been inspecting various roads in different parts of the southland; he examined the old San Gabriel Valley Rapid Transit line from Shorb to Alhambra, as well as the Redondo line. Other papers reported that Huntington was applying for street franchises and acquiring rights-of-way in many directions out of Los Angeles.[21] By October 1901, prognosticating about his plans was no longer necessary. Huntington's interurban line, the Los Angeles and Pasadena, began building an extension to Alhambra and San Gabriel, and the company secured a franchise for a line from Los Angeles to Monrovia.[22]

In order to obtain the financing to carry out his interurban plans, Huntington created a new company. Once he had a rough idea of the size and scope of the system, he went looking for investors. He had already determined that the new railroad's goal was to operate 452 miles of track. Bicknell, now attorney for the Los Angeles Railway, informed his boss that, according to California law, one thousand dollars worth of stock must be subscribed for every mile of track proposed in the articles of incorporation.[23] The Pacific Electric Railway came into being with a minimum amount of subscribed stock, 4,520 shares with a par value of one hundred dollars each. However, the initial amount paid on the stock amounted to only ten dollars per share. The remainder of the money due on each share could be called in when needed through stock assessments.[24]

Having received a substantial sum of money from his uncle's will, Huntington was a wealthy man, but he chose to take on partners in the interurban enterprise. All the investors Huntington pulled together for the PE venture possessed knowledge or abilities that would benefit the trolley company. The largest block of stock, 986 shares, or about 22 percent of the PE, was taken by Huntington. Hellman, Borel, and DeGuigne—the other members of the Los Angeles Railway syndicate—each subscribed to 678 shares. As bankers, these three investors could facilitate the sale of securities and thus raise needed capital for the new company. The remaining fifteen hundred shares were divided equally among John Bicknell and Epes Randolph, who had already proven their worth to Huntington, and Jonathan S. Slauson. Huntington likely brought in Slauson, owner of the seventeen-thousand-acre Azusa ranch, to tap into the landowner's resources of wealth and influence.[25]

The Pacific Electric's Articles of Incorporation, signed 29 October, and filed 10 November 1901, made the company's large-scale plans explicit. Its capital stock was set at $10 million, and bonds were to be issued as construction began. The PE was a consolidation of several streetcar companies Huntington had obtained earlier. It consisted of the Los Angeles and Pasadena, the Mt. Lowe Railway, the PE of Arizona, the West Ninth Street line, the Mateo Street line, and the Temple Street Cable Railway, which was being electrified.[26]

Huntington's boldness was illustrated by the articles' description of the PE's building program. Trolley routes were being planned to run from Los Angeles north and east—to Monrovia, Duarte, San Bernardino, Redlands, Riverside, Santa Ana, and Pomona. Other northeastern lines to be constructed included a route from Pasadena to Sierra Madre, South Pasadena, and San Gabriel. Heading southeast from Los Angeles, tracks were to be laid to Whittier, Santa Ana, and then north to Pomona. Plans also called for rails to run from Los Angeles to Long Beach, Santa Ana, San Pedro, and Covina, and from Los Angeles to San Pedro and Redondo. Indicative of the far-reaching streetcar network envisioned by Huntington was a proposed route that was never built, a 115-mile line from Los Angeles to Santa Barbara.[27]

Unlike the LARY's narrow-gauge track, which limited the size and speed of its trolleys, the Pacific Electric, largely because of Randolph's influence, operated more like a steam railroad. The PE's tracks were standard-gauge, four feet eight and a half inches, which permitted easy transfer of passengers and freight from the transcontinental steam railroads to Huntington's interurbans. Also similar to steam railways, the PE obtained private rights-of-way for many of its routes; with no cross traffic and few curves, the interurban cars could attain high speeds. Finally, plans on the PE drawing board called for many extensions running parallel to and competing with existing steam railroad routes.[28]

In modeling the PE after a steam railway, Huntington relied on his experience with the SP operations in southern California. From his many junkets in the 1890s to Los Angeles, he had become thoroughly familiar with the region. He was also well aware of the relationship between railroads and land development. Since the 1870s and the arrival of the railroads, settlement in southern California had followed the railways' tracks. As the SP and the Santa Fe rapidly laid rails through the southland, agricultural communities were founded in anticipation of a transcontinental connection and the easy access of shipping produce; these towns included San Bernardino, Riverside, Pasadena, El Monte, Pomona, and Long Beach.[29]

The railroad, then, was very effective in creating towns. With his Pacific Electric Railway, Huntington held an essential component to further real estate development in the entire region. His interurbans, combined with the area's increasing population, enabled Huntington to make a fortune in subdivisions. In 1902, he wrote of the southland's prospects and growth: "I don't think any bright young business fellow can make a mistake in coming to Southern California. Los Angeles is growing very rapidly; in 1880 they had a population of about 12,000; in 1890 a trifle over 50,000; in 1900 about 103,000, and they claim today 130,000."[30] In order to take advantage of his trolley cars, and the expanding population seeking new places to live, Huntington formed several land companies, adopting a strategy similar to that used by Borax Smith in the San Francisco Bay area.

His first land enterprise, the Huntington Land and Improvement Company (HL&I), was incorporated in 1902 and capitalized at one hundred thousand dollars, comprised of one thousand shares of one hundred dollars each. Although he actually owned all the company's stock, forty shares divided into ten-share increments, the minimum amount legally required for one to qualify as a director, were held under the names of his associates who served in that capacity. He chose as manager George S. Patton, an anti–Southern Pacific democrat. Patton, whose son, George S. Patton, became the famous World War II general, had served as manager of San Gabriel Wine Company, owned by Hellman and Shorb. On 30 April 1903, two weeks after it was announced that Patton was to head the HL&I, the *Los Angeles Herald* reported that Huntington had acquired a controlling interest in the wine company.[31] Over the seven years Patton worked for Huntington, the two men became close friends, and although Huntington continued to make the strategic decisions regarding his real estate properties, Patton was given charge of the day-to-day operations.[32]

Because many of the proposed PE routes were through the San Gabriel Valley and because this was the area that Huntington had intensively explored in his SP days, much of his early real estate investments were made in this northeastern section of the county. From 1901 to 1903, Huntington, largely through HL&I, purchased immense tracts of land in what is today Alhambra, Pasadena, San Marino, and South Pasadena. Unwilling to relinquish the long-range planning to his managers, he spent hours pouring over maps and passed days in the countryside contemplating land purchases and possible rail routes. He made frequent surveying trips by carriage, usually accompanied by his stenographer, Oscar A. Smith. After he had decided how an area might be developed, Huntington directed his associates to buy the property and lay out the most effective rail line to the region.[33]

Huntington's purchases in this area included the choice property he had first seen in 1892, the Shorb San Marino Ranch. In January 1903, through another of his land firms, the Los Angeles Land Company, he acquired the estate of approximately 490 acres from the Farmers and Merchants Bank for $239,730.[34] Huntington's son, Howard, who had joined the PE as Randolph's assistant in March, wrote his grandmother regarding his father's real estate buying spree: "He is certainly buying a great deal of real estate and ranches and seems to have the greatest faith in the future development of Southern California. It is certainly making a wonderful showing now."[35]

Huntington's faith in the area was reflected in the grand scale of his projects. Similar to other urban entrepreneurs who built impressive structures, Huntington constructed a larger interurban depot. Like James Phelan of San Francisco, who in the 1880s erected the Phelan Building, one of the city's first high-rise buildings, Huntington planned to build a nine-story structure to centralize the offices of the various Huntington concerns. Called the Pacific Electric Building, it was to be located on property that Huntington had acquired in March 1902 at the corner of Sixth and Main streets in downtown Los Angeles. When purchased, this land was in a residential district and far from the city's major business section around Spring and First streets. Just as the business district had shifted in San Francisco in 1875 when the Central Pacific moved its ferry landings, so Huntington believed businessmen in Los Angeles would relocate around the new interurban terminal.

As blueprints for the PE Building were being considered, Huntington, to hedge his bet and facilitate the shift of the business core to the south, worked closely with congressional lobbyist John Boyd to keep the Main Street post office in its present location. The post office required expanded quarters, and some people wished to see it moved, but Huntington's frequent letters stressed the importance of keeping it where it was. When the depot was completed, this thoroughfare would be the major artery for the interurbans. Huntington stated: "I am building several interurban lines running from the surrounding towns into Los Angeles and probabilities are that local mail in Southern California will be carried by electric lines. All interurbans lines [will] run past the present post office." [36] Huntington's efforts succeeded, and his move to the corner of Sixth and Main proved astute; the business district soon followed the PE Building into this section of downtown.

When the PE Building was opened in January 1905, it contained twelve acres of floor space, making it the largest office building west of Chicago. The Huntington companies occupied the seventh floor, and the top two floors were held by an exclusive men's organization, the Jonathan Club. [37]

Although Huntington was making large investments in southern California, the majority of his time was spent in New York. His extended stays there served two purposes. First, since Collis's will had divided many of the millionaire's extensive holdings between his widow and favorite nephew, Henry often worked with Arabella and the executors of Collis Huntington's estate overseeing their joint business interests. [38] These New York trips also provided an opportunity for Henry to continue his longstanding friendship with Arabella. Second, and related to his Los Angeles concerns,

Huntington often went to New York to obtain money for his southern California projects by selling and liquidating many of the stocks and bonds he held in major railroads and other corporations. As the PE's Joseph McMillan explained in 1907, "Year after year, Mr. Huntington goes to New York and comes back with money for building new lines."[39] When in New York, Huntington resided in the exclusive Metropolitan Club. When in Los Angeles, prior to the completion of the Jonathan Club, he stayed at the prestigious Van Nuys Hotel located at the corner of Fourth and Main streets.[40]

While Huntington was building street railways and snapping up large portions of inexpensive land along planned interurban lines, he did not forget his uncle Collis's advice about the value of entering another trolley-related industry, electric power generation. In July 1901, Hellman wrote Huntington regarding the purchase of electric power and mentioned Los Angeles entrepreneur William G. Kerckhoff, a man with whom Huntington had a long business association. The banker told Huntington that Kerckhoff had offered to sell electricity to the Los Angeles Railway, and, more important, that "Kerckhoff has now made [us] a proposition to form a new company to supply electric power from the Kern River."[41]

Kerckhoff and Huntington had become acquainted in 1893. Before Huntington and the SP purchased the San Gabriel Valley Rapid Transit Railway, Kerckhoff had been one of the railway's owners. Kerckhoff, who had arrived in southern California in 1878, had been involved in several ventures, including a lumber company and an ice business, before entering the electric power field. He first moved into the electric power industry in April 1894, with the incorporation of the San Gabriel Power Company. Three years later, on 24 May 1897, he and electrical engineer Allan C. Balch formed the larger San Gabriel Electric Company. This firm combined the former San Gabriel Power Company with the Sierra Power Company, which consisted of two hydroelectric plants, the San Antonio facility near Pomona, and the Sierra plant in the San Bernardino Mountains. Another hydroelectric power station was later built on the San Gabriel River. Known as the Azusa plant, it produced and transmitted current to Los Angeles, where it powered streetcars and manufacturing plants.[42]

Aware of the value of controlling hydroelectric power generation, Huntington willingly listened to the power entrepreneur's proposals. Eager to get the Kern River project off the ground, Kerckhoff wrote to Huntington: "My idea is, that we should organize the company, go over with our engineers all the estimates, plans, and surveys heretofore made, and obtain bids from the most responsible."[43] After some thought, Huntington agreed to join Kerckhoff and two others, Henry W. O'Melveny, a Los Angeles attorney associated with John Bicknell, and Kaspare Cohn, in the venture. As with his other companies, Huntington brought in his investment partners. On 6 March 1902, the Pacific Light and Power Company was incorporated. It was capitalized at ten million dollars; the Huntington group received 51 percent of the stock, which was held under the name of the Los Angeles Railway, and the Kerckhoff investors took the remaining 49 percent. Although the Huntington syndicate held the controlling share of stock, Kerckhoff, because of his experience, was named president of the new company.[44]

Just as he had done with the street railways, Huntington made the PL&P a consolidation of several smaller companies. It absorbed the former San Gabriel Electric Company, the Kern Power Company, and the Los Angeles Electric Company. The new firm owned the 1,600-horsepower Azusa water power plant, the 800-horsepower San Antonio water power plant, and the 3,000-horsepower Los Angeles steam plant. The company also owned sixty-three miles of transmission lines and a distribution system for the Los Angeles area.[45]

Since the PL&P was incorporated to provide motive power for Huntington's two growing street railways as well as electricity to the city, more and larger power plants were necessary. To meet demand, PL&P began building the 10,000-horsepower Kern River hydroelectric power plant, 11.5 miles down river from Kernville, and two sets of transmission lines, which ran 105 miles to Los Angeles. In addition, the company doubled the capacity of the Los Angeles steam plant; it was to be used to generate power in cases of emergencies or when problems occurred with the distant hydroelectric sites.[46]

Besides expanding through a building program, PL&P continued to grow by purchasing other power companies. In 1903 it acquired the Ontario Electric Company, the Ontario and San Antonio Heights Railway, which held water rights for a power plant, and the San Bernardino Gas and Electric Company.[47]

Huntington maintained active interest in PL&P, but this occupied only a small part of his time. A railroad man first, he guided the vast expansion programs of both the Los Angeles Railway and the Pacific Electric. Proud of his growing trolley and real estate empire, Huntington wished to be kept up to date on the latest development of his properties. In Los Angeles he spent much of his time in the field checking rail construction and contemplating future land development. In New York, at his office on Broad Street, he kept abreast of details by requiring his subordinates to send photographs of the most recent construction work.[48]

From 1901 to mid-1903, Huntington's major building efforts took place on his interurban PE, although the LARY was not altogether neglected. The city's population continued moving southeast and southwest of the central residential districts centering near Sixth and Main streets.[49] The LARY's extensions followed these migration patterns and helped disperse the population away from the city's former core.

In order to reach growing residential areas, the LARY struggled to procure street franchises. In 1901, Huntington encountered stiff competition for franchises from William and T. J. Hook and their Los Angeles Traction Company. On 27 May, the Traction Company was the highest bidder at the franchise auction for rights to build on West Jefferson Street from University to Arlington Avenue. In September, Huntington, represented by manager Randolph and attorney William E. Dunn, who had once served as Los Angeles city attorney, outbid Hook for the Echo Park franchise. Dunn soon retired from his other legal activities to act as Huntington's agent on the West Coast.[50] The disputes over franchises continued, and it was not until October that Huntington learned of a defeat that had actually occurred five months earlier. In October, Huntington wrote businessman Hervey Lindley regarding the franchise Lindley held on Eleventh Street, that ran from Georgia to Alvarado; this important franchise covered a street leading to the growing residential area of Pico Heights. Much to Huntington's chagrin, Lindley responded that Hook had already purchased the franchise in May.[51]

Regardless of these setbacks, the LARY completed many extensions. In 1901 the Pico Street line was expanded east from Harvard to Wilton Place. The following year there were two additions; a road was built on private right-of-way from the Washington line down La Salle Avenue to Western, and the Eastlake Park (now Lincoln Park) line was connected to the Maple Avenue line.[52]

Perhaps the most important change in these years was the introduction of an improved, standardized streetcar. Designed by Huntington engineers, these cars came to be called "Huntington Standards." Up to this time, the LARY used a variety of streetcar models. The Standards were especially well suited to the dry, southern California climate. The wooden cars consisted of barred, open-air sections at the front and back and a five-window enclosed compartment in the middle of the car.[53]

As a Huntington letter to the *Railroad Gazette* revealed, he was interested in the Los Angeles Railway and its growth, but he was excited about the Pacific Electric and its possibilities. On 20 February 1902, Huntington reported that the LARY held ninety-eight miles of track, but he provided a much more detailed description of his interurban firm. The PE, he noted, designed to carry passengers, freight, and mail, had forty miles of track stretching from Los Angeles to Pasadena and Altadena via Garvanza (now part of Highland Park), with a scenic extension winding its way up Mt. Lowe. Huntington added that a new line to Pasadena and a Los Angeles to Long Beach line were under construction.[54]

Once Huntington decided on a particular destination for the PE, he left the details of planning and construction to his civil engineer, Epes Randolph. The new Pasadena route, dubbed the "Short Line" because of its directness from downtown to the northeastern community, opened 21 June 1902 and quickly replaced the old Los Angeles and Pasadena as the commuters' first choice. The cities of Alhambra and San Gabriel were to be connected to the new Pasadena route by branch lines, and residents eagerly awaited the streetcars' arrival. The *Los Angeles Times* recounted the reaction in Alhambra to the advent of the trolleys:

> An electric shock struck Alhambra yesterday morning. It set the people agog. It almost completely depopulated the pretty suburban town. After many months of anxious anticipation, the new electric line of the Huntington syndicate opened for business at 6 o'clock. . . . The town turned out en masse to experience the novel sensation of riding to the city by electricity. . . . It is the first branch to be set in motion of the big broad gauge system of the Huntington-Hellman syndicate.[55]

Long Beach had previously been connected to Los Angeles by horse car and then by steam railroad. Yet the streetcar possessed an almost magical aura. People had seen land booms take place in Santa Monica and Pasadena, the two cities first reached by the interurbans. The belief that trolley access precipitated increased land values led many property owners to donate land to the PE along its proposed line to Long Beach. Over this land, combined with property the PE had purchased at nominal prices, Randolph constructed a double-track route on private, eighty-foot right-of-way. Earlier, Huntington had promised Long Beach residents that the interurban connection to Los Angeles would be completed by October. When acting as construction superintendent in the 1880s, Huntington had often beaten his own timetable. Emulating his employer, Randolph pushed work crews to complete the line three months ahead of schedule. On 4 July, the first trolley left Los Angeles for Long Beach. With high frequency service—cars ran every fifteen minutes—and high-speed transit over a first-class roadbed, Huntington called it "the finest road in the world." The Long Beach line was soon the system's most profitable run.[56]

Wherever the PE cars led, subdividers, development, and growth soon followed. And Huntington significantly affected how and where greater Los Angeles developed. The advent of the trolleys in Long Beach is illustrative. Prior to the interurban connection, an acre of land three blocks from the beach cost three hundred dollars in this town of about two thousand residents. Six months after the PE's arrival in 1902, an acre of land one mile from the ocean was advertised for seven hundred dollars. Furthermore, by 1910, the population of Long Beach had risen to nearly eighteen thousand, a rate of growth higher than that of any other U.S. city.[57]

Similar growth, if slightly less spectacular, occurred wherever and whenever trolley lines were built. The San Gabriel Valley town of Alhambra, for example, although founded during the boom of 1887, remained too small to be listed on the census reports of 1890 or 1900. In 1902 the PE reached the community, and by 1910 the town's population had risen to five thousand.[58]

Huntington's ambition to build an interurban empire and develop land along its lines fueled the PE's expansion. After the Pasadena and Long Beach lines were completed, extensions into the San Gabriel Valley centers of Monrovia and Whittier were finished in 1903, and by June of that year, the PE's tracks stretched over 170 miles of southern California.[59] The PE's rapid growth led many to speculate just how far and in what direction Huntington would build. Thinking in this vein, E. A. Adams, a Huntington secretary, wrote C. E. Graham in 1903: "There is a good deal of talk about Mr. Huntington running his trolley lines to Frisco. It looks like hot air, but I would hardly be surprised if such a thing did happen within the next year."[60] Ironically, it was the success and swiftness of his PE expansion that led to an internal conflict among Huntington and his associates and an external struggle with the steam railroad interests.

Huntington's partners became dissatisfied because of the constant demands for funds to finance the expansions. A stock assessment of 5 percent was levied on all shareholders in February 1902. Because the PE's building program did not slow down, the company issued one million dollars' worth of forty-year, 6 percent bonds through Hellman's Union Trust Company in San Francisco. The bond issue was oversubscribed by California investors, and plans were readied to issue more bonds.[61]

The sluggish economy made the immediate sale of more bonds difficult but Huntington adhered to his building program. Cash to finance construction was obtained by the PE stockholders' taking up the bonds themselves. By February 1903, the PE had $3,555,000 worth of bonds outstanding. Of that amount, Huntington held $400,000 by the end of 1902, and by the following December his total of PE bonds had risen to $1,468,000.[62]

When associated with Huntington in San Francisco, Hellman, Borel, and DeGuigne had seen Huntington manage a large street railroad that resulted almost immediately in high profits and healthy dividends. Yet in Los Angeles, these men found themselves providing money for Huntington's pet project, with no end in sight for the cash outflow. Following the first assessment, DeGuigne sold 427 of his 678 shares to the other three associates. Huntington took up 273 shares, and Hellman and Borel each bought 77 shares.[63]

Concerned about the costs of the PE, the three financiers were also displeased with its net earnings. Unlike the LARY's net earnings, which rose from $85,200 in 1900 to $366,100 in 1903, the PE netted $121,000 in 1902, but that amount dropped to a loss of $37,600 in 1903.[64] These figures proved fairly prophetic; over the next few years, the LARY continued to have strong earning power and showed a steadily increasing profit, but the growing PE constantly struggled to meet the break-even point.

Although the PE did not generate large profits, the already existing nucleus of a far-flung, standard-gauge network caught the attention of E. H. Harriman and the SP. Harriman feared that Huntington's electric system, which often ran cars more frequently and at higher speeds than the steam railroads, would drastically cut into the SP's passenger and freight business in southern California. The pattern of transportation connected with the annual Los Angeles Festival of Flowers in May 1903 indicated the reasons for Harriman's concern. Approximately 70,000 out-of-town visitors came into Los Angeles to see the pageant. Of that figure, 47,500 were transported by electric railways, and 30,000 were brought in by Huntington's PE. The SP, on the other hand, carried only 9,000 of the tourists.[65]

Huntington's first five years in southern California met with incredible success, but that success did not come without its costs. The PE's building program was tremendously expensive, and Huntington's partners began to worry about his policy of continued expansion. He also had to acknowledge an impending confrontation with the Harriman / SP interests.

During these years, Huntington drew upon his experience with the Market Street Railway and the SP to lay the foundation for a business empire based on street railroads, and in so doing, was soon shaping the growth of greater Los Angeles. He established two separate trolley systems, each for a distinct purpose, and entered the related industries of real estate and electric power generation. Day-to-day operations of these ventures were overseen by his hand-picked managers, but Huntington made the long-range decisions and was the guiding force behind his organizations.

Huntington then prepared for a period of unprecedented activity, which included rail extensions, real estate subdivisions, and the building of new power plants. These activities did take place but not in the manner, nor as rapidly, as Huntington had expected. Control over his railways—the key to his growing empire that Huntington had jealously sought to hold, became difficult to maintain. Hampered by associates unwilling to pour money into the PE, and confronted with a battle for the southern California transportation market, Huntington was on the brink of an era of intense struggle.

5

Shaping the Basin and Developing the Economy, 1903–1907

In 1908 Huntington mused about his activity in southern California: "When I came out here five years ago, my friends in the East asserted that I was too optimistic over the opportunities for growth and development. . . . They regarded my investments as visionary. My chief mistake is that I was too conservative."[1]

The period from 1903 to 1907 was Huntington's most active, when his business empire in southern California reached its apex. The *Los Angeles Financier*, a contemporary business periodical, described Huntington's activities: "He has in all his big operations in this southland had an immense advantage over the general market—he knew what he was going to do next." Huntington constructed trolley lines to areas where people could "build their country homes in his extension block by block in the outposts of the city, bringing in the dairies and alfalfa ranches and planting and paving and dotting them with bungalows."[2]

Huntington rarely released information about his business dealings. In May 1908, he was quoted in the *Los Angeles Examiner* as saying: "I will not tell you what I intend to do further, for I never talk about my intentions until they become facts. . . . What I am going to do must remain to be told by what I do do."[3]

During this half-decade, Huntington remained in charge of both of Los Angeles's largest streetcar companies. Meanwhile, his longtime associates sold off their interests in the Pacific Electric and later the Los Angeles Railway. For different reasons, neither of these railroads paid dividends.

The PE operated near the break-even point, and its revenues often failed to meet expenses. Huntington's partners had invested in his southern California trolleys believing they would reap returns similar to those generated earlier by the Market Street Railway. In 1904, alarmed by the PE's failure to pay dividends and by the steady cash outgo for assessments for continuing construction, the three associates divested themselves of their interests in the PE.

To Huntington, the PE and his other interurban firms were not isolated enterprises. The trolleys worked together synergistically with his power company and land firms. Huntington streetcars, powered by his Pacific Light and Power Company, rolled over tracks to property that was often already owned by one of his land companies or was under consideration for purchase. The acreage was eventually subdivided into communities designed for various socioeconomic groups and sold at a large profit. From 1905 to 1907, the return on investment for the Huntington Land and Improvement Company was 7.6 percent. Adding to this efficient development machine, Huntington bought or established water companies and, with the PL&P, his firms often provided these new communities with public utilities. As long as the triad of companies was ultimately successful, the profitability of the trolley firms was not his primary concern.

Hellman, Borel, and DeGuigne understood Huntington's logic, but they held no interest in the Huntington Land and Improvement Company. Although they all had substantial real estate holdings in the southland and frequently benefited from new PE lines, they did not wish to continue putting money into the interurban with no sight of a return on their transit investment. Unlike the PE, the LARY was very profitable, but, to the dismay of the minority stockholders, Huntington reinvested the profits in the company, believing that foregoing dividends would generate larger returns to the stockholders at a later date. Unwilling to wait, the three financiers sold their holdings in the Los Angeles Railway in 1907.

E. H. Harriman and the Southern Pacific superseded Hellman, Borel, and DeGuigne as Huntington's partners in street railways. Like Huntington, Harriman and his SP also desired to dominate southern California's mass transit business. To attain this goal, Harriman wanted to add electric rail lines, which were rapidly blanketing the southland, to supplement the existing SP regional steam railway network. Huntington's interurban system had become the largest in the area, providing stiff competition with the SP for passenger and freight traffic. Thus, Harriman believed that if he acquired a percentage of stock at least equal to Huntington's share in the PE, he could control the interurban's development and would be on his way to tightening his grip on the regional transportation business. At the same time, he wanted to eliminate the competition between the trolleys and the SP railroad in the Los Angeles market.

Harriman was ultimately successful in creating a unified transit system in the Los Angeles area. Although he did not live to see the SP gain complete control of the PE in 1910, under his leadership the SP obtained half-ownership of the trolley company by 1904. With this interest in the PE, the SP was eventually able to control where interurban lines were built. An SP veto, for example, kept Huntington from constructing a trolley line between Los Angeles and San Diego. Generally, however, the SP backed Huntington's interurban expansion program, and Huntington ultimately deferred to the Southern Pacific's control over the PE so he could concentrate on the Los Angeles Railway, real estate investments, and power development.

As Harriman expanded the SP's involvement in local mass transit, Huntington enlarged his rail empire by incorporating another company, the Los Angeles Inter-Urban (LAIU), and acquiring several existing railways, among them the valuable Los Angeles and Redondo Railway. While his rail systems were growing, Huntington purchased real estate in the southland. He did so by either incorporating new land development companies or by joining existing firms with other entrepreneurs already involved in a particular region.

Whether laying rails, surveying property, or inspecting cost sheets for new power plants, Huntington was constantly working on one project or another. Pacific Electric manager Joseph McMillan remarked: "He has inherited the building disease, the operating disease. It is in his blood."[4] Huntington recognized his need for constant work and continuous challenges. When the whirl of the business world slowed, he found solace making improvements on his San Marino Ranch. In October 1904, he wrote his mother: "I am doing some grading on the Shorb place; you know I can't well live unless I can be grading somewhere."[5]

Aware of this activity, the *Los Angeles Times* in 1903 reported that Huntington "will probably build a palatial estate on the Shorb [ranch], and part of that section will be built for millionaires to live."[6] The newspaper's prediction was accurate. In 1906 Huntington retained architects Myron Hunt and Elmer Grey to design and build a large Georgian-style mansion on the San Marino property. While making improvements on his ranch and when in Los Angeles, Huntington continued to reside at the Van Nuys Hotel until he moved in 1905 to a five-room suite in the Jonathan Club atop his newly completed Pacific Electric Building.

Huntington's need for continuous challenge and his rapid establishment of many important enterprises inevitably drew comparisons between the nephew and his late uncle. Isaac F. Marcosson noted in 1914 that "Henry E. Huntington is a sort of reincarnation of Collis P., with the same thrift, foresight, and constructive energy. . . ." Both men also exhibited tremendous patience with their businesses and were willing to wait for investments to become profitable. But Marcosson also observed a significant difference in the two men's personalities; while Collis apparently enjoyed attention, Henry was rather shy and reserved.[7] These personal characteristics, combined with his refusal to have his decisions dictated by others, account for Huntington's tendency to operate independently.

Spending more time in Los Angeles, Huntington saw less of his family, which had remained in San Francisco. His daughters and his mother, as well as his sister, Caroline, and her husband, Burke, frequently came south to visit Huntington and his son, Howard.[8] Yet Mary Huntington, who preferred San Francisco to Los Angeles, spent little, if any, time in the southland visiting her husband. On 21 March 1906, Mary's absences were explained when she filed for divorce, revealing that the couple had been separated since 1900. The divorce hearing took place the following day and lasted only seven minutes; Mary's alimony was set at forty thousand dollars annually, to come from a $1 million trust fund. Following the brief court appearance, Mary and her daughter, Marian, boarded the steamship *Korea* for a trip to Japan. Huntington returned to his business affairs in southern California.[9]

Although Huntington's drive to build an empire may have destroyed his marriage, it also took its toll on his relationship with his children. Clara, Henry's eldest daughter, later explained that business seemed to consume her father's life: "For my own part, I see how the few have to be sacrificed for the benefit of the greater number, meaning that we rarely saw father, and his ambitions, his dreams, [and] his plans that would have been interesting to hear about, we just didn't." [10]

Three years before his marital problems became public knowledge, Huntington was concentrating on becoming the undisputed leader in the Los Angeles transit market. As 1903 began, he proceeded with his planned rail extensions to Whittier and Monrovia.

He then began laying track from downtown to San Pedro to compete for freight and passenger traffic with the SP's steam railroads and the Hook family's new narrow-gauge interurban, the California Pacific, which connected downtown Los Angeles with San Pedro. In April he extended his railroad holdings eastward beyond the Los Angeles county line to the rich citrus-growing area known as the "Orange Empire." Huntington purchased stock in the San Bernardino Valley Traction Company and then gained control of the Riverside and Arlington Railway. The latter owned all the city lines in Riverside, a city about fifty miles east of Los Angeles.[11] These acquisitions led many people to believe that Huntington was preparing to connect the lines in this eastern region with his Los Angeles rail network.

The electric railway magnate was also interested in interurban companies in central California. Huntington's purchase of the Fresno Electric Railway, approximately two hundred miles to the north, and the streetcar lines in Stockton, about seventy miles southeast of San Francisco, prompted the *Los Angeles Express* to report that he was contemplating building a trunk line from Los Angeles to San Francisco through the San Joaquin Valley.[12] An electric line through California's central valley connecting the southland with the Bay Area was never built. The exact reason is unknown, but Harriman, who by mid-1903 had acquired a share of the PE, was on record of disapproving of the plan. If constructed, such a trolley route would have competed with the extensive SP steam railroad system, which already dominated the transit market in the agriculturally rich San Joaquin Valley.

The continued growth of Huntington's trolley system finally pushed E. H. Harriman to act more aggressively. Huntington's expansions and mergings with smaller trolley lines began to cut in on the SP's existing market, threatening Harriman's plan of dominating southland transportation. If he could not halt the PE's rapid growth, Harriman's other option was to acquire an interest in the electric railway and share in its success. Such a move was not without precedent. Throughout the nation, many steam railroads had found it advantageous to acquire interurbans, with which the railroads once competed, and to integrate the trolleys' passenger service and freight lines with the larger steam network. Although interurbans were not necessarily more efficient than steam railroads, they were often run at four to six times the frequency and at one-half to two-thirds the fare of their steam rivals. Thus, trolleys had an advantage over steam railroads for short-haul traffic, and they had their greatest success carrying passengers and freight for distances from ten to forty miles between outlying towns and major cities.[13]

Although a rivalry later developed between these two railroad men, it was not the bitter clash of millionaire titans so often described in contemporary accounts. Relations between the two men, in fact, remained amicable. Huntington, at Harriman's request, had stayed on as SP vice-president after leaving San Francisco in 1901. After he resigned that post in 1904, he continued to serve as a director of the SP. Although each man was loath to give up any advantage, the men came to a joint ownership settlement in May 1903 on the electric railroads in southern California.

In the months leading up to the agreement, the two men had tried to negotiate a settlement via telegrams, regarding the regional transportation market. Huntington stayed in close touch with William Herrin, SP attorney and Harriman's representative, but reaching an agreement was difficult. The major point of contention was Harriman's desire to gain, and Huntington's steadfast unwillingness to grant, equal interest in the Pacific Electric Railway. Huntington wrote Harriman in January 1903: "Like to get trade closed up. Have made arrangements to use the San Gabriel Valley Road from Shorb [an SP station in Alhambra] to LA, but not until we own it. . . . Spoke to Herrin, but he made the same request you did, that is, to allow you as much stock as myself, and which I told you on several occasions, I could not comply with." [14]

Meanwhile, Harriman had been jockeying for a stronger negotiating position. He not only wanted to share the Los Angeles market with Huntington but also to surpass his rival. The Harriman-backed activities were designed to provide the SP with an entrée into the Los Angeles interurban field either by obtaining its own lines or by prodding Huntington to the bargaining table. Such machinations in the first months of 1903 included the SP's three-cent-fare franchise proposal, the West Sixth Street franchise battle, and the SP's purchase of the Hooks' Los Angeles streetcar companies, which by the end of 1902 accounted for about 15 percent of the local market.

Senator William A. Clark of Montana, organizer of the San Pedro, Los Angeles and Salt Lake Railroad, and the Union Pacific / Southern Pacific had been partners since July 1902, when the Clark syndicate and Harriman agreed to share equal ownership of the Salt Lake City to Los Angeles line.[15] Acting for the SP, Clark applied to the Los Angeles City Council for eighty-three miles of street railway franchises. If granted, these franchises would provide the SP with the basis for a substantial streetcar system. The proposed trolley was to operate over the entire eighty-three-mile area, providing service for a three-cent fare, with free transfers valid for transit over the whole system. This differed from the five-cent fare of the Los Angeles Railway and the PE trolley fares, which were based on several distinct fare regions that radiated from downtown Los Angeles in concentric circles. Travel within a zone cost five cents, and movement into each new PE zone cost an additional five cents. If the three-cent plan was approved, Clark and Harriman believed Huntington might make concessions to them rather than try to compete with a system designed to parallel many of his companies' streetcar routes at a fare that promised certain losses. Huntington's PE countered this proposal by introducing a $6.25 coupon book valid for five hundred miles of streetcar transit. Although this move did not lower prices to the SP's proposed three-cent fare level, the plan cut rates on many trolley routes almost in half.[16]

In June the council denied the SP's application. Its action was based on the belief that adequate trolley service could not possibly be provided with such a low fare.[17] Further, if passed, the franchise would cause streetcar companies to restrict services to the most heavily trafficked routes where high passenger volume might make up for the minimal fare. Not surprised by the rejection of the SP proposal, Huntington said:

> The people don't want three cent fares. They would rather pay five cent fares and get good service than three cent fares and get unsatisfactory service . . . [N]o company can operate an electric road as it should be operated and maintained for three cent fares. It cost us 4⅓ cents the past year to carry passengers on the LA Railway Co.[18]

While the council considered the three-cent fare franchise, Clark and Harriman attempted to acquire the Hooks' streetcar holdings, which the Huntington group was also trying to obtain. The Hooks owned the Los Angeles Traction Company, operating twenty-eight miles of track largely in the southwestern portion of the city; the twenty-mile interurban California Pacific, which was the only trolley operating between downtown and San Pedro; and the Los Angeles Pasadena Traction Company. The last firm owned no track or rolling stock but held the rights to build a line between Los Angeles and Pasadena. The Hooks also held a one-half interest in the Los Angeles, Ocean Park and Santa Monica

Railway. Bids for the railway property came from both the Huntington and Clark / Harriman groups, but it was the latter syndicate that obtained the property. On 14 April 1903, the Hooks and Clark reached an agreement; Clark and Harriman purchased the streetcar companies for $1.75 million.[19] The *Los Angeles Times* reported:

> Senator W. A. Clark has positively purchased the Traction Company as a nucleus for the Southern Pacific syndicate's operation in competition with H. E. Huntington for supremacy in the local street railway field. . . . The transfer is an important move in the campaign launched by the powerful transportation operators [Clark and Harriman] . . . to overcome H. E. Huntington and possess themselves of the street railway traffic in Los Angeles and Southern California.[20]

The final confrontation, prior to the Huntington / Harriman meeting and accord, occurred over the city's sale of the West Sixth Street franchise. Huntington had applied for this franchise, considered to be worth a maximum of ten thousand dollars, with the idea of laying track from downtown to Hollywood.[21] On 3 May 1903, the franchise auction took place, and the bidding came from three camps—the Huntington group, the Hooks, and Harriman, who was represented by George G. Johnson, a local real estate man. The Hooks, having just sold out their existing properties to the Clark / Harriman group, hoped to reenter the market in another area of town. The opening bid was twenty-five hundred dollars, but the price quickly jumped to unrealistically high levels. The auction became a test of wills between Huntington and Harriman. Huntington's top offer was $100,000; Harriman's bid of $110,000 won the franchise.[22]

The sale of the Sixth Street franchise and the exorbitant amount Harriman was willing to pay for it led Huntington to believe that he had to bargain with the SP magnate. The next day, the two men met in San Francisco. Rather than engaging in a potentially ruinous streetcar competition with Harriman, whose financial resources exceeded his own, Huntington was willing to compromise. Three days later, an agreement was signed between the Huntington syndicate and Harriman. The accord called for the consolidation of the PE property and the SP's recently acquired street railways. Under its terms, the Huntington group's Los Angeles Land Company received the SP's San Gabriel Valley Rapid Transit Railway and track between Alameda, Los Angeles, and San Pedro streets. Harriman then agreed to transfer the Hooks' railroads and the Sixth Street franchise to the PE. In return, he was granted 40.3

percent of PE stock, an amount equal to Huntington's share. The May bargain shuffled PE ownership; Huntington and Harriman together held over 80 percent, with Hellman, Borel, and DeGuigne retaining a minority position. The owners of the PE, who now included Harriman, paid the remaining $1.5 million that was due the Hooks for the streetcar companies; they then reimbursed the SP for the $110,000 it had paid for the Sixth Street franchise and the $250,000 down payment it had made for the Hook properties. Each stockholder paid in proportion to his percentage of ownership in the Pacific Electric.[23]

Huntington desired continued PE expansion. From March 1902 to November 1903, the rapid growth of the interurban had consumed $8.4 million, which had become available through the issuance of bonds.[24] Further PE extensions required more cash, but a depressed bond market in California and New York made the sale of additional bonds difficult. Harriman backed the building program. Although he had initially acquired stock in the PE under his own name, Harriman had been operating for the SP, and in August the property was officially transferred to the Southern Pacific. But Hellman, Borel, and DeGuigne lacked Huntington's enthusiasm for continued expansion without the sale of new bonds. In June 1903 they asked that no new construction be considered until the depressed condition of the money market had changed, but Huntington brushed the suggestion aside. He told Hellman that pursuant to an agreement with Harriman, he had no intention of stopping "in the middle of the stream."[25]

Still hoping to build a vast trolley network, on 6 June 1903 Huntington incorporated another new company, the Los Angeles Inter-Urban (LAIU) Railway. Its articles of incorporation called for construction and operation of 350 miles of track with lines to La Habra, Redlands, and Riverside and branches to Colton and San Bernardino. Other proposed roads included rails reaching Santa Ana, Newport, and the San Fernando Valley. The LAIU was authorized to issue $10 million in bonds and was capitalized at $10 million. Like the PE, the first stock subscription was for the minimum required by California law to begin operations, $1,000 per mile of planned track, or $350,000.

Initially wholly owned by Huntington and independent of the Pacific Electric, the LAIU was Huntington's attempt to bypass his obdurate partners, who grudgingly agreed to assessments allowing electric railway construction to continue.[26] However, the LAIU soon became an appendage of the PE. The depressed bond market in New York and California made the sale of securities undesirable, and Huntington apparently made an agreement with the other PE shareholders that they would advance cash for the construction of rail lines and be compensated in a similar amount of LAIU 5 percent bonds. Funds thus received were used to begin construction of LAIU lines as well as continue building PE lines. The LAIU became, in essence, a construction arm for the growing interurban system. From 1903 to 1907, in return for LAIU bonds, Huntington and Harriman together provided the trolley company with $7.2 million. Before they sold their PE stock in December 1904, Hellman, Borel, and DeGuigne's combined contribution totaled $1 million. Although the LAIU operated its own rolling stock and maintained a semblance of a separate identity, it was intimately linked with the PE from its inception; by 1905 the officers of the two companies were identical.[27]

Because Huntington had retained many interurban lines in his own name, he was able to transfer these holdings to the LAIU, which he originally completely controlled, rather than to the PE, which he shared with Harriman. The LAIU completed the building of the PE's Whittier and San Pedro lines. Then, in March 1904, the LAIU absorbed the Los Angeles Traction Company and its subsidiaries. The growing trolley firm also acquired and finished constructing the Los Angeles and Glendale Railway. In June the LAIU assumed control of two more Huntington-owned roads, the Riverside and Arlington Railway and the Santa Ana and Orange Motor Railway.[28]

In 1904 the PE and LAIU built rail extensions to Huntington Beach and began building to Covina. Plans for additional tracks to Newport Beach, Balboa, and Santa Ana were also prepared. This construction was paid for by stockholder assessments. Although determined to continue building, even Huntington began feeling the financial pinch. He had sacrificed many opportunities to keep his personal funds flowing to the railroad. In April of that year, he wrote Patton: "I am throwing over my shoulder almost daily good investments simply for the reason that I am trying to have fewer investments instead of more. As you know, it is taking a great deal of money to carry on our railroad project, and I need all the money I can spare for the work."[29]

In November 1904, Huntington sent a letter to all PE shareholders stating that $250,000 was necessary to carry out LAIU construction and that each stockholder was required to pay the amount proportionate to his percentage of PE stock. Harriman's and Huntington's shares were identical: each paid $101,000, and the minority owners were obligated for a total of $48,000. Convinced that Huntington's ambition could not be contained, they were no longer willing to support any new rail projects. The PE and the LAIU were not paying dividends and seemed to be a tool for Huntington's land development companies. The three financiers were ready to quit the Pacific Electric altogether. Speaking for the group, Hellman wrote Huntington:

> You know very well that I am opposed to continued expenditures of money on these railways, but my views on this matter have been entirely ignored. I have concluded that I will make no further advances as a stockholder except under the compulsion of regular proceedings by way of an assessment. . . . I do not wish to be an obstructionist; I am willing to sell my Pacific Electric Ry CO. stock and bonds of the Inter-Urban Company, which represent advances I have made to you and Mr. Harriman at a fair price.[30]

According to the May 1903 agreement, which made the SP an equal partner to Huntington in the Pacific Electric, any PE shareholder wishing to sell an interest had to first offer it to the existing owners, giving them the option to divide the stock among themselves in proportion to their current ownership in the company. On 7 December 1904, Hellman, Borel, and DeGuigne agreed to sell their entire interest in the PE—19,346.68 shares of PE stock and $995,480 worth of LAIU bonds—for $1.2 million. One-half of their holdings were purchased by Huntington and one-half by Harriman, acting for the SP.[31] All the PE's capital stock was equally shared by Huntington and the Southern Pacific. Free of the interurban, Hellman, Borel, and DeGuigne retained their interest in the Los Angeles Railway, the downtown system, because they expected that soon it would begin paying dividends.

Under the expansive-minded Huntington, the Pacific Electric and Los Angeles Inter-Urban extended their rails and roadbeds into new areas. An equal partner in the PE, the Southern Pacific, led by Harriman, saw the advantages of an enlarged trolley system that could be integrated into its existing steam railway network, and the SP backed Huntington's building program. The *Los Angeles Examiner* commented: "Not withstanding his large interests in the Pacific Electric . . . Mr. Harriman has never been able to prevent H. E. Huntington from extending his lines as best suited his purpose."[32] By 1905, tracks reached Newport Beach and Santa Ana. In 1906 a branch was added to the Newport line connecting it to

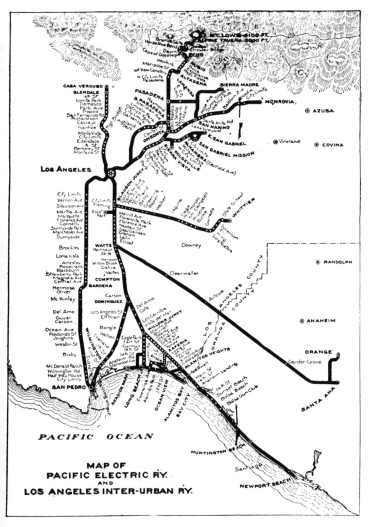

From the

Mountains

to the

Sea

TROLLEY

TRIPS

Through all this gorgeous and hustling southland, over perfect roadbeds in luxurious cars, at the speed of electricity.

Pacific
Electric
Railway

The Pacific Electric Railway and the Los Angeles Inter-Urban Railway system in 1905. Courtesy of the Huntington Library

Balboa. Midway through that year, the combined track of the two companies stretched over 449 miles of southern California; the LAIU operated 252 miles of track, and the PE held 197 miles. A line to Sierra Madre and an extension to the Oak Knoll section of Pasadena were completed in late 1906.

If the SP were to consider blocking construction of an interurban route, the line to Covina was the most likely candidate because it would parallel SP tracks and travel through a heavily trafficked corridor. Yet all Harriman said regarding this connection was: "All right, Huntington, if you want to build it, go ahead."[33] Covina was reached in 1907, and tracks were laid from Monrovia to Glendora that same year. By February 1908, the LAIU had increased its track mileage to 311 miles, and the PE operated 212 miles.[34]

Although Harriman was apparently willing to support his partner's interurban expansion program within the Los Angeles basin, when Huntington attempted to push into San Diego County, Harriman nixed the plan. The huge project involved the development of real estate in San Diego County—with transportation provided by a rail line from Los Angeles to San Diego and energy supplied by a locally built electric power plant.

San Diego County's population rose from 35,100 in 1900 to 61,700 in 1910. Huntington planned to take advantage of this expansion by extending his PE line from Santa Ana southward along the coast through thousands of acres that were to be acquired by a Huntington syndicate. Once in San Diego, it was proposed, the PE line would turn east and run to the fertile Imperial Valley. Power for this rail line as well as for the new homes was to be furnished by harnessing the San Luis Rey River at Warner's ranch in northeastern San Diego County.

In 1905 Pacific Light and Power purchased the forty-five-thousand-acre Warner's ranch and the riparian rights of the San Luis Rey River in order to develop hydroelectric power. Huntington and Kerckhoff, in association with Colonel Ed Fletcher, a San Diego developer, and Los Angeles businessmen C. A. Canfield and H. W. Keller, formed the South Coast Land Company and proceeded to purchase vast stretches of land from Oceanside to Del Mar. Having obtained land through which the PE could lay track, Huntington had Kerckhoff and Keller, with the assistance of Fletcher, obtain a franchise from the San Diego City Council that granted rights to construct a railway to extend from Del Mar to San Diego.[35]

Holding land, a rail franchise, and the right to build a hydroelectric plant, the Huntington group appeared ready to begin development. The Hayes Land Company, owners of property in Oceanside, made use of Huntington's name and his plans in the introduction of their subdivision advertisement:

Henry E. Huntington has purchased within the last two years over $2 million worth of property. The South Coast Land Company, represented by millionaires Keller and Kerckhoff, who are now building a railroad from San Diego to Los Angeles, have invested over $2 million. . . . Huntington now owns the entire riparian rights to bring his sytem of car service from Los Angeles to San Diego.[36]

But the key to the project, the rail extension from Santa Ana to San Diego, was vetoed by Harriman because it conflicted with the SP's large steam railroad interests in the area. From 1901 until his death in 1909, Harriman had been knitting together a vast railroad network. By 1902, his western railway empire included the Union Pacific (UP); the Southern Pacific; and a half-interest in the San Pedro, Los Angeles and Salt Lake Railroad. In fact, Harriman's only major rival in the southwest was the Atchison, Topeka and Santa Fe Railway (AT&SF).

To ease, if not end, the competition with the Santa Fe in the southwest, Harriman sought an understanding with the rival railway. When no cooperation was forthcoming, Harriman and a group of financiers, including Henry Frick, Otto Kahn, and Henry Rogers, purchased $30 million worth of Santa Fe stock in 1904. Owning about 14 percent of the Santa Fe, Harriman placed Frick and Rogers, who already served on the UP directorate, on the Santa Fe's board of directors. Because of his links to the Santa Fe, Harriman worked out a plan of compromise and cooperation between the SP/UP and the AT&SF. The agreements included an important pooling arrangement between the Harriman lines and the Santa Fe for the shipment of California's citrus crop. This accord eliminated the competition over citrus traffic. Thus, by 1906, Harriman had achieved a harmonious relationship between the two railroads, and he and his associates sold their Santa Fe stock.[37]

Having only recently settled the regional railroad rivalry, Harriman did not want to upset the delicate balance by participating in the construction of an electric line into the San Diego area, where the Santa Fe had a major investment. If the PE built a trolley line from Los Angeles to San Diego, it would compete for passenger traffic with the Santa Fe's existing line between the two cities. In addition, to attract freight as well as passengers, Huntington's group had proposed a branch of the PE's line to run from the San Diego coast eastward to the Imperial Valley. This planned track ran counter to the Harriman-backed plan for a steam line, the San

Diego and Arizona (SD&A) Railroad, which was to run through the same area. Harriman had become involved in the SD&A as a defensive move to keep this railroad from reaching its proposed destination of Yuma, which would give the city of San Diego a direct transcontinental rail linkage. All traffic out of San Diego had to travel the circuitous route north along the coast to Santa Ana and then east to San Bernardino. From there, shipments could be carried eastward over the SP line through Yuma or via the AT&SF route through Needles. If the San Diego to Yuma connection were made, the traffic on SP's southern transcontinental line running from Arizona northwest to Los Angeles would face competition from the proposed SD&A line from Yuma to San Diego. To avoid the threat of competition and disharmony because of a rivalry along the southern coast of the state, Harriman quashed the PE's plans to build to San Diego.[38] In addition to Harriman's opposition, Huntington also faced a fight with John D. Spreckels, a wealthy San Diego businessman who controlled much of the city's streetcar network and did not relish the Los Angeles trolley entrepreneur entering the area.[39]

Confronted with these obstacles, Huntington scrapped the whole San Diego project. The trolley line was never built; Huntington sold his interest in the South Coast Land Company; and in 1911 the PL&P sold Warner's ranch and the riparian rights to the San Luis Rey River to developer William G. Henshaw.[40]

With the exception of his failed San Diego scheme, Huntington directed where interurban lines were built. As had occurred earlier, towns reached by trolley lines grew rapidly. Santa Ana, for example, connected to Los Angeles by electric railway in 1905, saw its population rise from forty-nine hundred in 1900 to eighty-four hundred in 1910. Besides encouraging such expansion in existing cities, interurban routes also provided fertile ground along which new cities incorporated. In fact, because these transportation lines were viewed as essential to a community's success, all seventeen cities incorporated in Los Angeles County during the first decade of the twentieth century were located on trolley routes.[41]

Huntington's interurban system was praised for its size and quality. The Los Angeles Herald quoted "a New Yorker not prone to enthusiasm" as saying that

> the people in the east do not know what a first-class electric railroad is. The Metropolitan system in New York is a go-cart compared with the Huntington system in Southern California. . . . While putting down the

most enduring kind of roadbed, laying the heaviest of steel rails with welded joints, supplying the largest and most comfortable electric cars, and employing the best paid labor, Mr. Huntington has not forgotten that which appeals to the eye.[42]

Despite these accolades, the PE and LAIU were not profitable. Because many of Huntington's interurban lines were built ahead of demand and frequently passed through regions just beginning to grow, their earnings were generally poor. Between 1903 and 1907, the PE's most profitable year was 1905, when the company's net earnings were $90,711; in the LAIU's best year, 1906, the firm lost $93,032. However, when people later moved into these developing areas, Huntington was among those willing to sell them real estate, and the profits from the Huntington Land and Improvement Company made up for the poor earnings of the interurbans. The net earnings of HL&I, derived largely from land rentals and sales, increased from $151,000 in 1905 to $402,000 in 1907. The land company's return on investment rose from 4.8 percent in 1905 to 12 percent in 1907.[43]

Unlike his interurbans, Huntington's Los Angeles Railway, operating largely within the city limits, was profitable. This firm posted net earnings of $550,990 in 1904, $483,990 in 1905, $580,657 in 1906, and $370,264 in 1907; the railway's average return on investment for these four years was 7.8 percent.[44] Hellman, Borel, and DeGuigne had kept their 45 percent interest in the Los Angeles Railway, hoping this company, which had not yet declared dividends, would not require cash advances and would soon start returning profits back to the shareholders. Like the PE, the LARY continued to expand but on a much smaller scale. In 1903, it added eighteen miles of track.

On 8 January 1904, John Muir, the Los Angeles Railway's general manager, died. Huntington's twenty-eight-year-old son, Howard, who had been the assistant to general manager Epes Randolph on the PE, was given the post. On 15 January, Howard wrote his grandmother: "Much to my surprise, I was selected GM of LARY Co. I think I am taking up some of the detail work that father was attending to during Mr. Muir's illness, and I hope to be able to take more of the load off father's shoulders as time goes on."[45]

Howard Huntington served as the general manager from 1904 to 1911, when a mental breakdown forced him to curtail his activities. Although he retained the title until 1918, most of his work was taken over by the assistant general manager. Lacking the business skills of his father, Howard was an only adequate administrator. Unable to deal with complex situations, such as organizing the sharing of facilities between the PE and the Los Angeles Railway, Howard referred complicated matters to his father. Henry's reply to one of Howard's 1907 letters was typical; he told his son, who faced an unresolvable problem, to wait until he had arrived in southern California, when he would solve it.[46]

In spite of his mediocre managerial abilities, Howard carried out his father's expansion plans. New Los Angeles Railway routes were built to population centers developing northeast, south, and west of the central downtown area. A line from downtown to Garvanza (Highland Park) opened for service in May 1904. The Griffith Avenue line, several blocks east of the present campus of the University of Southern California, was extended south and reached Vernon Avenue by October 1905. Earlier that same year, in March, the company built northwest toward the growing residential section of Hollywood, using a private right-of-way from present-day Lafayette Park to Bimini Place.[47]

The laying of rails out of the downtown area was expensive. Although profits were reinvested in the company, the extensions frequently required more financing. The Los Angeles Railway often borrowed from commercial banks or the Huntington Land and Improvement Company. Hellman questioned the wisdom of making capital investments financed through short-term loans. In May 1904, he told Howard Huntington that he did not want the railroad to borrow any more money for construction. Hellman wanted to slow the growth of the system to coincide with the availability of funds generated from internal operations. Howard reported Hellman's views to his father; the elder Huntington, who considered the property his own and its policy his domain, angrily dashed off a note to Hellman:

> I hope that hereafter in all matters that pertain to the management of the property, you will take the matter up with me instead of with subordinates [Howard Huntington]. . . . There can be but one head in the management of the property, although of course I shall always be very glad to consult with yourself, Mr. DeGuigne, and Mr. Borel . . . but I think I understand the needs of the property and what is essential better than anyone else.[48]

With a tight grip on the company, Huntington added to this streetcar network during the next two years. A route to Eagle Rock, as well as the Cummings Street line extension southeast from the downtown core to Euclid and Indiana Street, were completed in 1906. The following year, Huntington extended the Garvanza line with two branches, one on York Boulevard and the other on North Figueroa Street. Later in 1907, the West Ninth Street line was built down Tenth Street from Vermont to Grammercy. Through this building program, the Los Angeles Railway, operating within a radius of eight miles of the city's center, nearly doubled in size, expanding from 99.6 miles of track in January 1903 to 180.1 miles in January 1908.[49]

The Los Angeles Railway's failure to declare dividends finally drove Hellman, Borel, and DeGuigne completely from the street-car magnate's fold. In January 1907, the *Pasadena Star News* and the *Los Angeles Evening News* reported that Harriman and the SP had purchased the three financiers' 45 percent interest in the Los Angeles Railway. In February, the former owners retired from the company's directorate and were replaced by W. F. Herrin, J. E. Foulds, and Hellman's son, I. W. Hellman, Jr.[50]

By 1907, Huntington and the Southern Pacific had become partners in the PE, the LAIU, and the LARY. Although each saw the Los Angeles Railway as primarily a downtown passenger transit system, Huntington and Harriman had different views on the electric interurbans. Because each partner wished to use the interurbans for his own purpose and each desired to dominate the southland's transit market, Huntington and the SP did not consolidate all their streetcar operations. To Huntington, the interurbans' main purpose was to promote the sale of his real estate. For Harriman, the trolleys were part of the larger Southern Pacific system and were to be operated mainly as transportation companies. The SP's aim was to establish a monopolistic, or at least a tight oligopolistic, market.

In July 1905, Huntington, operating alone, acquired the Los Angeles and Redondo Railway by purchasing all the outstanding stock, 3,770 shares, and assuming the bonded indebtedness of $500,000 from local railroader Leman Thomas Garnsey. The former owner stayed on as president and general manager of the railway. In 1907 he supervised 57.5 miles of track, including two lines running from Los Angeles to Redondo.[51] Huntington had bought and then operated this railway as part of his larger development plans for the subdivision and sale of property in Redondo.

Still desirous of obtaining trolley lines to unify electric and steam service in the area and prompted by Huntington's acquisition

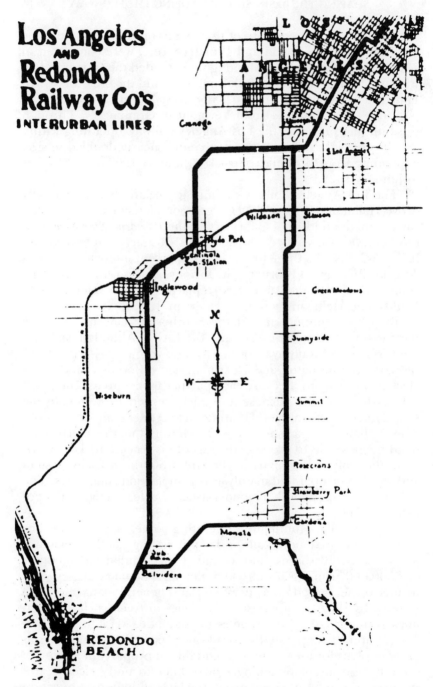

The Los Angeles and Redondo Railway, c. 1905. Source: *P. E. Topics* I (June 1906): 23

The Los Angeles Pacific Railway, c. 1906. Source: William A. Myers and Ira L. Swett, *Trolleys to the Surf: The Story of the Los Angeles Pacific Railway* (Glendale, Cal.: Interurbans Publications, 1976), 156. Courtesy of Interurbans Press

of the Los Angeles and Redondo, Harriman moved to obtain the only remaining interurban in the entire region still independent of Huntington. In 1906 he negotiated with the Los Angeles Pacific's (LAP) owners, Moses Sherman and E. P. Clark, for their railway. The LAP held approximately 180 miles of track and operated in the western section of the county, including the popular areas of Hollywood, Santa Monica, Venice, Playa del Rey, and Redondo. By March 1906, an agreement was reached, and Harriman paid a reported $6 million to the line's owners, securing a controlling interest in the company for the Southern Pacific.[52]

Huntington devoted vast amounts of time and money to his trolley companies because he saw them as essential to his development of real estate. Largely unhampered by land-use or zoning regulations, which did not become effective until the 1920s, Huntington freely chose the areas he developed as well as the subsequent form of each development.[53] As his trolleys were laying out the scope and shape of greater Los Angeles, his land firms were designing many of the region's communities. A large-scale subdivider, Huntington was involved in a myriad of land deals from 1903 to 1907, but several major real estate projects, each in a different part of the southland, illustrate his activities.

Sometimes Huntington designed communities with distinct classes of people in mind. Various controls and deed restrictions— including racial exclusion, lot size and price, and the setting of minimum construction costs—were used to determine the makeup of a subdivision's residents.[54] Three of his projects, all northeast of downtown Los Angeles—Oak Knoll, Oneonta Park, and Dolgeville—are representative of subdivisions planned for particular socioeconomic groups.

For the wealthy, Huntington built the Oak Knoll subdivision, which today is a fashionable area split between Pasadena and San Marino. Initially established in the 1880s, the tract opened when the real estate boom of the decade had subsided, and the development languished. In December 1905, Huntington and brokers William Staats and A. Kingsley Macomber formed the Oak Knoll Company and purchased the subdivision for $300,000.[55]

The winding roads and landscaping begun earlier were completed; a Huntington interurban line was extended to the property; and, to introduce the wealthy potential residents to the development, several acres were reserved for the construction of a luxury hotel, the Wentworth. Huntington opened the prestigious subdivision in 1906. Only Caucasians were to be allowed and Oak Knoll was reserved for single-family residences. Lots varied in size from one to ten acres; in price from $5,000 to $20,000; and, depending on size and location, minimum construction costs ranged from $6,000 to $15,000.[56]

Hailed as one of the most exclusive subdivisions in the West, the Oak Knoll tract sold well through the remainder of 1906. The financial panic of 1907 had a negative impact on sales, however, and Staats closed the subdivision's sales office. The partially completed Hotel Wentworth opened in February 1907; because of cost overruns, it soon encountered financial troubles, and less than six months later it was declared insolvent and closed.

Toward the end of 1909, lot sales in nearby residential areas began picking up, and the Staats's Oak Knoll sales office was reopened on 6 November. Three weeks later, Huntington purchased the ninety-three-acre Oak Grove tract between Oak Knoll to the west and his San Marino Ranch to the east.[57] The linkage of Huntington's name with the area encouraged purchases of property.

After the Oak Knoll lots began selling again, Huntington gave the tract another boost in 1912. Much like William Ralston, who had saved a faltering real estate subdivision by building the luxurious Palace Hotel in San Francisco, Huntington purchased the Hotel Wentworth and announced that Myron Hunt, the architect who had built Huntington's San Marino home, would double the building's guest capacity by adding two stories. With this demonstration of confidence in the area, Huntington assured the success of the Oak Knoll subdivision.[58]

West of the elite Oak Knoll, Huntington Land and Improvement laid out Oneonta Park—today an upper-middle-class section of South Pasadena—as a community for the middle classes. Connected to downtown Los Angeles by the PE, this subdivision consisted largely of one-third and one-half acre lots. Buildings could only be constructed for single-family residential use, and the homes' minimum worth was set at $3,500.[59]

Huntington also developed tracts of land for those of more modest means. In the present-day city of Alhambra, ten miles east of downtown Los Angeles, he established a model industrial town. This subdivision was linked to the Alfred Dolge Manufacturing Company, the felt venture Huntington had established in 1903 in an attempt to lure industry to southern California. Named Dolgeville, the town was laid out in a gridiron pattern with modest-sized, single-family residential lots selling from three hundred dollars to four hundred dollars each. The felt business was not very successful, but it did attract several other industries to Dolgeville, and as Huntington had planned, many of the homesites were purchased by employees of the town's manufacturing plants.[60]

Although Huntington's largest landholdings were in the San Gabriel Valley, his most successful real estate venture was in Redondo Beach. Incorporated in 1892 and situated along the southwest coast of Los Angeles County, Redondo Beach was originally a coastal development established by the firm of Vail and Freeman during the land boom of 1887. After the boom ended in 1889, the developers sold their interests in the undeveloped areas of the community to John C. Ainsworth and Robert R. Thompson of Oregon. The new owners incorporated three associated companies to develop the property: the Redondo Hotel Company, the Redondo Improvement Company, and the Los Angeles and Redondo Railway. The last was sold to Leman Garnsey in 1894.[61]

On 7 July 1905, Huntington announced his purchase of the Redondo Improvement Company, which owned 90 percent of the property in Redondo Beach, and his plans to spend millions on developing the area. Four days later, he obtained the Los Angeles and Redondo Railway. The association of Huntington's name with the coastal town and his expressed confidence in Redondo Beach set off a new speculative land boom lasting about two weeks. On 20 July the *Los Angeles Times* reported: "A couple of weeks ago . . . the magic name of Huntington awoke this dreamer by the sea and for several days there was enacted the wildest schemes of mad speculation by feverish and frenzied speculators. . . . With characteristic enterprise and liberal outlays of capital, Mr. Huntington will doubtless create here one of the finest resorts on the entire Pacific Coast." Then, explaining one of the reasons for the excitement in Redondo, the *Times* continued: "Mr. Huntington is already double tracking the railroad [the Los Angeles and Redondo] and maintaining the wise policy of not advancing the price of lots [approximately ninety dollars each] from his original offering."[62]

A buying frenzy ensued in which property often changed hands several times a day, and more than one hundred real estate offices set up shop on Front Street, some doing business out of hastily erected tents. As a result of the rash speculation, Huntington sold approximately $3 million of Redondo Beach property and almost immediately recouped his initial outlay for the real estate and the railway.[63] In the midst of the craze over the Redondo project, Burke Holladay, Huntington's brother-in-law, wrote Harriet Huntington:

> Redondo has been a dead town. . . . The hotel never paid. . . . The name Redondo made a Los Angeles capitalist shy like a horse at an auto. But on Friday last, it came out that Mr. H. E. Huntington had bought the entire townsite of Redondo from the Redondo Land Co. and that he would offer it for sale. Oh! What a change in the twinkling of an eye. Immediately the people of Los Angeles rushed in droves to Redondo— to buy, buy, buy. . . . [64]

By the end of July, the boom had subsided, but Huntington continued to pour money into Redondo Beach. By 1907, a three-story pavilion, which housed a giant ballroom, a restaurant, and a theater, had been completed, and in 1909 Huntington erected the largest indoor salt-water plunge in the world. Because the Pacific Ocean was too cold for comfortable swimming most of the year, the plunge, opened every day of the year, provided three pools with heated water and more than one thousand small dressing rooms and steam and Turkish baths, and could accommodate two thousand bathers at one time. The success of Huntington's Redondo Beach development was reflected in the city's expanding population: the number of residents rose from the 1890 figure of 668 to 855 in 1900; it then increased to 2,935 in 1910 and was 4,900 by 1920.[65]

Besides designing homogeneous communities or revitalizing areas like Redondo Beach, Huntington also participated in speculative large-scale land development projects. Unlike Huntington's other land ventures, one involved a rare collaboration with others of the Los Angeles business community and did not immediately include electric railways.

In November 1904, a group of prominent Los Angeles businessmen—including Huntington; Harriman; Kerckhoff; L. C. Brand, a developer of Glendale, a Los Angeles suburb; and Joseph Sartori, president of Security Trust and Savings Bank—purchased the sixteen-thousand-acre Porter ranch in the San Fernando Valley. Each of the ten stockholders received a one-tenth interest in the firm. Forming the San Fernando Mission Land Company, the developers first took an option on the property on 28 November 1904 and then assumed full control on 23 March 1905.[66]

Because it was widely known that Huntington preferred working "quietly and alone," the *Los Angeles Examiner* observed: "The mystery of the enterprise [the San Fernando Mission Land Company] is how it happened that Messrs. Huntington and Harriman, who let no one into their land purchasing schemes, but bought up everything for themselves, consented to let eight others in on the 'ground floor' so to speak."[67]

Considered a long-term investment, the purchase of Porter ranch was predicated on the belief that the city government would build an aqueduct at some future date and bring water from the Sierras to the southland. If such a project were undertaken, the arid San Fernando Valley would be transformed into a well-watered plain ripe for subdivision. A $23 million bond issue to finance the aqueduct was passed by Los Angeles voters in June 1907, and water from the Owens Valley reached Los Angeles in 1913. In this context, Huntington's decision to work with others in the project becomes clearer. He joined the nine other syndicate members, all major powers of the Los Angeles business community, because his participation could further his private interests. Subdivision in the San Fernando Valley would stimulate expansion and lead to an increasing population in the southland. Since this venture seemed likely to encourage general growth in southern California, Huntington would surely benefit.[68]

In 1909, Harry Chandler, general manager of the *Los Angeles Times*, who was a member of the earlier land syndicate, took an option on 47,400 additional acres of San Fernando Valley land. A year later, Chandler and thirty-nine other investors formed the Los Angeles Suburban Homes Company and purchased the property. In 1911, the new company prepared a large section of land for subdivision, and the PE began construction of an interurban line to the valley. Although the syndicate's projects proved very profitable, Huntington began to withdraw from some business interests and in June 1912 received $130,000 for his one-tenth share of the San Fernando Mission Land Company, for which he had originally paid $15,000.[69]

Often working with his real estate ventures, the Huntington-controlled Pacific Light and Power followed a strategy of rapid growth. As Huntington explained to Kerckhoff in July 1904, in some cases, expansion should precede demand:

> We cannot afford to lag behind in the procession and should rather keep always a little ahead of it [demand for power]. If we need more power, by all means, let us contract for it; for our aim should always be to give the very best service we can *and to give better service than anybody else does.* While this may cost money in the beginning, it will be very profitable in the end.[70]

Such expansion through construction and acquisition was expensive, and financing was constantly a problem. The PL&P's major project was the construction of a hydroelectric power station near Kernville on the Kern River, 120 miles northeast of Los Angeles in the Sierra Nevada Mountains. One of the largest power-generating sites undertaken in the country up to that time, this facility's completion was hampered by more than funding. In April 1903, work on the plant, which had only recently begun, was tied up by a lawsuit brought against the PL&P by two competing land companies, the Miller and Lux and Kern River firms. The former, established by Henry Miller and Charles Lux in the mid-nineteenth century, held a large land empire in the San Joaquin Valley and riparian rights on many parts of the San Joaquin and Kern rivers. The latter company owned property in the Kern River Valley.

The lawsuit charged that the PL&P's construction of a canal necessary to divert water to the hydroelectric plant would alter the normal flow of the Kern River and its flood waters, which annually fertilized and restored the valley's farmland. The Miller and Lux / Kern coalition asked for a perpetual injunction to disallow the diversion of water via the canal. Henry O'Melveny, attorney and stockholder of the PL&P, negotiated a settlement with the land companies in July 1904. The PL&P purchased water rights, promised to refrain from using water for irrigation purposes, and agreed to make the diversion canal watertight so that seepage would not affect the quality or quantity of the Kern River flow.[71]

The conflict with the central California land companies slowed the Kern power project, and the eventual settlement called for a much more expensive cement canal. However, Huntington conveyed his pleasure about the outcome to O'Melveny: "I think from what you say that we have made a very good trade with Miller, Lux, and Tevis [representing the Kern River Land Company]. Certainly having clear title is worth a great deal to us."[72]

The new, more stringent building requirements for the canal increased the PL&P's need for cash. In 1902 and 1903, attempts to sell Pacific Light and Power bonds to outside investors had not been successful. The stockholders ended up buying many of the bonds to provide funds for the construction costs; they hoped to resell them later on the open market when conditions improved. In January 1903, Huntington arranged for the cash-rich Los Angeles Railway, the company that held Huntington's PL&P stock, to purchase two hundred PL&P bonds, providing $200,000.

Then, on 23 July, Kerckhoff wrote Huntington of DeGuigne's suggestion to assess the stockholders one dollar per share for six consecutive months to raise the $600,000 required to complete the project. This suggestion came before the three minority owners expressed doubts about the constant need for funds to finance Huntington's various projects. But the assessment was not acted upon immediately. Soon afterward, Kerckhoff acknowledged a Huntington note telling him that the LARY would take $50,000 more of PL&P bonds; this purchase, when combined with the $75,000 in bonds Kerckhoff had taken, allowed the Kern River project to proceed. As they had done earlier, the major shareholders took the bonds with the understanding that they could later resell the securities so long as they did not dump them at less than par value. Such action provided PL&P with the cash necessary without the need for stock assessments through 1903.[73]

By July 1904, the Kern power station had already cost $1.8

million, but it was still not ready to operate. With the additional expense of the lined canal plus cost overruns, the plant required another $500,000 for completion. Kerckhoff believed the earlier idea about assessing the stockholders was now the best way to proceed. Huntington approved DeGuigne's original plan, and Hellman and Borel consented to the assessments. With the money thus secured, the Kern River project went forward. In December 1905, the plant commenced operations, supplying the Huntington companies, as well as parts of Los Angeles, with electricity.[74]

Although Kern River was the PL&P's largest project, the company also sought to expand by acquiring other power firms. Between the end of 1903 and 1907, PL&P added the Mentone Power Company, owner of a hydroelectric plant north of Redlands, and the Riverside Power Company. The former was originally a Kerckhoff / Balch venture before its merger with the larger Pacific Light and Power. With this enlarged generating capacity, PL&P sold approximately 90 percent of its electricity to commercial users, largely Huntington's railroads. It also provided current for lighting and other residential use in the southern and northeastern portions of Los Angeles County.[75]

After the Kern project was completed, Huntington and Kerckhoff made plans for another power plant. In December 1906, in conjunction with Huntington's real estate developments in the area, PL&P began constructing a fifteen-thousand-kilowatt steam plant at Redondo Beach, which was completed in March 1908. By that date it was clear that PL&P's expansion program was paying off: the company's net earnings in 1906 were $359,662 and in 1907 were $413,143.[76]

As the PL&P electrical generating capacity was growing, Huntington expanded his other public utility business, water distribution. His San Gabriel Wine Company already owned the Alhambra Addition Water Company, a small firm providing water to parts of the San Gabriel area. In September 1907, Huntington incorporated the much larger San Gabriel Valley Water Company (SGVW). Capitalized at $2.5 million, all its stock was held by the Huntington Land and Improvement Company. Often operated in tandem with HL&I, SGVW provided water to many of the newly opened subdivisions. In February 1908, Huntington consolidated his holdings by transferring all the property of the Alhambra Addition Water Company to the SGVW.[77]

To oversee the San Gabriel Valley Water Company, Huntington brought in George C. Ward, who had worked as chief engineer on Collis Huntington's Raquette Lake Railroad. Remembering the words of his uncle, "Stick to Ward; you can trust him," Huntington had hired Ward in 1902 as the superintendent of his London Water Works in Washington Court House, Ohio. With a promise of a better job, Huntington lured Ward to California in 1905. Prior to heading SGVW, Ward had served Huntington in several other capacities. Initially brought out to southern California as the assistant general manager of HL&I, Ward also worked for Huntington's street railways purchasing land and rights-of-way. Later, in 1910, Ward succeeded Patton as general manager of HL&I.[78]

From 1903 to 1907, Huntington labored to expand the southland's urban economy by extending his business triad. With his spreading operations, he molded the basin. Because the city and county lacked regulations or commissions overseeing land use and dictating how or where development should take place, Huntington became the metropolitan planner of greater Los Angeles. His trolleys diffused the population and nurtured the growth of many suburban communities, his land firms rapidly transformed rural landscape into a variety of subdivisions, and his power firm provided electricity for the growing region.

Although the Los Angeles Railway operated as a passenger-carrying transit system in the downtown area, the interurban PE was used primarily to promote land developments. Because Huntington wished to dominate the region's transportation market, the PE was rapidly expanded, but because of the area's sparse population, it was never profitable. The Los Angeles Railway, on the other hand, was profitable, but because Huntington reinvested all the profits back into the company, the LARY did not declare any dividends during this period. This lack of a return on investment combined with the PE's constant need for funds, finally drove Hellman, Borel, and DeGuigne to withdraw from both street railroad companies.

The three junior partners were supplanted by the SP, which, led by Harriman, pursued the goal of monopolizing the transportation market within southern California by building a unified steam and electric railway system. Concerned about the competition for passengers and freight provided by the PE, the SP acquired a half-interest in the interurban to control the trolley company's growth and make use of its extensive network of standard-gauge electric lines. Because it wanted to dominate the regional transit market, the SP generally approved of Huntington's rapid interurban expansion program within the Los Angeles basin. However, when it was detrimental to the SP railroad system, such as the proposed trolley route to San Diego, the plan was blocked by Harriman.

Attempting to sidestep the SP and act independently, Huntington incorporated a new trolley firm in 1903, the LAIU, and in 1905 purchased the Los Angeles and Redondo Railway. However, the LAIU did not remain independent of the PE. A depressed economy in 1903 created a soft bond market, and unable to move the new railway's securities at a desired price, Huntington could not finance LAIU construction projects. So that building could commence on the LAIU and continue on the PE, which was also having difficulty selling bonds, Huntington decided to use the newly formed LAIU to act as a construction arm of the PE. Beginning in July 1903, the PE shareholders advanced cash to build new PE and LAIU lines; in return, they received an equal amount of LAIU bonds. Unlike the LAIU, the Los Angeles and Redondo Railway remained a wholly controlled Huntington venture. In response to the acquisition of this railroad, Harriman, still wanting to see the SP dominate area transportation, and unwilling to allow his partner / rival to gain an independent share of that market, obtained a controlling interest in the Los Angeles Pacific, the only trolley firm remaining outside of Huntington's grasp.

As the powerful SP concentrated on the region's transportation sector, Huntington was involved in various land developments and electric power projects. His profitable real estate ventures during this period included the successful rehabilitation of Redondo Beach and his work with selected members of the Los Angeles business community in property acquisition in the San Fernando Valley. The growing power needs of Huntington's trolley lines and subdivisions were met by PL&P, which vigorously expanded its electrical generating capacity. The utility firm built a hydroelectric station on the Kern River and a steam plant in Redondo Beach.

From 1903 to 1907, Huntington's streetcar companies, including the PE, the LAIU, and the LARY, which he shared with the SP, plus his solely owned and controlled Los Angeles and Redondo line, expanded rapidly into new territories. In advance of railway construction, Huntington's land companies purchased real estate along the planned routes. Once tracks were laid, his properties were subdivided and sold, and his utility companies provided many of these new communities with water and power. Although Huntington knew where and when transit and power services would be extended to particular areas, he was not the sole beneficiary of his various projects. His courage and vision led him to pour vast amounts of capital into southern California, and his development of the area not only provided ample possibilities for others to profit from land speculation, but it also created thousands of job opportunities for residents of the Los Angeles basin.

By the end of the period, Huntington was prepared to acquiesce to the SP and build only trolley lines that fit into the transit giant's plans. Control in the interurban field was ultimately turned over to the SP, and Huntington focused on the more lucrative businesses of intraurban transit, real estate sales and power development.

6

Changing Course and Shifting Gears, 1908–1913

On 1 January 1908, the *Los Angeles Herald* applauded Huntington for his building of the Los Angeles basin:

> To Henry E. Huntington who is essentially a man who does things and does them well once he undertakes them, the city owes a large degree of its prosperity. He handles millions where the ordinary man handles dollars. He is not one of those who waits for a place to grow up in a favored locality before he builds a railroad to it. He first builds the road, and then puts his shoulder to the wheel with the rest of the people and aids in the upbuilding of the town and the development of its enterprises.[1]

Although Huntington's business career in southern California was at its peak in 1908, the entrepreneur had repeatedly said he wished to retire by 1910, and when that date arrived, he appeared ready to comply with his original plan. In April 1910, he told the *Los Angeles Times*: "I have been trying to get out of business during the past few years, and when my home [at the San Marino Ranch] is done, I am going to retire."[2] But once his home was completed, he failed to follow through with his retirement plans. Thriving on the process of creation, Huntington the builder once confessed: "After all the great joy in life is in the creating; I expect to get pleasure in the thing that is accomplished, but it is in the making of it that the real thrill comes."[3] This viewpoint made his early retirement improbable, and although he often contemplated such a move and began to delegate more authority to hired managers, Huntington remained actively in charge of his major commitments in southern California.

Rather than marking the beginning of a life of leisure, the years from 1908 to 1913 represented a period of transition and adjustment for this metropolitan entrepreneur. Huntington labored to improve and develop the region and, of course, to gain wealth. After the SP blocked his original plans for an interurban system stretching from southern California to the Mexican border, he sold his interest in the trolley firm and turned to other ventures.

The seeds for a new direction in his business career had been planted in 1903 and 1904, when E. H. Harriman acquired one-half interest in the Pacific Electric for the Southern Pacific. Huntington discovered that sharing ownership of the interurban with the SP worked well—the steam railroad company was prepared to spend millions of dollars to improve and extend the electric network—as long as the PE extensions he proposed did not conflict with the existing SP system or its long-range goals.[4] When potential conflicts arose, however, Harriman and the SP were quick to scuttle any unwanted PE incursions. Huntington eventually realized the futility of fighting his trolley partner and in 1907 began negotiations with the SP to consolidate all the streetcar lines under one management or to separate completely the ownership of the urban LARY and the interurban PE. The subsequent business deal, finally consummated in 1910, gave Huntington sole ownership of the Los Angeles Railway, and the SP received all the stock of the Pacific Electric.

Out of the interurban business, Huntington then became more involved in other enterprises. Now he reorganized the Los Angeles Railway to provide more financing for improvements and extensions and incorporated a subsidiary, City Railway, to act as a construction firm serving the parent company. But unlike previous years when his trolleys were unhampered by government regulatory agencies, from 1910 onward, Huntington's streetcar company had to adjust to operating under the scrutiny of both state and municipal agencies.

Meanwhile, Huntington remained active in real estate development, subdivision, and sales, and the HL&I continued to generate profits. However, the Panic of 1907 and the recession that followed slowed land sales; HL&I lost money in 1909 and 1910. Toward the end of 1912, the economy began to recover, and, in 1913, HL&I netted more than $2 million. In spite of that year's earnings, HL&I's net return on investment for this six-year period averaged only 3.8 percent.[5]

Yet, although HL&I did not record high profits on the basis of actual land sales, it did enjoy huge paper profit as the value of its unsold inventory of property skyrocketed. Because of HL&I's vast assets, which rose in market value from $4.3 million in 1908 to $10.9 million by 1910, Huntington was able to borrow large sums of money through the issuance of HL&I debenture notes and bonds. He then financed Pacific Light and Power's building of the Big Creek power station, the largest hydroelectric-generating facility in the country, and his most ambitious project of this period. In addition to expanding its production and distribution of electricity, PL&P also entered the natural gas industry by purchasing several small companies and merging them into a subsidiary, the Southern California (SoCal) Gas Company.

Huntington understood that electric railway profits were easily made by running trolleys through the more densely populated areas. In explaining to William Herrin why neither the LARY nor the PE should build a line on a particular street, Huntington wrote: "Wilshire Blvd. is laid out in large lots on which large houses will be erected. As you know, it is a street like Figueroa St. which is very unprofitable for street railways. It is the houses on 25 foot lots that bring in the nickels."[6] He realized that because the PE and LAIU operated hundreds of miles of track that connected small communities to the downtown core, they were not likely to be big money makers. Yet as long as Huntington could decide the destination of future interurban lines and as long as the trolley companies were operated in close cooperation with his land firms, profits from eventual real estate sales made up for the poor earnings of the railroads.

After the SP joined him in the ownership of the PE and the LAIU, Huntington was not always able to utilize the interurbans for the sole benefit of his own subdivisions, and the trolley became more of a tool of the SP's transit system in southern California. Pacific Electric rail expansions proposed by Huntington were only approved by the SP if the extensions did not injure the steam railroad's existing regional transportation network and, of course, seemed promising as transit ventures. As the electric railways became integrated into its network, the SP pushed to acquire full ownership of the PE/LAIU. Given the competitive situation, Huntington decided to negotiate with the SP.

Ever since the SP had obtained an interest in the PE and then acquired a majority interest in the Los Angeles Pacific in 1906, area newspapers began speculating about an imminent consolidation of the region's streetcar companies. In 1907, the *Los Angeles Express* reported that Huntington and Harriman's personal representative, William Herrin, had conferred, "signaling the merger between Huntington street railway companies and the Los Angeles Pacific Railway system, recently purchased by Harriman and undergoing improvements reaching into millions."[7]

Talks had begun between Huntington and the SP in the spring of 1907. The following year, some preliminary deals were made to pave the way for the eventual consolidation. In June 1908, all the lines of the LAIU were leased to the PE. The two trolley companies already shared the same ownership and management, and arrangements were made to expedite the integration of the two systems. The following year, Huntington further divested himself of the interurban business by selling the SP his trolley systems in Fresno and Santa Clara County.[8]

Negotiations continued intermittently for over two years, but the talks did not halt the PE expansion program. In 1908, an electric line reached La Habra, a citrus-growing community twenty miles southeast of downtown Los Angeles; work was also completed on another line linking the two Orange County towns of Santa Ana and Huntington Beach. The following year, tracks were laid from Covina eastward to San Dimas and from La Habra eastward about ten miles to Stearn, a trolley stop southeast of present-day Yorba Linda. Unlike previous extensions that were financed by PE stockholder cash advances to the PE in exchange for LAIU bonds, these expansions were paid for by loans to the PE from its two owners, Huntington and the Southern Pacific. By 1910, the PE, including the leased lines of the LAIU, operated nearly nine hundred miles of track. Earnings, however, remained poor. In 1909, the PE's net income was only $75,000; the following year it lost $22,000.[9]

As with the PE, Huntington expanded and improved the Los Angeles Railway. During 1908, the LARY extended the Seventh Street line northeast from Broadway to the Los Angeles River and built the Temple Street line in a northwest direction up Hoover Street to Virgil Avenue and then on to Monroe Street.

Although a few short extensions were added the following year, the most important change introduced in 1909 was a new design of streetcar—the pay-as-you-enter (PAYE) car. In New York City, Huntington had been impressed with the operation of these cars. Always ready to adopt an innovation or new technology that might improve his streetcar system, he ordered his engineers to build an experimental PAYE car and test it in Los Angeles. In use in Portland and Montreal as well as New York, most PAYE cars had a box at the rear for the payment of fares. Passengers entered via the rear door, deposited the fare in the box, and when they arrived at their stop, exited the trolley from either the front or rear door. This method of collecting fares allowed the conductor to remain at the back of the trolley while the motorman operated the car from the front. Most trolley accidents were caused by passengers trying to enter or exit a car while it was in motion, but the PAYE car made such mishaps less likely by placing employees at the front and rear of the car where they could insure that people did not try to get on or off the streetcar before it came to a complete stop. Satisfied with the success of the new car design, the Los Angeles Railway decided to transform thirty of its cars to PAYE type—the new Los Angeles Railway's PAYE cars did not have fare collection boxes; rather, entering passengers paid the conductor stationed at the rear door—and planned to convert more the following year.[10]

In 1910, the LARY expanded two of its east Los Angeles routes; the Seventh Street line was extended further east across the Los Angeles River to Indiana Street, and the Santa Fe line was lengthened a few blocks south to Randolph Street. By the end of that year, the LARY operated 222.5 miles of track and continued to be profitable. In 1908, the Los Angeles Railway's net income was $408,000, and the return on investment was 5.1 percent. Net earnings for the following two years are unavailable, but using the gross revenue figures for these years, less the operating expenses of 1908, the approximate net earnings for 1909 were $750,000 and $1,365,000 for 1910.[11]

By mid-1909, progress had been made in the negotiations to consolidate the streetcar companies in the Los Angeles basin, but on 9 September, E. H. Harriman died, and discussions were temporarily halted. In the spring of the following year, negotiations were reopened. Huntington and the SP were near a settlement in July 1910, but an agreement was held up because Harriman's successor at the SP, R. S. Lovett, considered Huntington's asking price for the Los Angeles and Redondo Railway too high.[12]

Both sides dickered through the summer, but an accord was finally reached on 27 September and announced in November 1910. The deal involved a complicated exchange of stock, bonds, and notes of the various street railways owned by Huntington and the SP. Turning over his 50 percent interest in the PE to the SP, Huntington received in exchange the SP's 45 percent interest in the LARY. This trade gave the SP complete ownership of the inter-urban PE. Because the Los Angeles Inter-Urban had become a wholly owned subsidiary of the PE by 1908, all the LAIU lines were now also part of SP.[13] Huntington, on the other hand, became sole proprietor of the urban Los Angeles Railway. The Los Angeles basin's electric railway market was now divided by two major operators. The SP owned the metropolitan interurban lines, and Huntington controlled the city lines in the downtown core.

Meanwhile, Huntington conveyed the Los Angeles and Redondo to the SP for $750,000; then, to obtain the city lines of the Los Angeles and Redondo which were to be integrated into the LARY, he paid the SP $153,000 ($930,000 minus $777,000 of the Los Angeles and Redondo bonds, which the SP agreed to assume). For the PE's downtown lines, Huntington paid $3,500,000 minus the PE notes he held—representing loans he had made to the interurban company amounting to $3,276,000—which he surrendered to the SP. In addition, since Huntington agreed to assume the $500,000 in outstanding bonds of these downtown lines, that amount was also subtracted from the purchase price. When these complex dealings were worked out, the SP owed Huntington about $113,000. Furthermore, Huntington received new consolidated PE bonds in exchange for $3,170,000 of Los Angeles and Redondo bonds and $2,563,000 of LAIU bonds.[14]

Once the Southern Pacific had outright control of the PE and the LAIU, it merged them with its other regional streetcar properties—the Los Angeles Pacific, the Los Angeles and Redondo, and several smaller lines in San Bernardino County. On 1 September 1911, in a move that was subsequently dubbed "The Great Merger," the SP incorporated a new PE firm, consolidating its southern California trolley companies. Now owning the largest electric interurban system in the world, with over 1,000 miles of track, the SP worked to integrate the trolley into its steam railroad network. In order to improve the interchange of passengers from the steam lines to the interurbans, the PE honored SP tickets for local service.[15]

The SP began concentrating on the interurban's freight-carrying ability to take advantage of its many miles of standard-gauge trackage. Following its takeover of the PE, the SP actively began to solicit local freight business. Major products carried included citrus fruit, grain, gravel, hay, lumber, nuts, oil, sand, and vegetables. Already hauling the U.S. mail, the PE also started to operate a daily milk train. This freight operation soon became a significant source of the interurban's income. In 1911, the PE's freight revenue was $519,226; in 1912, it was $1,164,654. By 1915, the PE's gross income from its hauling business had climbed to $1,203,956, or 13 percent of total revenue.[16] The trolley also played an important role as an intermediary between the SP's steam railroads and ocean-going traffic. George W. Hilton and John F. Due, who have studied the nation's interurbans, noted that "the Pacific Electric served as a vast switching network for the Southern Pacific, and did a heavy carload business between Los Angeles and the port facilities at San Pedro."[17]

Although the enlarged PE was considered a valuable addition by the Southern Pacific, it was not as financially successful as the original PE. In 1912, its first full year of operation, the new PE's net income was $71,000; the following year its net income rose to $478,000. However, in 1914, the railroad lost $610,000, and the PE showed a profit only once during the next twenty years.[18]

Huntington's turning over full control of the PE to the SP seemed to represent a local victory for the Harriman forces. Yet the SP victory did not necessarily mean Huntington had been defeated. On the contrary, Huntington also came away from the 1910 deal a winner. At the time of the settlement, the PE operated a large first-class trolley system that maintained rail routes radiating out in all directions from the downtown core to various suburbs of the Los Angeles basin. Because the PE had previously promoted many of his subdivisions and already had lines to areas where future Huntington real estate developments were planned, Huntington assumed that the trolley had served its purpose and saw no benefit in battling the SP for control of the PE. Whether or not he managed the interurban, the trolley system would still carry passengers to Huntington subdivisions. Besides, he correctly assumed that the SP would continue expanding the PE. On 11 November 1910, speaking about the streetcar settlement and the PE's future, Huntington said:

> The Southern Pacific is now in control of the Pacific Electric. The Harriman interest in the LA Railway has passed. I was assured by R. S. Lovett, head of the Southern Pacific, in New York, that the same broad policy that had dominated the management of the PE in the past will be continued under the new regime, and I believe it. The people of Southern California may be assured of fair and liberal treatment in the future.[19]

Finally, in giving up his interest in the financially draining PE, Huntington had more time and money to devote to his profitable Los Angeles Railway.

Following the agreements of 1910, Huntington emerged with an enlarged Los Angeles Railway. From the PE, the LARY took over several miles of city rail routes, including lines on West Temple, Angeleno Heights, Crown Hill, West Sixth Street, and Brooklyn

Avenue. The LAIU transferred to Huntington's urban railroad the former Los Angeles Traction lines on West Adams, West Jefferson, East Fourth, and East Eighth streets. In addition, the LARY received the lines of the Los Angeles and Redondo north of 116th Street. In addition to gaining 73 miles of track from the PE/LAIU and 49 miles from the Los Angeles and Redondo, the Los Angeles Railway obtained an additional 147 streetcars. Huntington's city transit system now comprised 345 miles of track, 25 percent of which were located on private right-of-way, and it had a fleet of 525 cars.[20]

To consolidate the new properties with the old and to provide funds to improve and expand the system, Huntington incorporated the Los Angeles Railway Corporation on 7 November 1910. Then, in early December, he established City Railway of Los Angeles to finance and construct rail lines to be operated under lease by the parent company.[21]

With these new organizations, Huntington expanded and upgraded his transit system. From 1911 to mid-1914, trackage operated by the Los Angeles Railway, capitalized at $20 million, increased from 345 to 386 miles. Similarly, Huntington added over 400 cars to his fleet. By June 1914, the Los Angeles Railway owned a total of 926 streetcars, 876 of which were passenger vehicles.[22]

Possessing more miles of track, serving a larger area, and having a larger number of streetcars, the LARY's patronage dramatically increased. In 1908, the Los Angeles Railway carried 71 million revenue passengers; in the fiscal year ending June 1914, it transported 140 million. In addition to doubling its passenger business, the net operating earnings per car mile—before interest payments on the bonds were deducted—rose from $0.055 in 1908 to $0.073 in 1914. However, the company's bonded indebtedness also vastly increased: prior to the formation of the Los Angeles Railway Corporation, the firm's outstanding funded debt was $5 million; afterward, it rose to $20 million. This hike in the company's debt expanded the annual interest payments from $250,300 in 1908 to $1,064,500 in the fiscal year 1914. The enlarged debt and corresponding high interest payments kept net earnings down, and the Los Angeles Railway's annual net income remained at approximately the same level it had been before the reincorporation in 1910. Hence, the Los Angeles Railway netted $575,445 in 1912; $536,673 in 1913; and $582,142 in 1914. Based on the reported capitalization of $20 million, the LARY's net return on investment over this three-year period was only 2.8 percent.[23]

Yet the LARY was actually much more profitable than it appeared on the company's financial statements. When the Los Angeles Railway Corporation was created in 1910, it had an authorized bonded indebtedness of $20 million. After assuming the $5 million in bonds of the Los Angeles Railway Company and the $500,000 bonded indebtedness of the lines Huntington had purchased from the PE, the new Los Angeles Railway still had authority to issue $14.5 million in bonds. These remaining bonds were issued to Huntington's Los Angeles Railway Company for the property it transferred to the new corporation.[24]

In 1911 Huntington issued $9.86 million of Los Angeles Railway bonds and placed them in his personal account. Earning 5 percent interest, the bonds paid Huntington approximately $490,000 in 1912. He thus held a large block of Los Angeles Railway bonds for which he had advanced no cash, yet on which he received interest payments. If the interest Huntington earned is added to the net income for 1912, the year's net return on investment rises from 2.9 to 5.2 percent. Using the same calculation for the following two years, a period in which Huntington apparently sold $4 million of LARY bonds, the Los Angeles Railway's net return on investment was 4.7 percent in 1913 and 4.3 percent in 1914.[25]

Several factors may account for Huntington's actions. In taking the bonds, he guaranteed himself a constant inflow of cash. Even if the railroad's net earnings declined in future years, the company was obligated to pay the interest on the bonded debt prior to paying the stockholders any dividends. As a bondholder, Huntington had a first lien on the Los Angeles Railway and assured himself a constant source of cash, which helped him finance his purchases of rare books, manuscripts, and artwork.

For example, in 1911 he purchased a Gutenberg Bible, an acquisition that prompted a humorous exchange of letters between Epes Randolph and Huntington. Randolph wrote: "I have known for years that you were sadly in need of the influence imparted by a constant use of the Holy Writ, but I did not suppose that on short notice you would feel the need of $50,000 worth of it in a bunch." Huntington replied: "I note what you say about the Holy Writ. I certainly should not have paid $50,000 for that Bible if I had not needed it very much, although, as a matter of fact, I found that I could buy one for 10 cents, the contents of which would probably have done me as much good as the one I have."[26] In addition to financing his book and art collecting, Huntington sought—in disguising profits by taking revenues as interest—to strengthen the position of his company against the city that had recently acquired the power to regulate streetcar fares and was contemplating a reduction.

Huntington also removed cash from the company by directing the LARY to declare dividends for the first time. As the sole stockholder, he was paid the first dividend of $400,000 in fiscal year 1912. This declaration was followed by a dividend of $800,000 in 1913 and $300,000 in 1914. Yet, as his West Coast manager William Dunn reported to the California Railroad Commission, Huntington took the three-year total of $1.5 million in dividends in the form of City Railway bonds.[27] This transaction allowed Huntington to keep the $1.5 million in cash in the company and provided him with securities that collected interest and could be used for collateral in any future borrowing.

Until 1910, Huntington's street railroads were largely unrestrained by governmental authority, and he was relatively free to manipulate the company's finances to his personal advantage. Although the California Railroad Commission had existed since 1880, it did not have authority over street railways until 1911. The same was true of the city's Board of Public Utilities, which had been established in 1902 but was not given any real regulatory power until 1909. Then, reporting to the city council, the Board of Public Utilities was empowered to examine the financial records of utilities companies, investigate charges brought against such firms, and recommend just and fair rates for utilities providing service in Los Angeles.[28]

In early 1911, the city council commissioned the first study to examine Los Angeles transportation and offer recommendations to relieve downtown congestion. Bion J. Arnold, a municipal transit expert, was retained to conduct the investigation. As part of the study, an Arnold employee requested the earnings record of the Los Angeles Railway for 1900–10. General manager Howard Huntington believed it was best to cooperate with the Arnold people and provided the railway's gross earnings for the previous ten years. When Huntington was informed of his son's actions, he expressed consternation over divulging information:

> I would of course have preferred not to give Mr. Damon [manager of Arnold's Los Angeles office] the earnings for the year 1910, and I don't see how the back earnings could have been obtained when we did not have the books to refer to. Of course, I want you to treat Mr. Damon with a good deal of courtesy . . . but I don't like to give the earnings for the back years because I can see where a great deal of harm can come from it.[29]

Huntington had good cause to hide the LARY's profits. In the latter half of 1911, the city council was considering an investigation of the LARY's earnings to determine whether a fare reduction was in order. By the summer of 1912, at the council's request, the Board of Public Utilities prepared to examine the railway's financial records.[30]

At the same time, the city council considered the possibility of purchasing the Los Angeles Railway. In March 1912, Councilman Haines Reed proposed that the city pay from $35 million to $40 million to acquire the railroad. Two months later, the council appointed a committee to negotiate the acquisition of the Los Angeles Railway. Huntington met with the committee in May, indicating that he was prepared to sell the railway to the city, but $15 million separated Huntington's $40 million price and the city's $25 million offer. On 12 July, the Los Angeles Railway asked the city council to appoint an expert to make a valuation of the streetcar company's property to facilitate talks. To make this study, as well as examine the books of the LARY, the Board of Public Utilities again hired the Bion Arnold Company.[31]

The Arnold report, completed by the company's Los Angeles representative, George Damon, was presented to the Board of Public Utilities on 9 January 1914. Unaware that Huntington had taken almost $10 million in Los Angeles Railway bonds without paying any cash, Damon accepted the net earnings recorded in the company's annual reports as the railroad's actual income. Because that figure was never outrageously high, the study concluded that the streetcar company was just becoming profitable; therefore, a reduction of the five-cent fare rate was not justified. Hence, Huntington's scheme of removing cash from the company by accepting interest on bonds helped protect the nickel fare. By making the net income to the sole owner appear substantially lower than it was in reality, Huntington thus disguised the true earnings of the LARY.[32]

The report also provided the first independent valuation of the LARY. Considering the property and franchises of the firm as of 1 January 1913, Damon set the value at $19,762,389. But the estimate did not help in bringing the city council and Huntington to an agreement on the proposed sale of the railroad. By the time the study was finally completed, the city's interest in purchasing the Los Angeles Railway had subsided. Then, on 5 February 1914, Councilman Reed, the major proponent of a municipal purchase of the Los Angeles Railway, resigned from the council because of poor health. With Reed's retirement, the city's efforts to purchase the streetcar company subsided.[33]

During this time, Huntington continued developing and selling real estate. The Panic of 1907 ushered in a recession, and the economy was generally sluggish through 1913. The weak local economy hurt land sales. The usually very profitable Huntington Land and Improvement Company struggled through these lean years with comparatively low earnings. In 1908, the HL&I's net income was $182,117 but declined over the next three years. Net earnings for 1909 fell to $32,562; in 1910, HL&I lost $49,110, and the following year it lost $5,988. The next two years however, real estate sales picked up, and earnings rebounded. In 1912, the company netted $109,750, and in 1913, net earnings escalated to $2,102,275.[34]

Huntington's biggest real estate sale during these years was in commercial rather than residential property, and much like Thomas Burke had done in Seattle, it was the result of successful land speculation. In January 1902, Huntington had wisely purchased the nine-acre homestead of Orzo W. Childs, an early Los Angeles developer, located in the block of Main, Hill, Eleventh, and Twelfth streets in downtown Los Angeles. At the time he bought the property, for $200,000, it was in the heart of the older, wealthy residential area of the city. Aware that the business district was gradually moving in a southwesterly direction, Huntington correctly assessed that this property would eventually become part of the city's business section and vastly increase in value. In March 1913, he cashed in on his foresight and sold this land to an investment company for $3 million dollars.[35]

Huntington found it expedient to use the HL&I to borrow money to finance his other undertakings. From 1908 to 1913, he focused on the Pacific Light and Power Company, which entered the natural gas business and constructed the first phase of its massive Big Creek hydroelectric power project 240 miles northeast of Los Angeles in the Sierra Nevada Mountains.

Until 1905, the natural gas industry in the Los Angeles area was dominated by a single firm, Los Angeles Gas and Electric Company. Hoping to break up the monopoly, Thaddeus S. C. Lowe, an inventor, pioneer hot air ballooner, and builder of the Mt. Lowe Railway, formed the People's Gas and Coke Company. But Lowe's firm was too small and undercapitalized to compete with Los Angeles Gas and Electric, and it soon went bankrupt. Following an extremely cold winter in 1906, in which the local gas companies could not meet the local demand, a group of prominent businessmen, led by wealthy reformer John R. Haynes and banker J. F. Sartori, formed the City Gas Company in 1907. Capitalized at $1 million, City Gas was established to compete with Los Angeles Gas and Electric and then to be sold to the city for cost plus 10 percent. However, the organizers of City Gas soon lost interest in the project. In August 1908, the Domestic Gas Company, a subsidiary of Huntington's Pacific Light and Power, purchased the property and franchises for $1,350,000.[36]

Huntington and Kerckhoff sought to expand the Domestic Gas Company as they had their other PL&P projects. To do so, they needed to increase the firm's supply of natural gas and extend its distribution system. Because of their work with the PL&P's hydro-electric facility on the Kern River, Huntington and Kerckhoff knew of the rapid development of large oil fields in Kern County between 1905 and 1910. While drilling for oil, vast deposits of natural gas were also found in Kern County's Buena Vista and Midway fields. Kerckhoff thought this natural gas could provide the PL&P sub-sidiary with the additional supplies it needed to increase its market share of the Los Angeles gas business. In 1909, Domestic Gas fur-nished about 10 percent of Los Angeles's natural gas, and the Los Angeles Gas and Electric provided almost 90 percent.[37]

Plans to build a 120-mile pipeline to bring natural gas from Kern County to Los Angeles were prepared by PL&P engineers. Because of the project's estimated high cost of $1.5 million, plus the expenses of the proposed betterments and extensions of the distribution system throughout the Los Angeles basin, Huntington and Kerckhoff formed Southern California Gas Company, a larger subsidiary to succeed Domestic Gas. Capitalized at $10 million and having an authorized bonded indebtedness of $10 million, the firm was incorporated on 5 October 1910.[38]

With additional capital available from sales of bonds—$6.4 million was outstanding by December 1911—Southern California Gas proceeded to lay high-pressure gas mains in Los Angeles and Orange counties. Because Los Angeles Gas and Electric already controlled the downtown market, SoCal Gas concentrated on ob-taining new business on the fringe areas of the city and in its sub-urbs. In March 1911, it purchased Edison's Riverside Light and Fuel Company, and in August the parent PL&P transferred the gas business of its San Bernardino Gas and Electric to SoCal Gas. In addition to an expanding distribution system in Los Angeles and Orange counties, the PL&P's gas division was extended to Riverside and San Bernardino counties as well.[39]

On 18 November 1911, PL&P formed another subsidiary, the Midway Gas Company, to build a pipeline to transport natural gas from Kern County to Los Angeles. Once the line was completed and gas was first delivered to the southland, on 28 April 1913, Midway Gas acted as a wholesaler, purchasing gas from Honolulu Consolidated Oil's Midway field or the SP's Buena Vista field and then sending it to Los Angeles. Although Midway Gas could sell its gas to any retailer in Los Angeles, it was under contract to first meet the natural gas needs of SoCal Gas.[40] By 1914, the aggressive expansion of SoCal Gas had proved successful. When organized in 1910, the firm's share of the Los Angeles gas market was slightly less than 10 percent; four years later, it had risen to 20 percent.[41]

Although he was diversifying his energy holdings by moving into the field of natural gas, Huntington remained primarily interested in developing electric power. His entrance into electric power production was originally motivated by his desire to guarantee a source of power for his streetcars. But with the rapidly expanding population of the Los Angeles basin, he believed that electric power generation and distribution could become very profitable. From 1908 to 1910, the gross earnings of PL&P rose from $1.8 million to $2.1 million, but a larger amount of outstanding bonds increased interest payments and cut down net earnings. In 1908, PL&P's net income was $377,352, but by 1910, it had dropped to $248,366.[42]

In order to provide electricity for more consumers and for the additional trolleys necessary to accommodate the growing area, Huntington decided to expand the steam plant at Redondo. When the $1 million addition was completed in December 1910, the generating capacity had been doubled, but this enlarged plant was only a stopgap measure. By the time the Redondo expansion was finished, PL&P was preparing to undertake a massive hydroelectric development project designed to generate electricity at Big Creek, a branch of the south fork of the San Joaquin River in eastern Fresno County, and then to transmit the electrical current approximately 240 miles southwest to the Los Angeles basin.

Aware of the potential of hydroelectric power, Huntington and Kerckhoff realized it was more efficient and thus cheaper than steam-generated electricity. For example, the cost of a kilowatt-hour of power provided by the state-of-the-art Redondo steam plant was about four cents; the same amount of hydroelectric-generated electricity was about 10 percent of one cent. Such a tremendous cost advantage led PL&P to investigate the likelihood of further hydroelectric development.[43]

Huntington and Kerckhoff were introduced to the Big Creek area in 1902 by John S. Eastwood, hydroelectric power pioneer and engineer. Eastwood had told Kerckhoff of the tremendous possibilities for power development in the Sierra Nevada Mountains in east Fresno County. When Huntington was informed of Eastwood's ideas for Big Creek, he promptly put the engineer on the PL&P payroll and sent him to make additional surveys and studies of the area. In 1905, Eastwood filed his report and proposed designs for hydroelectric power facilities with the PL&P. Busy expanding his trolley systems, Huntington lacked the time and capital to consider the vast power project.[44] But by 1910 Huntington had sold his interest in the financially draining PE. In addition, the city's demand for electricity continued to grow, and PL&P wanted to increase its generating capacity to meet that demand. The time was propitious for Huntington to launch an enormous power venture.

In January 1910, Huntington and partners Kerckhoff and Balch incorporated a new Pacific Light and Power Corporation. Established to absorb the property of the earlier PL&P, the firm was capitalized at $40 million, and it had an authorized bonded indebtedness of $40 million. Kerckhoff explained that the larger company was formed "to give us additional capital. Our old company was too small." One month after its incorporation, the new PL&P laid the groundwork for the Big Creek development. On 23 February, PL&P acquired the water rights to Big Creek by purchasing the company that held this franchise, Eastwood's Mammoth Power Company.[45]

Ready to develop Big Creek, Huntington placed George Ward in charge of the project. In November 1910, PL&P hired the Boston engineering firm of Stone and Webster to oversee the Big Creek venture. Plans called for creating a reservoir by building three concrete dams to close off the outlets of a natural basin near the headwaters of Big Creek. Below this reservoir, a series of powerhouses were to be constructed. Water from this artificial lake would flow via pipeline downward more than 2,100 feet to a powerhouse. After turning two waterwheel generators in this plant, the water would drop another 1,900 feet by pipeline to a second powerhouse. Initial estimates for the first phase of the venture were $9.3 million.

The capital was difficult to obtain. By October 1911, only $2.5 million of a $10 million PL&P bond issue had been sold. The trustee of the mortgage, United States Mortgage and Trust Company, called on investment bankers William Salomon and Company to set up a syndicate and take the remaining $7.5 million of the PL&P bonds at 85 percent of their face value. The syndicate was formed and purchased the bonds for $6.375 million; Huntington was a member and subscribed for $2.5 million of the securities. Meanwhile, because the PL&P had had difficulty raising money, the financially strong HL&I borrowed $1 million by issuing two-year, 6 percent notes and loaned the money to PL&P to complete its Redondo steam plant expansion.[46]

When capital became available, preliminary work on the project began, but PL&P had to surmount the lack of a good transportation system. The Big Creek area was fifty miles from the nearest railroad, and the only existing means of transporting the heavy equipment and tons of material was by mule teams. But, as PL&P learned during the construction of the Kern River hydroelectric station, that means of transit was slow and expensive. Huntington and Ward's solution was to build a spur line off the SP track from Fresno to Big Creek.[47]

Stone and Webster began building the Big Creek Railroad on 5 February 1912. The railway was to start at the SP station at El Prado, about twenty miles northeast of Fresno, and wind its way fifty-six miles further northeast to the site of Big Creek power station No. 1. After construction started, PL&P incorporated the subsidiary San Joaquin and Eastern Railroad (SJ&E) in March 1912. Four months later in July, the railroad was completed.

With the rail connection in place, the pace of construction on the Big Creek power facility rapidly increased. Powerhouse No. 1 was originally scheduled to open in July 1913, but progress was slowed for several reasons, and the facility's debut was postponed. Because of the continuing steady growth of demand for electricity in the Los Angeles basin, PL&P management decided to increase the initial capacity of its Big Creek development from 40,000 to 60,000 kilowatts. To finance the larger generators, PL&P issued $2.5 million of one-year, 6 percent notes in May 1913. But one month earlier, prior to the sale of its bonds, PL&P experienced a setback when a fire broke out in powerhouse No. 2. The blaze caused the building's just-poured concrete ceiling to collapse, resulting in major damage to the structure.[48]

The extensive repairs necessary on powerhouse No. 2 created another capital shortage. William Dunn, Huntington's West Coast manager, tried to solve the cash problem by negotiating for a $4 million loan for HL&I. On 14 July 1913, he told C. E. Graham, the East Coast manager, about the dilemma: "We shall be obligated to stop work on Big Creek unless we get additional large sums of money. It is impossible to raise it here unless I am able to put through a HL&IC debenture loan, which we are working on now." Noting that stopping work at Big Creek would cost PL&P "at least a half million extra," Dunn said that completing the project required a total of $2.5 million; beginning in August, $500,000 would be spent in each of the succeeding five months. In addition to the immediate cash needed at Big Creek, HL&I had to repay $1.5 million of loans due in September.[49]

Fortunately for the PL&P, Dunn closed the $4 million loan deal with the banking house of E. H. Rollins and Sons by the end of July, and work on the Big Creek venture continued unabated. On 2 September 1913, HL&I issued $4 million in 6 percent debenture notes, with maturities scheduled in equal $1 million installments over the next four years. The deal called for E. H. Rollins and Sons to purchase the $4 million in bonds at 92.5 percent of face value. This gave HL&I $2.2 million—$3.7 million minus $1.5 million that Rollins had advanced HL&I to meet its maturing loans and notes due in the fall—to invest in the Big Creek construction. The balance received from the loan was funneled to the project by the HL&I's purchase of PL&P first preferred stock.[50]

Thus financed, the Big Creek project neared completion. On 14 October, a generator in powerhouse No. 1 began delivering electricity to local circuits near the facility. But power from Big Creek could not be sent to southern California until 241 miles of transmission wires were strung from the hydroelectric station to the Eagle Rock substation in northeast Los Angeles. The transmission lines reached Los Angeles the first week of November. Then, on 8 November, a failure at the Redondo plant caused it to shut down, and to make up for the power shortage, electricity from Big Creek's powerhouse No. 1 was sent to southern California for the first time. By mid-December, the two-year, $13.9 million project was completed. The three remaining generators of Big Creek's initial development were activated, and the new hydroelectric facilities provided the Los Angeles basin with 60,000 kilowatts of electricity, or a total of 80,400 horsepower. With the two additional power stations, PL&P had more than doubled its previous operating capacity of 75,000 horsepower.[51]

During construction of its Big Creek facilities, PL&P net earnings began to increase. With the modern, efficient Redondo plant in operation, PL&P's net income was $594,634 in 1911 and $619,136 in 1912. The first dividend declared in 1912 amounted to only $72,232. Despite this first dividend payment and the likelihood of more payments once Big Creek was in operation, Kerckhoff and Balch tired of waiting for a substantial return on their sizable PL&P investment of approximately $1.3 million. In addition, the bonds were difficult to move at low rates. Kerckhoff and Balch worried about the continuing problem of financing the massive power project. However, Huntington was sanguine about the prospects of Big Creek, the future of electricity, and the considerable return on investment he felt PL&P would eventually generate.

Kerckhoff and Balch's anxieties ran counter to Huntington's optimism and led to a deal that separated the partners' power interests. Because Huntington believed in the future of hydroelectric power and wished to pour all available resources into Big Creek construction, he saw PL&P's subsidiary, Southern California Gas Company, which was not yet very profitable, as a drain on PL&P funds and thus a liability. Besides earning a return on investment of only 1.8 percent in 1912, SoCal Gas was largely financed by PL&P which held $4 million of its bonds and over thirty thousand shares of its stock. To free Huntington of the costly natural gas holdings and his nervous partners, his staff worked out an agreement, which divided up the holdings of the three and broke up the power triumvirate established in 1902.[52]

On 14 August 1913, the settlement was concluded. Huntington purchased the 33,000 shares of common and 1,250 of preferred SoCal Gas stock owned by PL&P. He then exchanged this stock, as well as his holdings of Midway Gas stocks and bonds, for Kerckhoff and Balch's interest in the PL&P. This interest consisted of 985 shares of first preferred, 12,601 shares of second preferred, and 43,995 shares of common stock, as well as the SJ&E Railroad. The deal left Kerckhoff and Balch in control of SoCal Gas and the subsidiary Midway Gas, and Huntington gained sole control of PL&P.[53]

Following this stock exchange, Huntington left his southern California business interests under the watchful eyes of his lieutenants—Dunn, Graham, and Ward—and headed for Europe to enjoy a few months of vacation. While in France, the sixty-three-year-old Huntington once again followed in his Uncle Collis's footsteps. But this was not the usual type of business venture. Rather, on 16 July 1913, Huntington married his deceased uncle's widow, sixty-one-year-old Arabella Huntington, at the American Church in Paris.[54]

Like the other transitions Huntington went through during this period, his marriage did not signal a retirement from business.

While he remained active in the financial end of his various enterprises in southern California, he increasingly relied on his managers to run his many concerns.

His marriage and the opening of the Big Creek hydroelectric
development did, however, mark the close of another period in
Huntington's business career. The years 1908–13 were ones of
retooling and reorientation in southern California. Because the
Southern Pacific, Huntington's equal partner in the Pacific Electric,
wanted to use the interurban for its own advantage by integrating the trolley lines into its regional transit network, Huntington
was no longer able to use the PE as a vehicle for his new subdivisions. Deciding that the trolleys had already largely served their
purpose in providing transportation lines to many of his developments, Huntington exchanged his interest in the PE for the SP's
share of the LARY.

Free of the PE, Huntington concentrated on expanding his
profitable Los Angeles Railway amidst the first attempts of government regulation of the streetcar industry. Aware of the continued
population expansion of the Los Angeles basin, he entered the
area's natural gas business and embarked on the enormous Big
Creek hydroelectric power project designed to provide cheap electricity to meet increasing demand.

Thus, unable to carry out his original trolley scheme, the ever-
versatile and optimistic metropolitan entrepreneur altered his business strategies in southern California. Yet he remained the guiding
force behind his various enterprises and a key developer of the Los
Angeles basin's economy.

Young Henry Huntington, c. 1870s.
Courtesy of the Huntington Library

Arabella Huntington, c. 1890. Courtesy
of the Huntington Library

Henry Huntington, c. 1880s. Courtesy
of the Huntington Library

Collis Huntington, *left*, with Henry Huntington and newsboy in New York City, 1895. Courtesy of the Huntington Library

Henry Huntington and his first family, Oneonta, New York, 1901. Seated at center are his mother, Harriet, and his first wife, Mary. Standing at left is his son, Howard. Henry is in the middle, surrounded by his three daughters. Courtesy of the Huntington Library

Northbound Los Angeles Railway car no. 275 on Spring Street looking north from Second Street in downtown Los Angeles, c. 1901. Magna Collection, courtesy of Richard J. Fellows

The Pacific Electric Railway Glendale station. Note the various businesses already established along the trolley line. Courtesy of the Huntington Library

The Pacific Electric Railway Building. Note the emerging trolley. Courtesy of the Huntington Library

Pacific Light and Power Company's Kern River power station, 1909, named the Borel Hydro Plant in honor of Huntington's associate Antoine Borel. Workers are standing by the original generators. Southern California Edison Company Historical Collection

Pacific Electric Building, 1910. Courtesy of the Huntington Library

Outbound Los Angeles Railway car on Main Street at junction of Main, Spring, and Ninth streets in downtown Los Angeles, c. 1910. Collection of William A. Myers

Los Angeles Railway "Huntington Standard" car, c. 1910. Collection of William A. Myers

The Pacific Electric Sierra Madre junction at San Marino, 1910. Courtesy of the Huntington Library

Center, Henry Huntington and his son, Howard, at an employee baseball game during the annual Los Angeles Railway employees' picnic at Redondo Beach, 1912. Courtesy of the Huntington Library

Pacific Light and Power Corporation's Redondo Beach steam plant operating at full capacity, 1912. Southern California Edison Company Historical Collection

Left to right, George Ward, Henry Huntington, and banker E. H. Rollins inspecting the Big Creek facility, c. 1913. Courtesy of the Huntington Library

The Huntington Hotel. Courtesy of the Huntington Hotel and Cottages

Henry Huntington in his New York library, 1917. Courtesy of the Huntington Library

Pacific Light and Power Corporation's Big Creek powerhouse No. 2, 1917. Southern California Edison Company Historical Collection

Left and center, Henry Huntington and art dealer Joseph Duveen, c. 1920. Courtesy of the Huntington Library

Huntington's San Marino mansion, c. 1920. Courtesy of the Huntington Library

7

Twilight of the Business Triad, 1914–1917

Even though the San Marino mansion was ready to be occupied by 1914, Huntington spent about half of his time away from southern California. He and Arabella planned to divide the year roughly into thirds: four months in the mansion Collis had bequeathed to Arabella on New York City's fashionable Fifth Avenue at Two East Fifty-seventh Street; four months at the five-hundred-acre Chateau Beauregard estate Huntington had leased for ten years near Versailles, France; and the remainder of the year in San Marino. However, the couple did not make the trip to France annually, and most years were divided equally between New York and California.[1]

Over the period 1914 to 1917, Huntington retired from active participation in his southern California business empire. He turned over the daily supervision of his companies to his key managers, William Dunn and Charles Graham, but insisted on being kept informed about the disposition of his holdings and never relinquished the ultimate decision-making power.

Like many other street railroads around the country, the Los Angeles Railway had been a money-making success from 1898 to 1913. But beginning in 1914, the LARY, as well as the streetcar industry in general, began to experience difficulties. Inflation associated with the economic boom created by World War I caused prices to rise. Operating expenses as well as trainmen's wages increased, but because the street railway's fare—five cents—was regulated by the California Railroad Commission, it remained unchanged.[2] The Los Angeles Railway's situation was further exacerbated by fewer riders because of an increase in the number of private automobiles in use and competition from jitneys (automobiles usually operating along trolley routes and charging a five-cent passenger fare). Declining ridership and revenues meant lower profits, and the Los Angeles Railway, with a large debt outstanding, needed a new way to finance required improvements and planned extensions.

Like the LARY, Pacific Light and Power also needed cash, but for a different reason. With the opening of the Big Creek power stations, PL&P was capable of generating surplus electricity. To take advantage of this excess power, the firm expanded its distribution system and continued development of its Big Creek hydroelectric facilities.

Dunn attempted to acquire the needed financing through two different means. He first petitioned the railroad commission for permission to reorganize the Los Angeles Railway and double its bonded indebtedness. Dunn then worked to obtain a $14 million loan for the Huntington Land and Improvement Company that would disperse the funds to the appropriate Huntington firms.

But even with Dunn and Graham at the helm of his enterprises, Huntington still wished to extricate himself even further from business affairs. He expressed a willingness to sell his companies to buyers offering a fair price. In September 1916, Huntington told the Los Angeles Examiner: "I am now out of business. I would like to sell all my interests and get clear of it."[3] Nine months prior to this statement (although not publicly announced until December 1916), Huntington, through Dunn, had closed a deal merging his Pacific Light and Power Corporation to Southern California Edison. The two firms petitioned the California Railroad Commission for permission to merge; the consolidation was approved in May 1917, and Huntington became SoCal Edison's largest shareholder, owning 38 percent of the stock.

Thus, by delegating control to his staff, Huntington eased himself out of the responsibilities of the business world and devoted his time to "fooling away money on books and other things that give me pleasure."[4] As the aging streetcar magnate focused less on his southern California enterprises, he relied more heavily on William Dunn, who had begun working for him in 1901. Much like the other general managers, Randolph and Patton, Dunn and Huntington became close friends. Always important within the management team, Dunn grew to be Huntington's right-hand man. Placing complete trust in this man, whom he once referred to as the "soul of honor," Huntington refused to make important decisions without first discussing them with Dunn and granted this associate absolute power of attorney.[5]

While Huntington was in Europe on an extended honeymoon throughout the fall of 1913, Dunn began working on both the Los Angeles Railway reorganization and the $14 million HL&I loan. In December 1913, articles of incorporation were filed for the new Los Angeles Railway Company. The proposal was to merge the properties of Los Angeles Railway Corporation and its subsidiary, City Railway of Los Angeles. Under the plan, the company was capitalized at $20 million, and its authorized bonded indebtedness was $50 million. The new Los Angeles Railway intended to issue $23,544,000 in new bonds to retire the outstanding bonds of the two constituent companies. An additional $26,465,000 of bonds could be issued to cover future improvements. Dunn explained the reasons for the reorganization: "With the opening of the Panama Canal and the coming of people in 1915, this company must be ready for a greatly increased population. New cars must be built and lines extended. New substations must be built. Pacific Light and Power Co. must be in a position to go ahead with Big Creek development."[6]

The Los Angeles Railway's application for reorganization came before the California Railroad Commission on 9 January 1914. The hearing opened with a discussion of the railroad's valuation because the company's ceiling for bonded indebtedness was based on the firm's assets. But the hearing was postponed until commission engineers could make an independent valuation of the LARY. A disparity existed between the company's estimate of the railway's value, placed at $26 million, and the city's engineers' estimate of $19.7 million.

While the reorganization petition was stalled before the commission, Dunn and Huntington succeeded in obtaining the large loan for the HL&I. The Huntington Land and Improvement Company was authorized to issue $14 million in 6 percent notes— secured by more than $40 million par value of Huntington-held stocks and bonds, including all the stock of the Los Angeles Railway and City Railway of Los Angeles—due serially from December 1914 to December 1927. The bond issue was jointly underwritten by the two investment banking firms headed by E. H. Rollins and Torrance Marshall. Huntington apportioned the incoming cash among his various companies. By May 1914, $8.4 million of HL&I notes had been sold; PL&P received $3.9 million, Los Angeles Railway obtained $150,000, and HL&I retained $967,000. Then, to repay personal loans he had earlier made to HL&I, Huntington assigned $3 million to his personal account. During the remaining seven months of 1914, another $2.5 million HL&I bonds had been sold.[7]

In August 1914, the railroad commission's engineering department completed its study of the LARY and set the value of the property at $22.3 million. The commission also thoroughly investigated the firm's equipment and financing. Although it found the LARY's rolling stock and track to be in "excellent physical and working condition," the company's financing remained clouded. The financial records of the two companies to be merged had been destroyed because company officials believed they were no longer important. However, Edwin Edgerton, the commissioner who wrote the report on the Los Angeles Railway, noted: "I think the conclusion is justified therefore, that these books were either destroyed or allowed to be destroyed in order to avoid public revelation of their contents."[8] Whatever the reason for the books' destruction, the action did hide the fact that Huntington had credited his personal account with almost $10 million of the LARY's bonds without transferring any cash to the company. Thus, uncertain of the value of Los Angeles Railway bonds that Huntington held or how he obtained them, and believing the firm's general condition satisfactory, on 3 March 1915 the California Railroad Commission denied the proposed merger of City Railway with the Los Angeles Railway.

While the commission considered the reorganization, the LARY encountered a new type of competition from automobiles known as jitneys. First appearing in Los Angeles in July 1914, they usually operated parallel to trolley tracks, picking up and carrying passengers for fares of five cents each. Unfettered by government regulation—they paid no taxes, licensing fees, or street maintenance assessments—jitneys rapidly increased in popularity; by November, over eight hundred were operating in Los Angeles.[9]

The street railways were affected immediately by the growing number of jitneys. In November 1914, Dunn claimed that "under present conditions, we [the Los Angeles Railway] cannot borrow any money for extensions or improvements. We have been trying to take care of these out of earnings, but these are reduced $600 per day or $219,000 per year." He added that current construction on extensions would cease and unprofitable lines would be abandoned because of jitney competition.[10]

By January 1915, competition for passengers had intensified as the jitneys' receipts reached an estimated $8,400 daily.[11] The Los Angeles Railway was forced to lay off 100 men and stop construction of 250 of the new center-entrance style cars. In addition to the approximately 1,800 jitneys that were carrying about 150,000 people daily, ownership of private automobiles in Los Angeles was also rising. Autos registered in the city rose from 17,000 in 1914 to 47,000 in 1917. With more transportation choices, people rode streetcars less, and LARY's patronage fell from 140 million revenue passengers in 1914 to 117 million in 1916 before rebounding to 123 million in 1917.[12]

The material shortages and inflation brought about by World War I further worsened its situation. As operating revenues fell because of shrinking ridership, operating expenses rose, and interest payments on bonded debt remained steady. Employee wages, which had averaged from twenty-five to twenty-seven cents per hour from 1910 to 1916, increased to thirty-six cents per hour by 1918. These factors combined to decrease Los Angeles Railway's net income from $588,094 in 1914 to $312,712 in 1915, and $250,744 in 1916. The following two years, the firm operated in the red, losing $13,368 in 1917 and $501,225 in 1918.[13]

Before the jitneys' advent and the onset of World War I, the LARY management had continued to follow Huntington's expansion policy. In May 1914, the Los Angeles Railway extended its crosstown north-south Vermont line from Adams Street north to First Street. In July, it received a franchise to extend the Brooklyn Avenue line to the eastern city limits in Boyle Heights. Building on the line commenced because, as promised, the citizens of Boyle Heights had paid to reduce the grade and thus had prepared the way for the roadbed. But by October 1915, when it was clear that bonds to cover the cost of construction could not be sold, Huntington told Dunn: "Conditions have changed very materially, and I gave instructions that no further work should be done." He acknowledged that Dunn would have to renege on his promise made two years ago to the people of Boyle Heights. Although they had upheld their part of the bargain and graded the route, Huntington wrote Dunn emphatically: "I do not want another foot of track laid or any franchise accepted until we can receive bonds for work already done."[14]

Work on this line, the only extension being built by the LARY in 1915, was stopped until February 1916, when the railroad commission approved the City Railway's petition to issue $280,000 in

6 percent bonds to the Los Angeles Railway in payment for extensions already built by the parent company for its subsidiary. City Railway bonds were credited to the Los Angeles Railway, and the firm completed the Brooklyn Avenue line eastward to the city limits later that year. But the LARY, which estimated that it lost $500,000 in revenue to jitneys in 1915, constructed no further extensions through 1916.[15]

As early as fall 1914, when jitney competition had emerged as a threat to the streetcars, the LARY and the PE sought legislation from the city council regulating the jitneys as public utilities. Making their case against the jitneys, the trolley firms presented several persuasive arguments. Jitneys ran almost exclusively along streetcar lines and only rarely made forays into lightly populated areas. This angered the trolley companies, which viewed this action as stealing patrons. Furthermore, unlike the streetcar companies that were required to pay licensing fees and taxes, jitneys were covered by no ordinance and paid no fees. Finally, as specified in their street franchises, the trolley firms paid for the maintenance and upkeep of the streets adjacent to their tracks. According to a 1919 report done jointly by the California Railroad Commission and the Board of Public Utilities, Huntington's railway paid over $500,000, or about 8 percent of its gross revenue, annually, for the paving and upkeep of streets over which its trolley lines operated. Moreover, the report corroborated the company's claim that auto traffic, and not streetcars, were responsible for pavement damage.[16]

With the powerful streetcar firms demanding a law regulating the jitneys, the city council began examining the issue in November 1914. Four months later in March 1915, the council unanimously passed a jitney ordinance. Operators of jitneys were required to carry insurance and obtain a permit from the police that granted each driver a specific territory and route. Jitney owners responded by filing a referendum petition asking that the ordinance be put before the public in the upcoming June election. Huntington's companies mounted a vigorous campaign to convince the electorate to uphold the new law. Pacific Light and Power, for example, issued a letter to all its employees extolling the virtues of the streetcars and disparaging the jitneys.[17]

The public voted to retain the ordinance. Its enforcement lessened jitney competition but did not entirely eliminate this transit service. Surveying the situation, Dunn wrote Huntington in August 1915: "The jitney fight is looking better all the time, and I hope within the next six months or a year the people will realize the effect of this menace and finally get completely rid of it."[18] Although Dunn was optimistic, the LARY's operating revenue continued to decline, falling from $7 million in 1913 to $5.9 million by 1916.[19]

The Los Angeles Railway's poor performance led to a decrease in Huntington's cash income as well. To conserve cash in the company, the interest due on Huntington's Los Angeles Railway and City Railway bonds went unpaid in 1914. Because the financial situation did not improve, from 1914 through 1917, Huntington received none of the cash due on his railroad's bonds. In June 1917, Dunn explained to Graham:

> Conditions with the LA Railway are such that the only way we can keep our heads above water is by not paying Mr. Huntington's coupons. . . . I do not believe the coupons for last year, this year, and perhaps for several years to come, will ever be paid. The return of the company will show the exact figures to the government and also the absolute inability of the company to pay this bond interest.[20]

By May 1917, LARY employees joined management in seeking stricter regulations of the jitneys. Two months earlier, in March, a committee of trainmen asked Howard Huntington and assistant general manager George Kuhrts for a pay increase to keep wages in line with wartime inflation and the rising cost of living. Management decided to grant a seven and a half percent wage increase and promised another seven and a half percent pay raise if the employees helped eliminate jitney competition. Employees and their wives circulated initiative petitions seeking to place on the ballot a law forbidding jitneys from operating in the heart of the downtown business district. They obtained 35,000 signatures, and the election was held 5 June. The proposal passed, and starting 1 July 1917, jitneys were no longer allowed to operate in the commercial zone bounded by First, Main, Eighth, and Hill streets. Although the new ordinance drastically cut the number of jitneys in Los Angeles, the final act completely eliminating this competition came in summer 1918. In July, the Los Angeles Board of Public Utilities ordered that, beginning 1 August, all existing licenses for jitneys operating next to trolley tracks were no longer valid. Because driving along the streetcar lines provided the jitney drivers with their only chance to attract enough passengers to earn a profit, this ordinance put an end to the city's jitney automobile passenger service.[21]

During 1915 and 1916, the years of intense jitney competition, the LARY built only one extension. But in 1917, when the number of jitneys dramatically declined, the company expanded several

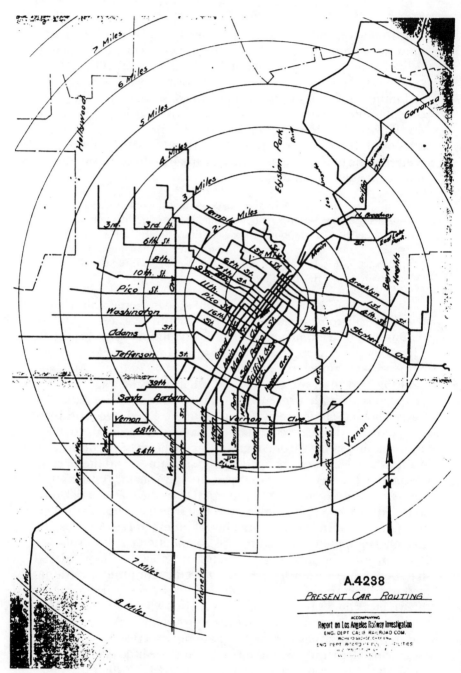

The Los Angeles Railway in 1919. Source: *Report on Los Angeles Railway Investigation* (Los Angeles, 1919). Courtesy of the Los Angeles City Archives

lines. The San Pedro Street line was extended south on South Park Avenue to Sixty-first Street, and the West Jefferson Street line was continued west from Fourth to Ninth Avenue. Operating revenue, which had been falling annually since 1913, rose to $6.6 million in 1918.[22]

Meanwhile, Huntington's land development firm had also been experiencing financial difficulties. A depressed real estate market in the Los Angeles basin curtailed the property sales and profits of Huntington Land and Improvement Company. The fluctuations of the volatile real estate market were reflected in the number of new subdivisions opening each year. Between 1904 and 1913, Huntington had rapidly expanded the regional trolley network largely for the purpose of developing land and selling property. The development was fueled by the expanding population of Los Angeles, which rose from 175,000 to 500,000, or a mean of more than 30,000 people per year. Consequently, the real estate market boomed, and approximately five hundred new subdivisions were opened each year in the Los Angeles basin. But from 1914 to 1916, when the city's population growth slowed somewhat, increasing by 15,000 annually, the number of newly opened subdivisions fell to approximately two hundred per year.[23]

In this slowing market, HL&I occasionally took a less active role in selling its real estate and chose to establish exclusive contracts with real estate firms to improve and then market particular properties. Realtor William M. Garland generally served as Huntington's chief sales agent, but over the years, several companies— such as Burbank and Baker, Henry S. Judson, and Frank Meline and Company—were used by HL&I to dispose of various properties. Because Huntington wished to maintain control over how his land was to be developed, contracts between HL&I and sales agents were very specific, laying out exacting building restrictions for each subdivision.[24]

In addition to facing sluggish real estate sales, HL&I was required to make substantial interest payments on $14 million in outstanding loans. From 1914 to 1917, HL&I's interest payments averaged approximately $700,000 per year. With this large outflow of cash, HL&I's balance sheets recorded losses of $260,000 in 1915, $428,000 in 1916, and $519,000 in 1917. In addition to paying interest, the principal matured serially each year. In 1914 and 1915, $1 million was paid on the maturing notes; in 1916 and 1917, the figure rose to $2 million.[25]

However, the financial statements did not reveal the complete story. Because commercial banks of the time did not provide long-term financing to individuals purchasing homes or firms purchasing property, HL&I frequently acted as a mortgage banker. When real estate was sold, HL&I often received a down payment and then fixed a payment schedule that included an interest charge plus principal. A buyer could thereby stretch the payments on the property purchased over a period of up to ten years. Because real estate profits were not recorded until final payments had been made to HL&I, it is difficult to judge accurately the company's performance in any year. Yet, the HL&I's statements of lot sales from 1914 to 1917 provide an estimate of the firm's activity. Huntington Land and Improvement and its subsidiaries—Dolgeville Land Company, Los Angeles Land Company, Huntington-Redondo Company, Redondo Improvement, and San Gabriel Valley Water—sold $489,000 worth of land in 1914; $192,000 in 1915; $458,000 in 1916; and $1.3 million in 1917.[26]

Regardless of the profits HL&I eventually recorded, once all the payments for a given property were received, the firm, burdened with a large debt, had cash shortages. The company had at one time obtained cash for Huntington's other enterprises through the issuance of its own notes and bonds, but when those securities came due, HL&I often did not have the cash required to meet these obligations. In July 1915, Dunn reported the financial straits of Huntington's Los Angeles operations to Graham and requested aid from New York:

> Our big trouble is going to come December 1st, when we have principal and interest of the Huntington Land & Improvement Company of $1,000,000 to pay. This absolutely must be met by sales of property or securities or by loan in New York. . . . It is taking everything we can raise to meet payments in the way of interest, new rails for the Los Angeles Railway, and extension of service for the Pacific Light & Power. There is absolutely no sale of real estate, and under these conditions I cannot depend on any help from home.[27]

Despite Dunn's dire forecast, HL&I met the principal and interest due in 1915 by selling another $1 million of bonds. However, the following year it was unable to obtain the cash needed to pay the maturing securities, and Huntington advanced the company $1 million to help pay the bonds due.

Unlike Huntington's railroad and land companies, his Pacific Light and Power Corporation was successful during this period. Once the first phase of the enormous Big Creek hydroelectric project was completed, the company upgraded older equipment and expanded its distribution system through construction and acquisition of smaller power companies. These changes facilitated sales of excess electricity generated by the new High Sierra power facility.

After the Big Creek station opened in December 1913, PL&P expanded its distribution system into new areas of the Los Angeles basin. To the northeast, Huntington's power company purchased the distribution system in Glendora; to the northwest, it obtained the distribution networks of the town of San Fernando and the lines of the San Fernando Mission Land Company. PL&P also bought distribution systems in the towns of Compton and Huntington Beach.[28]

With Big Creek's enormous generating capacity, PL&P needed access to other areas to market its electricity. George Ward, the PL&P vice-president, sought to do this by purchasing control of Ventura County Power Company. Incorporated in 1906, VCPC owned utility networks in Ventura, Oxnard, and Santa Paula. In addition to providing electricity to this region, approximately sixty miles northwest of downtown Los Angeles, the diversified utility also supplied natural gas and water throughout Ventura County.

Owning an electrical distribution system in a growing area, Ventura County Power appeared to be the outlet PL&P required for its Big Creek electricity. Because Huntington's utility already had a substation in San Fernando providing power for PE trolleys in the western end of the valley, Ward and Huntington saw the possibility of building transmission lines west from the substation through Chatsworth and Simi Valley to link up with the distribution of Ventura County Power.[29]

In early 1914, Ward began talks with VCPC management about the purchasing of their assets. By March an agreement was reached, and Ward acquired a controlling interest of Ventura County Power. Huntington traded forty-six dollars of PL&P first preferred stock for every share of Ventura County Power preferred stock. Then, for every share of preferred stock purchased, he received approximately two shares of the Ventura common stock. Two years later in June 1916, he acquired a central California outlet for PL&P's abundant electricity. In a deal similar to one it completed with Ventura County Power, Huntington purchased a controlling interest in the southern San Joaquin Valley firm of Mt. Whitney Power and Electric.[30]

In addition to these new markets and outlets for sales, PL&P

sold excess electric power to Southern California Edison and Los Angeles Gas and Electric, the other two major utilities operating in the Los Angeles basin. Selling more electricity, PL&P's net earnings rose from $308,000 in 1914 to $651,000 the following year. The return to investors also escalated; PL&P declared dividends of $186,000 in 1914 and $300,000 in 1915.[31]

As PL&P increased its delivery system, management also became interested in developing the Big Creek region as a recreation area. Huntington Lake, the reservoir PL&P had created to store water for the hydroelectric power stations, provided a beautiful setting for an outdoor vacation retreat. Because the area lacked a hotel, PL&P decided to establish a nonutility subsidiary to build and operate an inn on the southwest shore of the High Sierra lake. The rustic Huntington Lodge opened for business on 4 July 1915, and Huntington installed H. M. Nickerson, assistant manager of the Huntington Hotel in Pasadena, as manager of the new retreat. However, because of heavy snows in winter and poor access roads, guests had to take buses to the lodge from the end of the rail line, and the lodge was only open for the summer season. Not very successful, the hotel never met the high expectations of Huntington and PL&P executives.[32]

Regardless of PL&P success, several factors led Huntington to consider selling the growing firm. By nature an organizer and consolidator, he had had a longstanding desire to merge the three major power companies of the Los Angeles basin—SoCal Edison, PL&P, and Los Angeles Gas and Electric—into a giant utility corporation. In 1915, he was pushed to attain this goal by two key events With its Owens Valley Aqueduct Project underway, the city of Los Angeles decided to build hydroelectric power stations along the aqueduct route. The city planned to supply this municipally generated power to its residents either by purchasing the distribution systems of the three power companies in Los Angeles or by building a parallel delivery network. These plans acted as the catalyst for merger talks between SoCal Edison and PL&P. As the discussion of consolidation between the two firms continued, Huntington became seriously ill, and his declining health led his staff to concentrate on selling the power company.

In December 1916, the date of the eventual consolidation between SoCal Edison and PL&P, John B. Miller, president of the former company, said: "Many times in the past ten years, negotiations toward consolidation of these properties have been taken up but only recently has an understanding been reached by which Mr. Huntington, principal owner of Pacific Light and Power stock, and I have been able to work out a satisfactory basis for a merger." [33]

But talks toward combination had begun even earlier than Miller recalled. As early as 1902, when Huntington and Kerckhoff first incorporated the PL&P, they considered buying SoCal Edison and Los Angeles Gas and Electric. However, no deal could be made with the former, and the latter's proposal—the insistence on selling both its electric and gas business together as a package—was unappealing to PL&P.[34] The following year, Huntington and Kerckhoff discussed the possibility of uniting PL&P with SoCal Edison. In June 1903, Kerckhoff noted that SoCal Edison was developing a large amount of water power, "below us at Kern River," and explained that additional hydroelectric stations would be valuable suppliers of electricity to Huntington's growing railway system. Furthermore, Miller was "anxious for consolidation if it can be carried out along fair lines." Yet, Kerckhoff saw problems with the merger and wrote Huntington: "Mr. Miller suggests a new corporation to take over the two companies. Owing to the fact that you always wanted a majority of the companies you are in, I do not believe a proper recognition could be made of your desires or of the value of your business if a new corporation were formed."[35]

Nothing came of these talks, but Huntington tried several more times to put together a larger utility company that could be operated more efficiently and be free from competition. In 1908, PL&P made another bid to acquire SoCal Edison. This time, however, both Huntington and Harriman—who, because the SP held 45 percent interest of the LARY, which in turn owned 51 percent of PL&P, had some influence over management of PL&P—believed the price Edison was asking for its common stock was too high. Setting aside the idea of combining with SoCal Edison, PL&P management considered a proposition from C. O. G. Miller, president of Pacific Lighting Corporation, to sell its subsidiary, Los Angeles Gas and Electric.[36]

In February 1909, a proposal was drawn up to consolidate PL&P and its subsidiaries—Kern River Power Company and Domestic Gas—plus the Kerckhoff-controlled San Joaquin Light and Power Company with the Pacific Lighting Corporation and its subsidiaries—Los Angeles Gas and Electric and Pasadena Consolidated Gas. The plan called for the creation of a $50 million corporation, with Huntington and Kerckhoff leading the new enterprise.

For some reason, the deal was called off, and another Huntington attempt to combine the electric utilities in the Los Angeles basin failed.[37]

Merger talks were not taken up until 1915, when PL&P and SoCal Edison were driven into negotiations by the city's plans to sell its own hydroelectric power. In 1910, the city council, at the Los Angeles Board of Public Works' request, placed a $3.5 million project proposal before the electorate. The proposal was to construct a hydroelectric power station in the San Francisquito Canyon, about forty miles northwest of downtown Los Angeles along the Owens Valley Aqueduct route. Over the strident opposition of Los Angeles's three privately held power companies, which feared municipal competition, voters approved the proposition by a wide margin of seven to one.[38]

Local government officials entered into negotiations with the three power companies in 1912 to purchase their distribution systems within the Los Angeles city limits in order to market their municipal electricity to residents. Unwilling to surrender their customers in Los Angeles, the power companies refused to sell their delivery systems but offered to purchase and distribute city-generated electricity. This proposal was unacceptable to the city; negotiations stalled, and the following year a $6.5 million bond issue was placed on the ballot to provide funds for Los Angeles to construct its own distribution network within the city. Uniting against the proposition, PL&P, SoCal Edison, and Los Angeles Gas and Electric put together an aggressive campaign that stressed the expense of a municipal distribution system largely paralleling their extant private networks. The power companies then reiterated their offer to purchase municipal generated electricity and lease their distribution systems to the city. The utility firms' efforts proved successful, and the proposal failed to receive the necessary two-thirds majority. But the city government refused to give up, putting another plan to construct an electrical distribution system before Los Angeles voters the following year. Supporters emphasized the $3.5 million already invested in the San Francisquito hydroelectric facility, and the bond issue passed.[39]

Los Angeles then possessed the funds to construct its own distribution system, and the power companies, with the threat of municipal competition looming on the horizon, reopened negotiations with the city. The electric firms proposed leasing their networks to the city as the first gradual step toward outright municipal ownership. Desiring an immediate transfer of the companies' systems, the city rejected the offer, but talks continued. Then, deciding to concentrate on acquiring only the SoCal Edison distribution network—which, excluding the railroads, supplied approximately 47 percent of the electricity in Los Angeles—the city council asked the California Railroad Commission to set a price on the company's system.[40]

As the railroad commission began to assess the value of its distribution system and severance charges, SoCal Edison president John Miller, concerned that the loss of business in Los Angeles might bankrupt SoCal Edison, sought to enlarge his market outside the city limits. He reopened merger talks with PL&P in 1915. Miller's timing was propitious; the sixty-five-year-old Huntington's strategy of divestment remained the same as it had been since 1910 when Charles Graham, his East Coast agent, wrote a prospective buyer about another Huntington company: "Mr. Huntington's policy is that anything he has can be bought at a price."[41]

Negotiations began in the spring of 1915 and continued through the fall. In October, when Huntington was stricken with a serious illness, his staff redoubled its efforts to arrive at a settlement with SoCal Edison. The deal had been held up by Huntington's refusal to trade his PL&P stock and bonds without receiving some type of guarantee about the continuance of cash dividends on SoCal Edison stock. In December, Miller broke the logjam by proposing to create a new class of SoCal Edison second-preferred cumulative 5 percent stock. This offer quelled Huntington's worries, because the new preferred stock would actually yield a higher annual return than he had received on his PL&P preferred stock and bonds combined. Huntington's income from his PL&P securities in 1915 was $527,000; the 5 percent earnings of the SoCal Edison stock were anticipated at $601,000 per year. Dunn closed the deal with Miller, selling PL&P to SoCal Edison on 30 December 1915.[42]

According to the terms of the consolidation, Huntington turned his PL&P securities—46,175 shares of first-preferred stock, 96,602 shares of second-preferred stock, 104,685 of common stock, $5 million PL&P bonds, and $1.4 million in PL&P notes—over to SoCal Edison. In exchange, Huntington became the largest shareholder of the utility firm, receiving 120,299 shares of $100 par value SoCal Edison second-preferred stock, which included full voting rights plus $4 million in cash due in installments in 1916 and 1917. Huntington's staff arranged this cash payment schedule, providing timely funds for HL&I notes maturing during the next two years.[43]

Details of the merger were worked out in the ensuing months. In December 1916, PL&P and SoCal Edison applied to the California Railroad Commission for the right to consolidate operations, and the city continued its drive to build or acquire a distribution system to market its electricity. In June 1915, the railroad commission fixed the value of the SoCal Edison distribution system at $4.75 million and set severance charges—the estimated loss of business SoCal Edison would sustain by surrendering distribution of electricity to the city of Los Angeles—at approximately $1.65 million. The city council felt the price for purchasing SoCal Edison's distribution system was too high and began constructing a municipal distribution network. By October 1916, the city again had tried to acquire the distribution system of the three major power companies in Los Angeles by offering them $10 million. But the power firms insisted on $12 million, and no deal was made. With settlement unlikely in the future, one electric company, Los Angeles Gas and Electric, withdrew from negotiations with the city.

In December, directors of both PL&P and SoCal Edison met to discuss another city proposal to pay $8.27 million for the two companies' distribution systems in Los Angeles plus $1.145 million in severance damages. Over the next few months, the city added more money to the pot. In addition to the purchase price, which with interest totaled nearly $12 million, the agreement called for the two power companies to operate the distribution systems under lease for a period of five years, sharing the revenue with the city. In addition, the city would not be producing enough electricity to supply Los Angeles even after the San Francisquito hydroelectric station began operating in mid-1917. Therefore, the offer committed the city to purchase, over each of the next two years, 58,814,000 kilowatt-hours of electric power at a rate varying from 0.5 cents to 1.22 cents per kilowatt-hour for a minimum annual payment of not less than $717,000. On 30 April 1917, the city and the two power companies signed the agreement.[44]

Three weeks later, the railroad commission approved the merger of PL&P and SoCal Edison. The enlarged SoCal Edison had a capitalization of $75 million and served more than 100 cities, towns, and rural communities in southern California. Company president John Miller said: "By the merger of these companies great economies can be effected; waste eliminated; the stockholders and investments stabilized and the consumers will . . . share in all the above benefits, but will, with the unification of the two systems with their large and diverse sources of power, have guaranteed service in excellence and continuity the peer of any of the world." [45]

Free of the electric power business, Huntington devoted more time and money to enlarging his library. By 1917, he had amassed a huge private library of rare books and manuscripts. Although his major foray into book collecting began after 1900, Huntington's interest in books was apparent by the 1870s when he had assembled a library of the major nineteenth-century authors, which was then worth approximately $1,800. Although forced to surrender this collection before the end of the decade, he remained interested in books. [46]

While residing in San Francisco during the 1890s, Huntington became more serious about collecting books, but it was after the turn of the century that his book purchases increased significantly. His taste in books was eclectic, and he acquired, for example, early editions of Chaucer and Montaigne and first editions of Issak Walton's life of Dr. Sanderson (1678) and Bishop Burnet's death of the earl of Rochester (1680). [47]

In 1904 Huntington obtained the Charles Morrogh collection of fine printing and the John Morschhauser library. Huntington's next major block purchases took place in 1908 and 1909 when he acquired one-quarter of the Henry W. Poor library. Concentrating mainly on early British and American literature, Huntington then bought the 2,100-volume E. Dwight Church library and the Robert Hoe library in 1911. From 1914 to 1917, he added several major private collections. In 1914, he bought the Kemble-Devonshire collection of English plays from the Duke of Devonshire. The following year, he obtained the 20,000 volumes of the Frederick Halsey library; in 1916 he acquired part of the Pembroke library; and in 1917 he purchased the Bridgewater library. [48] A builder, in railroads, the power industry, and real estate, Huntington moved rapidly, combining many smaller holdings into large consolidated enterprises. These characteristics carried over into his career as a collector of rare books and art.

Although relying on prominent book dealers such as Isaac Mendoza, George D. Smith, and A. S. W. Rosenbach to assemble his library, Huntington decided which collections to purchase, basing his decisions on what he liked: "I buy books simply for my own pleasure, and it is merely a case of buying whatever I do not have, whenever the opportunity is offered." But his purchases were soon based on more than personal whim; pouring over catalogs and studying the subject, Huntington became an educated collector. In fact, the last book he looked at before he died was the *Short-Title Catalogue of Books Printed in England, Scotland, and Ireland, 1475–1640*.[49]

In addition to determining what would be part of the collection, Huntington worked rapidly to piece together an unequaled library, establishing one of the largest libraries of English literature in the world.

Huntington also purchased a number of eighteenth-century English paintings, mainly through art dealer Joseph Duveen. He appears to have liked British art, but this taste seems to have been influenced by Arabella. Although the two were not married until 1913, their correspondence from 1908 until their wedding indicates they were operating closely together, selecting various works of art. Once begun, the collection focused on British portraits by such painters as Gainsborough, Reynolds, and Romney.[50]

In addition to building fine collections of books and art, Huntington built beautiful gardens at the San Marino estate. Landscape architect William Hertrich was hired to develop the land. Overseen by Huntington, Hertrich created lily ponds, a cactus garden, and palm garden, and laid out a Japanese garden on the grounds.[51]

Thus, between the years 1914 and 1917, Huntington retired from active participation in his southern California business empire. Remarried in 1913, he began spending less time in greater Los Angeles because his new wife preferred living in New York, and his southland business triad was now managed largely by William Dunn with the assistance of Charles Graham. Although he had moved away from the business world, Huntington remained a builder even in retirement. Days once spent planning railroad routes, preparing subdivisions, or contemplating power stations were devoted to planning library acquisitions, purchasing paintings, and expanding his botanical gardens at the San Marino estate.

8

Organized Labor, 1900–1920

Many aspects of the southern California economy lured Huntington to the region. The area possessed a warm, dry climate conducive to a tourist industry; its citrus orchards were booming; tremendous potential existed for growth and expansion; and, thus, large profits were a possibility. Equally as important in enticing Huntington to the Los Angeles basin was its lack of strong labor organizations and therefore its relatively low labor costs. "One reason Mr. Huntington invested heavily in the southern part of the state was his dislike of labor conditions in San Francisco and his preference for the open shop. He was a quiet but determined opponent of any outside interference in business and had no use for . . . labor organizations, and no sympathy for strikes."[1]

During the first two decades of the twentieth century, Huntington, the largest employer in the rapidly growing Los Angeles basin, squared off with his workers in a series of confrontations over unionization. The conflict pitted his dictatorial paternalism against labor's desire for recognition in the sprawling Los Angeles metropolis. In his continuing drive to stamp out unions, Huntington, whose widespread southern California business empire employed more than five thousand workers, used several tactics utilized by other entrepreneurs of the time. He fired workers who were involved in unions, made use of strikebreakers, joined other employers in local and national anti-union organizations, and tried to placate his work force with various paternalistic programs.

The vastness of the Los Angeles basin also helped shape Huntington's labor strategy, for he encouraged internal divisions among his workers, counting on their diffusion throughout the southland

135

to frustrate attempts to resolve differences and unite against him. This dispersal, however, eventually thwarted Huntington as much as his workers, because he found it impossible to stamp out worker unrest spread over such a large geographical area. The ultimate outcome was no resolution of the conflict between Huntington and his employees.[2]

Huntington adhered to a "no concession to labor" policy, which had been shaped by his experiences during the Pullman Strike in 1894. He had come to believe that negotiating with a union was tantamount to turning over the running of a company to organized labor, and brought this anti-union attitude with him when he entered the Los Angeles basin's trolley and electric power businesses. His ventures in the vast, sparsely settled area required a decentralized organizational structure, with workers operating out of numerous carhouses and power substations.[3]

Huntington's first encounter with labor in southern California came in 1901 when the Los Angeles Railway's platform men—conductors and motormen—demanded that their hourly wages be increased from twenty cents to twenty-two and a half cents per hour. In June these employees accepted the company's counterproposal of a progressive wage scale based on seniority—men with under four years' experience were paid twenty cents per hour, those with four years received twenty-one cents, and workers with five or more years at the LARY earned twenty-two cents per hour.[4] These graduated pay levels tied to seniority became an obstacle to a unified labor movement. Rather than identify with other platform men, many individual workers focused on their own situation and endeavored to remain with the company so as to increase their wages. Their views were reinforced by Huntington's announcement that he would fire any employee who joined a union.[5]

Later in 1901, the Los Angeles Council of Labor tried to organize streetcar workers in the Los Angeles basin. Created in 1890 as a representative body of labor in Los Angeles, the council's goal was to form new unions and gain the affiliation of established ones. This attempt to unionize trolley employees, as well as another in 1902, was put down by Huntington and other street railway owners by firing those who joined the organization.[6]

Although anti-union, Huntington did not view himself as anti-labor. He maintained a benevolent attitude toward employees. In 1902, the trolley magnate wrote to the Los Angeles Railway's Committee of Trainmen: "It is the duty of every employer to endeavor to treat those whom the fortune of life has made his employees, with as exact a measure of fairness and justice, as the limitations of human nature and intelligence permit, and such has been and always will continue to be my own determination."[7] Despite such rhetoric, once in southern California, Huntington allied himself with other major "enemies of organized labor." A chief member of this camp was Harrison Gray Otis, owner and publisher of the *Los Angeles Times*. Huntington heartily approved of Otis's bombastic anti-unionism and frequently corresponded with the newspaper publisher on the subject of labor. He also provided generous monetary support to various employers' associations pledged to smashing unions in Los Angeles.

Otis had been conducting the fight against organized labor since the 1880s. His primary aim was to keep the *Los Angeles Times* union-free. Leading the city's struggle against unions, Otis viewed strikers as deserters who should be "denied a job," "blacklisted," and "driven from the community."[8] He used his newspaper to spearhead the business community's effort to make Los Angeles a model open-shop city, helping to create an atmosphere of battle between capital and labor. Whether for protection or to threaten others, Otis rode through the city in a luxury automobile with a cannon mounted on it.[9]

When Huntington came to the Los Angeles basin, he instinctively sought out men whose conservative views paralleled his. Both he and Otis were convinced that honest American laborers were being led astray by radical, un-American "dictators—otherwise known as labor leaders"—who sought to undermine an owner's rightful control of a company. In addition to the almost-daily publication of bellicose anti-union editorials, the *Los Angeles Times* frequently quoted the views of powerful businessmen on the labor situation in the southland. In June 1904, Otis printed Huntington's position: "I believe in free labor, and I shall employ no man who owes allegiance to a labor organization. . . . There is not a union man on our payroll now. I cannot trust a union man because he is not a free agent."[10]

Huntington also collaborated with other prominent labor foes, including David Parry, the president of the National Association of Manufacturers (NAM). Established in 1895, the NAM originally promoted trade and commerce, but by 1903 it had turned stridently anti-union. Huntington agreed with the ideas of the NAM, and he joined Parry in demanding legislation outlawing boycotts and protecting strikebreakers and nonunion workers.[11]

Huntington became an active member and generous supporter

of national and local anti-union employer associations that stressed the open shop. Nationally, he belonged to the NAM and the National Street Railway Association; locally, he did battle against organized labor as a member of the Los Angeles Merchants' and Manufacturers' Association and the local branch of the Citizens' Alliance. The Merchants' and Manufacturers' Association, or M&M, was formed in the 1890s to encourage business and industry in the Los Angeles basin, and it was initially neutral in disputes between employers and workers. But in 1902, after observing a union-orchestrated boycott against the *Los Angeles Times*, the M&M began to look less favorably on labor organizations. A year later it hardened its position against labor, publicly condemning boycotts and pledging both moral and financial aid to members under union attack.[12] It also pressured unwilling businessmen to follow its open-shop policies. With membership as high as 80 percent or more of the Los Angeles business community, the M&M coerced firms by withholding bank credit, denying advertising space in the *Los Angeles Times*, delaying shipments of needed supplies or raw materials, and encouraging people to buy from rival companies.[13]

Working closely with the M&M was the Citizens' Alliance, established in Dayton, Ohio, and originally known as the Order of the Bees. Citizens' Alliances were part of a national open-shop movement that rapidly spread to hundreds of cities across the United States. The alliance was brought to Los Angeles in 1904 by Herbert George, who had already set up such groups in Denver and San Francisco. Once established, the Los Angeles Citizens' Alliance (LACA) grew quickly.[14] Two months after its founding, the LACA had approximately six thousand members making it, in proportion to the area's population, one of the strongest alliances in the country. Membership was open to any company, employer, or citizen who did not belong to a labor union; most of the city's major businessmen joined the Citizens' Alliance. Huntington, however, did much more than sign on with the organization; he made an initial contribution of $1,000 and promised to provide, if necessary, another $250 annually. This money, along with other donations, went into a war chest used to support members who became victims of a strike or boycott. The LACA gave members one dollar per day for each worker who walked off the job.[15]

With these alliances, Huntington hoped to crush unions in southern California, but in 1903, he found himself battling labor on several fronts. Following the Council of Labor's unsuccessful unionization attempts, San Francisco organizers came to Los Angeles, created Local No. 203 of the Amalgamated Association of

Street Railway Employees, and soon claimed two hundred members. Huntington responded by firing all employees who joined the union.[16] In March when some of the dismissed employees attempted to call a strike, Huntington obtained police help to break up the assembled workers, and, to avoid further trouble, ordered his managers to fire any employee seen talking to labor organizers. The following month, the union asked the Los Angeles Railway for recognition, reinstatement of the dismissed workers, and reasonable wages and hours. When the company refused, a strike order was issued for 29 April, but Huntington once more averted major trouble by asking the police for help. Officers went aboard streetcars and deterred most motormen from walking off the job. Thirteen LARY employees were fired. Then, after hiring detectives to spy on the local street railway union and prevent its revival, Huntington rewarded his loyal employees with a wage hike of nearly 10 percent.[17]

Huntington utilized similar tactics to put down attempts to organize a union among trainmen employed by the interurban Pacific Electric in 1902 and 1903. In May 1903, after Huntington fired those involved and rewarded nonstrikers, a group of thirty-five trainmen on the Long Beach line issued a statement of allegiance: "It is our desire to be always faithful in the discharge of duty; and [we] trust, that should the circumstances be repeated, you will feel assured of our unchanging loyalty and personal interest in the advancement of all that pertains to the PACIFIC ELEC-TRIC RY. Co."[18]

This momentary quieting of the trainmen did not end Huntington's labor problems with the PE. The Amalgamated Association of Street Railway Employees decided to assist the Mexican laborers working in the Huntington construction gangs to organize a separate union. Mexican laborers had long been hired to lay track in the southwestern United States because their wage rate, $1.00 to $1.25 for a ten-hour day, was significantly less than other minorities, such as the Chinese, who demanded up to $1.75 per day for the same work. Although in 1901 PE officials had initially paid Mexican workers $1.85 per day to guarantee themselves a sufficient supply of labor to carry out the planned expansions, by mid-decade, as construction of the interurban lines slowed, large numbers of track layers were no longer needed, and wages fell to the level that other railroads were paying. In 1904, for example, Huntington noted that a Mexican laborer, costing $1.25 per day, was much cheaper than a white laborer who averaged from $2.00 to $2.50 per day.[19]

On 23 April 1903, Lemuel Biddle, secretary of the Los Angeles

Council of Labor, announced the formation of the Mexican Federal Union. Within a week the new organization boasted nine hundred members and a $600 bank account. The morning after its creation, union representatives went to a PE superintendent and demanded a wage increase for the Mexican track layers on the Main Street line. Laborers were working day and night to complete this line for the annual Los Angeles Fiesta to be held in early May. The 1903 Fiesta was especially important because President Theodore Roosevelt was expected to attend. Caught off guard by the union's demands, PE management agreed to its wishes: wages were raised from seventeen and a half cents per hour to twenty cents per hour for week days, thirty cents per hour for night work, and forty cents an hour for Sundays. But when Huntington, who was in San Francisco on the morning of the agreement, learned of the concessions, he abrogated the deal. The union promptly called a strike, and all seven hundred Mexican laborers working on the Main Street line walked off the job.[20]

The PE retaliated by firing the strikers and replacing them with Japanese, black, and white laborers whom it paid twenty-two and a half cents per hour. Again, Huntington received police protection for strikebreakers. The strike quickly collapsed, and the Main Street line was completed in time for the Fiesta.[21]

Despite his swift action against strikers, Huntington was faced almost immediately with yet another labor dispute. On 1 May 1903, the International Brotherhood of Electrical Workers, represented by Local No. 61 in Los Angeles, issued demands to the Home Telephone Company, Sunset Telephone and Telegraph Company, Southern California Edison Company, and Los Angeles Traction, as well as Huntington's Los Angeles Railway, Pacific Electric, and Pacific Light and Power Company. The union called for a closed shop, wage increases, an eight-hour workday with time-and-a-half overtime pay, and the establishment of union regulations for apprentices. When the companies rejected the union's demands on 5 May, about five hundred Los Angeles linemen struck. The strike quickly spread from the Los Angeles basin to much of southern California. The dispute dragged on into the fall of 1903 before a settlement was finally reached.[22]

Huntington, however, was unwilling to have his companies brought to a standstill and, rather than wait for negotiations to end the strike, decided on individual action. The Los Angeles basin lacked a large reserve of qualified laborers ready to assume the positions of the skilled workers on strike, but Huntington tapped into labor pools as far away as the East Coast. He operated much like a large corporation, transferring workers into struck plants or jobs from non-union facilities.[23] To induce these workers to come to the Los Angeles basin, Huntington offered to pay their transportation costs, promised the linemen the same three-dollar-per-day wage they received in the East, assured them free room and board, and agreed to pay their fare home if they wished to return.[24] He successfully quashed the strikes in his firms, noting in 1905 that "this country is having marvelous growth and yet quite healthy. . . . Our people here stand together and work together, and we are practically free from Union domination. Our different companies have between four and five thousand men employed and not a union man among them. Once in a while one joins a union, but he does not remain with us long."[25]

Huntington's strategy of employing vigorous anti-union tactics and allying himself with like-minded businessmen proved successful. From the end of 1903 through 1909, he had no clashes with labor. His constant efforts to weaken unions in southern California led the Central Labor Council in 1907 to single out the trolley magnate: "In the city of Los Angeles is gathered some of the most notable and powerful enemies of organized labor in the United States, and probably the most wealthy and vindictive among them all is Henry E. Huntington."[26]

The council's statement notwithstanding, Huntington followed a paternalistic policy in dealing with his work force, a policy that he used to strengthen his stand against unions. Like many other wealthy businessmen of the era, he realized the importance of lessening the sense of impersonality brought on by increasing plant size and tried to maintain close contact with his employees.[27] When in Los Angeles, he spent hours talking to his workers and riding his streetcars, seeking ways to improve the system. In a 1930 interview, Myron Hunt, one of the architects who designed Huntington's San Marino home and library, remembered: "Mr. Huntington derived much pleasure from talks on the back platform with conductors or on the front platform with the motorman while riding into town. He would get suggestions on the system or just exchange a few words with his men."[28]

Concerned with his workers' well-being, Huntington offered laborers several employee-benefit programs. Similar programs were already in place in many firms throughout the country; companies such as H. J. Heinz, National Cash Register, and International Harvester led the way with welfare plans that were

fairly successful in limiting union activity. These benefit pack-
ages often provided housing, hospitals, athletic facilities, movie
theaters, schools for employee children, profit sharing, and pen-
sions.[29] Huntington's policy of welfare capitalism was an attempt
to improve the workers' quality of life, increase their loyalty, improve their attitude toward the job and the company, and, most
importantly, avoid unions.[30]

One of the earliest aspects of Huntington's paternalism was a
voluntary medical insurance program for employees of the Los
Angeles Railway. To participate, workers had fifty cents taken
from their paychecks each month. The company physician not only
treated sick employees but also kept a check on malingering. The
plan's benefits included "medical and surgical treatment, medical
and surgical dressings, artificial limbs and appliances, and treatment for serious injury or illness." Through the health program,
Huntington also hoped to mold better employees and create moral,
upright citizens. Toward this end, the LARY did not extend medical benefits to ailments resulting from activities considered either
improper or immoral. Maladies such as venereal disease or injuries
caused by intemperance or fighting were not covered by the insurance plan.[31]

Another element of the LARY's fringe-benefit scheme, and
possibly the most important, was the establishment of recreational
facilities for employees. Like many other entrepreneurs, Huntington had at least two reasons for building recreational clubhouses.
First, out of a sense of guilt, employers occasionally felt obligated
to reward employees who worked long and grueling shifts. To improve the motorman's life, Huntington set up indoor and outdoor
recreational facilities. Second, Huntington reasoned that after the
workday ended, employees had some free time, time that might
be detrimental to the firm if workers engaged in drinking and
gambling. Worse still, they might attempt to organize a union. To
occupy workers' free time and channel their energies away from
destructive activities Huntington considered it an inexpensive and
wise investment to provide a variety of diversions.[32] The *Los Angeles
Herald* in 1908 commented approvingly on the firm's recreational
program: "This way of looking after the ease of the employees is
one of the best investments of the management because it is realized that this little recognition of the men and their comfort has
been the means of winning their loyalty and securing the best work
from the best class of men."[33]

Clubhouses were built at several division headquarters, adjacent to carbarns. The recreational centers included libraries, card rooms, swimming pools, movie theaters, pool tables, tennis courts, and restaurants where food was served at cost.[34] Because the facilities were established at scattered locations, workers of the various divisions were prevented from fraternizing and possibly creating a union or organizing a strike.

In addition to these employee recreational complexes, the Los Angeles Railway organized an interdivisional baseball league. Designed to create team spirit within each division, the league also boosted company morale. Management reinforced employees' ties to their individual divisions by holding annual competitions to see which division could maintain the best trolley safety record with the fewest accidents.[35] This creation of a competitive atmosphere among divisions also inhibited workers from cooperating with one another to form a union.

Another reflection of the LARY's paternalism was its company-sponsored employee organization. Called the Los Angeles Railway Recreation Association, the group was strictly a social club. All employees and officers were eligible to join the organization, which sponsored a company band and put on events such as monthly dances, discussions, picnics, and "smokers" (informal social gatherings for men). Although the organization was companywide, events were most often held separately within each division.

The struggle between capital and labor was renewed, however, in the explosive year of 1910. In June, Los Angeles experienced its largest strike to date when workers engaged in the metal trades walked off their jobs. To assist metal trade employers and encourage them not to compromise with the strikers, the M&M promised financial aid. Along with many other area employers, Huntington was concerned with the outcome of this strike and, according to Socialist leader and trade union lawyer Job Harriman, contributed $100,000 to the M&M's fund to support struck employers.[36]

Probably to placate his railway work force during the conflict (it continued for two years and resulted in only modest gains for strikers),[37] Huntington held a large company picnic at Redondo Beach for all LARY employees. The outing, which became an annual event thereafter, was sponsored by the Los Angeles Railway Recreation Association, and all the costs—including PE trolley transportation to and from the festivities—were borne by Huntington. Typically, the picnic involved a baseball game, aquatic sports, and a dance, with music provided by the Los Angeles Railway Company band.[38]

Following the strike of 1910, tensions between employers and workers increased, and the Amalgamated Association of Street Railway Employees strove to take advantage of this rift by organizing Los Angeles trainmen and creating Carmen's Local No. 410. The new organization joined with the Central Labor Council in 1911 to lobby for a state law limiting the workday to ten hours on both local and interurban railways. Local 410 failed to gain many adherents from the Los Angeles Railway, because management made it clear that workers who joined the union would be fired.

Yet labor leaders remained determined. By 1913, Amalgamated, using the same issue of a shorter workday, renewed its efforts to organize Huntington's carmen. This time the company fended off the attempt by obtaining between two thousand and three thousand trainmen's signatures on petitions against the proposed legislation. In 1914, however, it was disclosed before the U.S. Commission on Industrial Relations that the carmen had been coerced into signing the petition out of fear of losing their jobs if they refused.[39]

Because the call for a shorter workday failed to gain union members, labor organizers took up the issue of wage rates. In 1914, hourly pay of the Los Angeles Railway trainmen started at twenty-five cents an hour; then, from the workers' second through their sixth year of service, wages were increased a penny annually. The maximum wage was thirty cents per hour. In appearances before the Commission on Industrial Relations, a Los Angeles Railway spokesman claimed that the firm paid high wages. Its pay scale was comparable to lines in other large cities such as St. Paul, Minneapolis, Chicago, Denver, and Portland; however, the LARY paid lower wages than the local street railroads in San Francisco and Oakland, two California cities with strong trainmen's unions.[40]

Attempting to improve this situation, the Amalgamated Association of Street Railway Employees continued its drive to organize the workers of the Los Angeles Railway in 1915. This effort failed when company management again made it clear that employees who joined the union would be fired. The firm then moved to ameliorate the growing labor unrest by adopting the company union, a strategy being used by a number of employers around the country.[41] Known as the Cooperative Association of Employees of the Los Angeles Railway, it was organized in early 1917. Huntington chose General Manager George Kuhrts as the group's president, and the other officers were elected by the workers. The union established a board selected by workers to air employee grievances and make recommendations to management. Although it made employee desires known to management, the union had no administrative authority, and it served in a purely advisory capacity. It did, however, create a fund that combined company contributions with the annual one-dollar union dues to purchase employees' uniforms and watches, expenses previously borne by individual workers, and it established a voluntary life insurance plan.[42]

The company union, however, did not address the problem of inflation that accompanied World War I. In an attempt to keep their employees' pay on a par with the rising cost of living, and thereby prevent union gains, the LARY raised wages between 1915 and 1918. By mid-1918 the hourly minimum of twenty-five cents had been increased to thirty-eight cents, and the maximum of thirty cents per hour had been raised to forty-four and a half cents.[43] But the pay increases averaged only 50 percent over a period when the cost of living had risen nearly 75 percent. The loss of the workers' purchasing power encouraged unions to organize trainmen.

The Amalgamated Association of Street Railway Employees made significant gains in 1918 among LARY's platform men when the organization's vice-president, Ben Bowbeer, arrived from San Francisco to launch a major unionization effort. With the support of wage adjustment boards and the Mediation Commission, established under President Woodrow Wilson in 1917, the federal government moved toward upholding workers' right to organize. Armed with such backing, labor leaders redoubled their efforts to set up unions, and in Los Angeles, Bowbeer succeeded in gaining adherents to Amalgamated Division 835. The union applied to the National War Labor Board (NWLB) in the fall of 1918 for an increase in wages and an eight-hour workday. The Los Angeles Railway, however, claimed that because it was only an intrastate firm, the national board had no jurisdiction over it, and it would not be bound by the agency's decisions.[44]

Before the NWLB made its recommendation, Huntington was looking ahead to a strike. Still implacable about negotiating with unions, he explained how he wanted the possible walkout handled:

> If the Los Angeles Railway employees strike, and are violent, I would attempt to run as few cars as possible. I have no doubt but that we will receive protection from the Police Department. If say two-thirds of the men remain loyal, I would discharge every agitator, and see to it that they never have another day's work with the Railway Co. We have always treated our men fairly, and now when it comes to a fight, if it is a fight, I want you to stay with them to the finish.[45]

In the spring of 1919, the NWLB handed down its decision. It called for wage increases and the institution of collective bargaining but rejected the eight-hour day. The Los Angeles Railway stood by its earlier statement and declined to act on the board's recommendations. By July, however, in an attempt to fend off a strike, officials decided to grant a wage increase, which was higher than the NWLB's suggestion, for the company's conductors and motormen. They raised the beginning salary of platform men to forty-one cents per hour and the maximum to forty-seven cents. But the union remained dissatisfied because the Los Angeles Railway did not establish a plan for collective bargaining.[46] The union then sent a list of additional demands—including an eight-hour day with time-and-a-half for overtime, and seventy-five cents per hour for conductors and motormen—to general manager Kuhrts. Management refused the wage increase but agreed to talk to a committee representing the workers themselves and not Amalgamated Division 835. Fearing a strike, the company hired 50 special law enforcement officers and began training 150 of its managerial personnel in streetcar operation. The workers did not accept the company's offer, and in August approximately one-third of the streetcar motormen and conductors walked off the job.[47]

Following Huntington's "no concession" policy, Los Angeles Railway management insured the continuance of the open shop by using managerial staff, as well as hiring additional motormen to maintain streetcar operations, and refusing to negotiate with the union. The strike was broken and full service restored by mid-September.[48]

Although Huntington rarely played an active management role after 1917 because he was devoting more time to his art collection and library, he continued to promote the open shop. In 1922, he told the New York Chamber of Commerce that there was no fight between capital and labor. The problem was the union organizers: "There would be but little difficulty between the employer and the employed if it was not for the pernicious influence of men who seek to control all workingmen, and so control the industries, and so control the country."[49]

Yet Huntington failed to crush his employees' will to fight for a permanent labor organization. Regardless of the tactics he employed to counter labor activities, his workers continued seeking union representation to obtain increases in payscales and better working conditions.

9

Conclusion: The Huntington Legacy

Like many other wealthy men of the era, such as Andrew Carnegie, J. P. Morgan, and Henry Frick, Henry Huntington spent his last years accumulating a priceless library and art collection. Along the way, he also established and endowed an institution that made his treasures available to scholars and the public. From 1917 until his death in 1927, Huntington concentrated on enriching the aesthetic, cultural, and intellectual landscape of southern California. Having amassed a fortune with his business triad, he wanted to build a monument to himself and his wife as well as return some of the fruits of his wealth to the people of the area. He once explained to financier and later Secretary of the Treasury Andrew Mellon: "I give my whole thing, my collection to California. I made money with the streetcars; I made money with the subdivisions; and I want to leave my money to America in memory of my wife and me."[1]

Huntington spent several months each year in New York and was undoubtedly impressed by the many philanthropic monuments being established by the city's wealthy entrepreneurs. Some, like the Rockefeller Foundation, were devoted to eradicating disease and aiding education; others, like the Morgan Library or Frick Museum, presented collections of great literary masterpieces and valuable artwork to both scholars and the public.

As early as 1906, Huntington was thinking about the future of his expanding rare book and manuscript collection. He had already considered giving his library to the public but was not sure of the method of disposition. It was George Ellery Hale, solar astronomer and creator of the Mount Wilson Observatory, who

147

convinced him to build the Huntington Library and Art Gallery in San Marino.

Hale had left his faculty position at the University of Chicago and the directorship of the Yerkes Observatory in Williams Bay, Wisconsin, to set up and take charge of the Carnegie Institution's Mount Wilson Solar Observatory in the mountains just north of Pasadena in 1904. Once in southern California, he also worked to strengthen the area's arts and sciences. Hale first labored to transform the Throop Polytechnic Institute in Pasadena (renamed the California Institute of Technology in 1920) into a major scientific research-oriented university. But he was also interested in the region's facilities for studies in the humanities and hoped to establish a first-class library in the southland.[2]

On 3 October 1906, at a dinner given in Huntington's honor by the city of Pasadena, the trolley magnate was seated next to Hale. That evening, the two men discussed book collecting, and Huntington asked Hale whether he should donate his library to a New York institution or install it in southern California. Hale, seeing an opportunity to fulfill his dream of making Pasadena a center for the arts and sciences, favored bringing the collection to the West Coast. Huntington listened carefully to the scholar's recommendations but made no commitments, and the two did not discuss the topic again for six years.[3]

In 1912, Hale and a group of culturally minded citizens organized an art and music association in Pasadena, and Huntington was named to the group's board of directors. Huntington tried to attend the meetings whenever he was in southern California, and Hale was given numerous opportunities to coax the millionaire to bring his library west. Hale also decided to talk with members of Huntington's family. On 14 February 1914, he wrote Arabella praising her son Archer's creation of the Hispanic Society of America Museum in New York and asked to be introduced to him. (Collis Huntington had adopted Archer, Arabella's son by a previous marriage.) The correspondence led to a meeting on 16 April. After seeing Archer in the morning, Hale was accompanied to the Hispanic Museum by Henry Huntington in the afternoon. As they toured the collections, Huntington surprised the scientist by describing a provision in his will that left the San Marino estate, including his art and book collections, to the people of southern California. The institution was to be administered by the Los Angeles County Board of Supervisors.[4]

Although pleased with Huntington's decision to set up his library in the Los Angeles basin, Hale did not approve of the county supervisors overseeing the institution. To dissuade Huntington from leaving his library in the hands of politicians, Hale played on Huntington's prejudices against organized labor. Stressing that the current board of supervisors knew little or nothing about rare books or fine art, Hale wrote Huntington on 17 April: "The outlook for the future is little better, and it would be much worse if by any unfortunate chance the labor leaders acquired any such power [municipal political office] as they have in San Francisco." As an alternative, Hale offered the idea of a board of trustees selected by Huntington to supervise the library and art collection. Three days later, Huntington responded to Hale, noting: "Some of your suggestions are most excellent, and I will take them under consideration."[5]

Encouraged by Huntington's note, Hale followed up with several other letters explaining the advantages of forming a board of trustees similar to those overseeing such organizations as the Rockefeller Foundation and the Carnegie Institution. In May 1914, he emphasized the international importance of Huntington's collections to the fields of art, history, and literature and tried to convince the millionaire to build a research library. Several months passed before Huntington returned Hale's letter. Then, in October, Huntington wrote the scientist: "Your letter of May 11th reached me as I was sailing to Europe, and during the summer I have given your suggestions some thought. I am not ready to reply, but it is quite possible that you have planted a seed."[6]

After Huntington returned from Europe in late 1914, Hale spoke with him several times about the library. He also discussed his ideas with Huntington's close business associates Patton and Dunn, whom he felt might be able to influence the millionaire. In March 1916, after again speaking with Huntington, Hale sent an outline of what he termed a "concrete plan" for the creation of the research library and a board of trustees.[7] Pleased with the recommendations, Huntington responded: "The mode of organization is in line with my ideas, and I hope, with the aid of Mr. Archer Huntington, to develop and formulate some such plans."[8] Two years passed uneventfully, then in March 1918 Hale met with Huntington to discuss further the library plans. Three months later, the scientist presented a lecture on Huntington's library to the Pasadena Art and Music Association. After a general discussion of book collecting, Hale praised Huntington for acquiring the Church, Chew, and Hoe libraries, which he collectively termed "the crown jewels of

English literature." After the talk, he sent Huntington a transcript
of his address.[9]

Fourteen months after this speech, the scientist's lobbying finally
paid off; Huntington informed Hale of his plans to establish the
library in San Marino and asked the astronomer to be one of the
trustees. On 31 August 1919, the first trust indenture creating
the Henry E. Huntington Library and Art Gallery was signed.
The institution was to be a "free public library, art gallery, museum,
and park, containing objects of artistic, historic, or literary interest,
and its object was to advance learning in the arts and sciences, and
to promote the public welfare." Its original trustees were Howard
Huntington, Archer Huntington, William Dunn, George Hale, and
George Patton.[10]

From 1919 until the founder's death in 1927, several additional indentures were signed preparing for the library's status as
a public institution. In 1922, Huntington transferred all his books
and manuscripts as well as his paintings, sculpture, tapestries, and
antique furniture, to the trustees. Two years later, the Board of
Trustees formally accepted the art gallery, the library, and the contents of the two buildings, which in 1924 had an aggregate value
of $4,043,964.[11]

In 1923 the board created a permanent endowment, and Huntington provided the library with numerous securities. The fund
held 2,550 shares of the Huntington-Redondo Company, 1,350
shares of Rodeo Land and Water Company, 10,000 shares of
Southern California Edison preferred stock, and 3,664 shares
of the Hammond Lumber Company. The endowment was also
given a sizable number of bonds. Listed at face value these included $1,092,000 worth of City Railway of Los Angeles bonds,
$2,830,000 worth of Los Angeles Railway bonds, $142,000 worth
of PE bonds, and $3,000,000 worth of Newport News Shipbuild-
ing and Dry Dock Company bonds. The market value of these
securities was between $9 million and $10 million.[12]

Meanwhile, as work progressed on the library building and
plans were laid to create a research staff and prepare the institution
for scholars, Huntington lost two immediate family members and a
close business associate. On 27 March 1922, he was shaken by the
death of his only son, Howard. One week after the death, Dunn
told Graham of Huntington's sadness: "Mr. Huntington is taking
the loss terribly hard, but is, I believe pulling up a little all the
time."[13] Henry M. Robinson, president of First National Bank of

California and a trustee of Caltech, succeeded Howard Huntington as a trustee of the Huntington Library.

Two years later, Huntington lost his wife. Arabella, who had been ill since December 1923, died on 16 September 1924. Describing Huntington's state following her death, George Hapgood, a personal secretary of the millionaire, wrote to art dealer Joseph Duveen about Huntington's trip to New York: "We arrived yesterday after a rather trying trip, but Mr. Huntington stood the strain better than I thought he would. The house seems desolate, and it will be a long time before he becomes adjusted to the new conditions." [14] Eleven months later, in August 1925, William Dunn, Huntington's right-hand man and close friend, died. Robert A. Millikan, a Nobel prize winner in physics and president of Caltech, succeeded Dunn on the Huntington Library's Board of Trustees.

Emotionally weakened by these deaths, Huntington's health rapidly deteriorated. His prostate problems, which had bedridden him in 1915, recurred in 1924. In the fall 1925, he was taken to see a specialist at Philadelphia's Lankenau Hospital by the chief surgeon of the Los Angeles Railway, Ernest A. Bryant. Huntington underwent what was believed a successful operation and returned to southern California to recuperate in late November.[15]

The seventy-five-year-old Huntington did not recover rapidly but remained optimistic. In February 1926, he wrote the wife of J. E. Brown, a deceased employee: "While I am still under the doctor's care [a full-time nurse had moved in to take care of him], I expect soon to be up and about and as active as ever, but it has taken a long time for the wound to heal, and until it is fully closed, I prefer to be cautious." [16] By May, Huntington was still convalescing in the upstairs portion of the San Marino house and had not yet ventured downstairs. Although Huntington's condition improved somewhat in the summer, and he began to receive visitors, he never fully regained his health.

In late April 1927, Huntington decided to return to Lankenau Hospital for a consultation to see why a complete recovery had not taken place. It was decided that a second operation was needed, but the situation did not appear life threatening. On 4 May Huntington wrote: "I am to be operated on tomorrow, but there is very little danger of it not being successful. I do not know how long I will be in the hospital but not probably more than two or three weeks." [17] Huntington never rebounded from this second operation, and three weeks later, on 23 May 1927, he died.[18]

Thus ended the life of Henry Huntington, a builder who capped a lifetime of creation by establishing the library, art collections, and botanical gardens. Although not the entrepreneur's greatest achievement, the institution remains his most visible and best-known contribution to metropolitan Los Angeles.

In 1908, Huntington had explained why he chose to build his many enterprises in the southland: "When I went to California years ago, I traveled east, north, and south from one end of the state to the other, even going off the beaten paths by team and studying every section carefully. I came to the conclusion then that the greatest natural advantages, those of climate and every other condition, lay in Southern California, and that is why I made it my field of endeavor."[19] Although this statement reveals that Huntington had shown foresight in investing in the Los Angeles basin, it does not tell the whole story.

By 1900, Huntington was a middle-aged man who had distinguished himself in the railroad business and, because of a huge inheritance from his uncle, was also quite wealthy. Many people quite properly believed he would retire to a life of luxury and philanthropy. But Huntington appears to have been a builder by nature, a man driven to create, and the evidence suggests that the shadow of Collis weighed heavily upon him.

Huntington's close ties to his uncle during their nearly thirty-year association were undoubtedly instrumental in shaping his subsequent career. Besides acquiring important administrative skills, Huntington thought these years with Collis were the best of his life.[20] He spoke frequently and fondly of his early railroad days, particularly when discussing his uncle. Journalist Otheman Stevens remembered: "I found his [Huntington's] dominant emotion concerned his uncle C. P. Huntington. He invariably spoke of him with a certain degree of awe, almost reverence. He showed me some portraits of C. P. Huntington one day, and regarded them almost as a zealot would look at a saint's picture."[21] These photographs most likely included the two of Collis that adorned Huntington's office in the Los Angeles Railway Building.[22]

Success at several positions with Collis's railroads aided the nephew's climb up the managerial ladder, and it appeared that Huntington would eventually attain his dream and succeed his mentor as president of the Southern Pacific Railroad. When Collis died unexpectedly in 1900, Henry explained the tremendous loss this way: "The shock of his death was the severest blow I have ever received, for I loved him as a boy loves his own father and received

from him the kindest treatment that any son could possibly get."[23]
The loss was compounded, however, by the majority stockholders
of the SP, who were unwilling to see the Huntington influence continue at the railroad, and dashed Henry's hope of following his
uncle as company president.

Yet Huntington remained influenced by the memory of Collis.
Either driven to get out from under his uncle's shadow and succeed by himself, or merely pushed by his own creative energy,
Huntington worked obsessively to establish a business kingdom that
might eclipse that of his famous relative. Whether or not his many
business successes in the Los Angeles basin could be considered a
memorial to Collis, one of his other endeavors was specifically to
honor his deceased associate. Upon his death in 1927, Huntington
left a sizable endowment for the establishment of the Collis P. and
Howard E. Memorial Hospital to be built in Pasadena.[24] And several years earlier, in 1913, perhaps in a subconscious attempt to
mirror his life, Huntington married his uncle's widow, Arabella.

Although it is debatable whether Huntington's achievements
actually surpassed those of his uncle, his role in developing the
Los Angeles basin is clear. In 1917, John B. Miller, president of
Southern California Edison, provided the best contemporary assessment:

> Mr. Huntington has been the direct means of bringing more money
> to this community than any other person. He built the great Pacific
> Electric Railway system, which linked Los Angeles to the surrounding
> towns which, with transportation abreast with the best in the world, be-
> came places of importance and the homes of thousands of prosperous
> people, aiding to make Los Angeles the Metropolis of the Southwest. . . .
> Mr. Huntington [later] concentrated his Southern California interests in
> the Los Angeles Railway. . . . He is principal owner of the Huntington
> Land and Improvement Company, one of the great real estate developing
> organizations of the region, and he has many other interests interwoven
> with the very fibre of our financial and industrial life.[25]

Indeed, as Miller had suggested, Huntington's contribution to the
creation of metropolitan Los Angeles was enormous. His many
enterprises and far-reaching influence shaped urban life of southern California. So prevalent were his southland projects and so
successful were his ventures that he became linked with prosperity
and progress. The Huntington name and the perceived image
of boosterism, investment, and development in the Los Angeles
metropolitan area were virtually interchangeable terms between
1902 and 1917.

Town/Area	1890	1900	1910	PE Arrives
Alhambra	—	—	5,021	1902
Azusa	—	863	1,477	1907
Burbank Township	2,996	3,048	12,255	1904–1911
Glendale	—	—	2,746	1904
Huntington Beach	—	—	815	1904
Long Beach	564	2,252	17,809	1902
Monrovia	907	1,205	3,576	1903
Newport Beach	—	—	445	1905
Pomona	3,634	5,526	10,207	1909–1912
Redondo Beach	603	855	2,935	1903[a]
San Fernando Township	1,110	1,326	2,134	1911
San Gabriel Township	1,713	2,501	8,550	1902
Santa Ana	3,628	4,933	8,429	1905
Santa Monica	1,580	3,057	7,847	ca. 1896[a]
Whittier	585	1,590	4,550	1903

[a] Dates mark the arrival of a streetcar line but not the PE.

Source: Glenn Dumke, "The Growth of the Pacific Electric and Its Influence upon the Development of Southern California to 1911" (M.A. thesis, Occidental College, 1939), p. 121.

Huntington built his business empire upon a foundation of an extensive trolley system that covered the downtown core of Los Angeles and radiated outward to neighboring settlements. Because growth and development followed the spreading trolley tracks, Huntington controlled how, when, and where the Los Angeles basin expanded. The positive relationship between a trolley link and community growth is shown by historian Glenn Dumke's chart (above) indicating how the population of selected suburbs rose after the PE's arrival.

Taking advantage of his trolleys, which were rapidly carrying the growing population to the suburbs, Huntington formed several land companies and power firms. A major landholder in southern California, he purchased vast stretches of rural land along the PE's planned routes; once the interurban tracks were laid, he subdivided, creating a variety of communities designed for different classes of home buyers.

His utility firm, Pacific Light and Power, supplied approximately 85 percent of the electricity it generated to the street railroads. But PL&P also furnished electricity for business and residential use; in 1913 it provided the city of Los Angeles with 20 percent of its electrical needs besides serving cities in the San

Gabriel Valley. Southern California Gas, a PL&P subsidiary, supplied nearly 20 percent of the natural gas consumed in Los Angeles when Huntington sold it in 1913.[26]

Thus, Huntington's major interests in southern California were in the critical sectors for regional growth. The three legs of his business triad—trolleys, real estate development, and electric power generation and distribution—determined the spatial layout of greater Los Angeles. Operating this well-oiled development machine in an era when land-use and zoning statutes were largely absent, Huntington became the Los Angeles basin's metropolitan planner.

In addition to frequently deciding the direction of development and its subsequent form, Huntington was also involved in a number of other businesses that promoted growth in the southland. He became involved in local agriculture, industry, the hotel business, and many leading civic and social organizations. With these various enterprises, he was one of the region's largest business employers. An ardent advocate of the open shop, Huntington employed strikebreakers and hired labor spies and provided employee-benefit programs to keep his companies free of union organization. Thus, he became a dominant force in thwarting attempts of organized labor to gain a foothold in the Los Angeles basin. Because the business community was successful in keeping strong unions out of Los Angeles, labor costs were approximately 30 percent lower than in closed-shop San Francisco. This was undoubtedly a factor in attracting businessmen to the Los Angeles basin.

Directly involved in so many different large-scale projects during the first two decades of the twentieth century, Huntington was by far the foremost urban developer in the area. Theodore Dreiser's depiction of his protagonist, Frank Algernon Cowperwood, and his many enterprises in *The Titan* could be used to describe Huntington's varied commercial ventures in southern California. "How wonderful it is that men grow until, like colossuses, they bestride the world, or, like banyan trees, they drop roots from every branch and are themselves a forest—a forest of intricate commercial life, of which a thousand material aspects are the evidence."[27]

Huntington and other entrepreneurs shared an "appetite for risk," invested in a number of different businesses, and had the fortune of being in the right place at the right time.[28] But Huntington was also exceptional in that he possessed a fine management background secured during his years of railroad service under the guid-

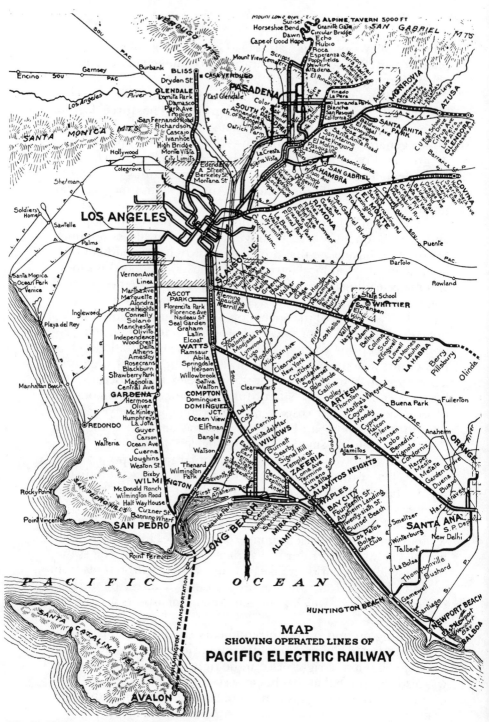

The Pacific Electric in 1910. Compare the layout of the trolley system with southern California's current freeway network. Courtesy of the Huntington Library

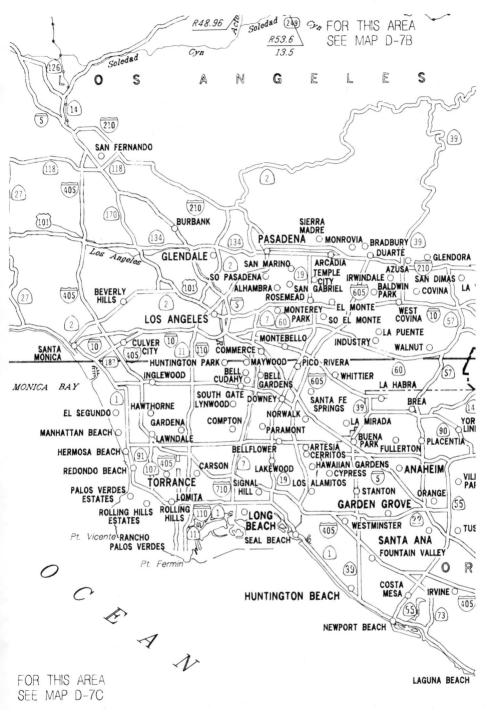

The Los Angeles basin's freeway system as of 1984. Courtesy of the California Department of Transportation

ance of Collis Huntington. Clearly, his connection with his uncle was important for Huntington's career. However, without the assistance of his uncle, with his determination, drive, and energy, Huntington likely would have been a successful businessman, possibly remaining a merchant in the hardware business. Rarely making a poor investment, he had a keen sense of timing and astute business skill. Huntington used these abilities to quintuple the market value of the fortune he had received from his uncle's will. In August 1928, his estate was appraised at $43 million, a figure that did not include the Huntington Library and Art Gallery in San Marino or his boyhood home in Oneonta, New York, which he had converted into a library and public park. Although the value of the Huntington Library and Art Gallery is difficult to ascertain, in 1927, for insurance purposes, the contents of the art gallery alone were valued at $15.1 million, and the library collections were worth at least another $15 million.[29]

Huntington's years with the railroads also taught him to think on a grand scale and in terms of building entirely integrated systems. These views, combined with the large inheritance, led to the creation of his southern California business triad that was unique in its scope, impact, and success. Although Huntington rarely discussed his business strategies, it is apparent that he came to southern California with the notion of transforming the basin into a thriving metropolis, a master plan to accomplish this goal, and the financial resources to carry it out.

Although many businessmen worked in specific ways to expand their respective urban economies, Huntington arrived in the Los Angeles basin with a vision for developing the entire area. To avoid possible interference from associates, he almost always chose to operate alone or in small syndicates that he dominated through control of a particular firm's stock. Because Huntington believed Los Angeles could "extend in any direction as far as you like," he proposed joining the "whole region into one big family" by blanketing it with trolley lines, transforming the landscape into neat suburban communities, and providing for future growth by constructing huge hydroelectric facilities to produce excess power.

Although other businessmen, such as Moses Sherman in Los Angeles or Borax Smith in Oakland, had used streetcars to promote real estate projects, their operations did not approach Huntington's in size or success. Sherman had operated several interurban lines in southern California over the years. However, none was profitable—in fact, most of his trolley firms went bankrupt—

and the largest system he ever operated was the 180-mile Los Angeles Pacific. In northern California, Smith established the extensive Key Route interurban network. Although successful in the borax business, he was not familiar with railroads, and because of some poor financial decisions lost control of his trolley empire and fell into bankruptcy.

However, Huntington's operations were so much larger in scope —spanning the entire Los Angeles basin—and were established in such a short period of time that they did not merely design and promote Huntington subdivisions, they designed and promoted metropolitan Los Angeles. Although the southland would have expanded into a major urban center without Huntington, because other entrepreneurs lacked his bold blueprint for overall regional development or the ability to carry it out, the area would have grown more slowly. With slower growth, vast suburban sprawl would have awaited the automobile and may have resulted in a differently shaped basin dominated by a downtown core.

His enterprises were so huge and his impact on the Los Angeles basin so great that Henry Huntington remains in a class by himself, the metropolitan entrepreneur. Sketching the outline of the area, Huntington directed the development of greater Los Angeles; then, involved in a number of other businesses, acted as a catalyst for its rapid economic expansion. He was the person with the right training, managerial skills, and financial resources who arrived in the right area at the right time. Huntington inherited vast wealth, but was no rentier; he used those resources to fund increasingly ambitious projects. The vast outlays of capital that he put into the southland's infrastructural industries in such a short period of time, combined with his vision, managerial expertise, and business acumen, provided the impetus that propelled southern California into the leading population, commercial, and cultural center on the West Coast.

Today, the Huntington name remains prominent in southern California. Examples include the Huntington Library, Art Collections, and Botanical Gardens, Huntington Drive, the Huntington Hotel, Huntington Beach, and Huntington Park. In addition, many people in the area still have fond memories of riding the Pacific Electric trolley cars. Yet these namesakes and recollections of the interurbans fall short of conveying Huntington's importance to the southland. Henry Huntington must be remembered as the entrepreneur who envisioned and then established the modern contours of metropolitan Los Angeles.

Appendix A

Henry E. Huntington's Net Worth

The following figures are the only data available. They come from Huntington's personal balance sheets. Huntington's net worth rose considerably from 1900 to 1902 because of his inheritance following Collis Huntington's death in 1900 and the final settlement of the estate in 1903 / 1904. After 1919, Huntington's personal wealth decreased because of philanthropic activities. That year he established the library as a separate institution and provided it with a healthy endowment of stocks and bonds. From 1919 until his death in 1927, Huntington transferred the San Marino Ranch, his house and the library building, his book and art collections to the trustees of the library.

In addition to Huntington's major investments in southern California, he held and traded large blocks of stocks and bonds in major U.S. corporations. Over the years, these included U.S. Steel, Newport News Shipbuilding and Dry Dock Company, the Chesapeake and Ohio Railroad, Iowa Central Railroad, the Colorado and Southern Railroad, and the Baltimore and Ohio Railroad.

Year	Net Worth	Amount of Increase	Percentage Increase	Percentage Derived from SoCal Business and Investments
1898	$ 738,000			
1901	8,037,900			
1902	14,277,300			
1903	14,319,800	$ 42,500	.003	.075
1907	16,546,700	2,226,900 a	.13	.49
1908	24,107,600	7,560,900 b	.31	.69
1909	25,446,000	1,338,400	.05	.63
1910	50,483,000	25,037,000 c	.49	.84
1911	57,770,400	7,287,400 d	.26	.85
1912	59,238,900	1,468,500	.02	.87
1913	60,918,500	1,679,600	.03	.77
1914	62,145,700	1,227,200	.02	.82
1915	63,260,900	1,115,200	.02	.85
1916	64,432,600	1,171,700	.02	.84
1917	64,825,000	392,400	.006	.85
1918	65,138,800	313,800	.005	.88
1920	62,530,900			
1921	45,548,900			
1923	45,115,100			
1924	40,447,500			
1925	37,777,100			
1928	42,613,000	appraisal of Henry E. Huntington estate		

Total percentage increase from 1907 to 1918—the period after Huntington had inherited all the securities and properties from his uncle and prior to his establishment of the library trust—was 393 percent over eleven years, or an average increase of 13.2 percent per year.

a Figure represents increase over four-year period.

b Large increase due to carrying LARY stock on personal balance sheet for first time in 1908 and a doubling of the stock in 1907.

c Extraordinary increase resulted from a reincorporation of the LARY following Huntington's deal selling the PE to the SP and a tripling of the LARY's stock.

d Large part of increase due to LARY bonds taken by Huntington.

Appendix B

Chronology of Henry E. Huntington's Major Projects in Southern California

Date

1898 Huntington syndicate purchases Los Angeles Railway and merges other small local lines with it

1901 LARY Pico Street line built to Wilton Place
Huntington syndicate incorporates Pacific Electric Railway and plans to build a system of 452 miles

1902 LARY Washington line built to Western
PE Pasadena "Short line" opened
Long Beach line opened
Huntington syndicate incorporates Pacific Light and Power
Huntington incorporates Huntington Land and Improvement Company
Huntington purchases Orzo W. Childs property in downtown Los Angeles

1903 PE Monrovia and Whittier lines finished
Huntington acquires stock of San Bernardino Valley Traction Co.
Harriman acquires Hook's streetcar system—the Los Angeles Traction Co., largely operating in the southwest portion of Los Angeles and the interurban California Pacific running between downtown and San Pedro—and outbids Huntington for Sixth Street franchise
Southern Pacific granted 40 percent interest in PE
Los Angeles Inter-Urban Railway incorporated
PL&P acquires Ontario and San Bernardino Gas and Electric
Huntington buys San Marino Ranch

1904 LARY Highland Park line opens
PE extension reaches Huntington Beach
Huntington and syndicate buy Porter ranch in San Fernando Valley

1905 LARY Griffith Avenue line reaches Vernon Avenue
      PE lines reach Newport Beach and Santa Ana
      PE Building opens at Sixth and Main Streets in downtown Los Angeles
      PL&P Kern Power Station opens
      Purchases Warner ranch in northeast San Diego County
      Huntington buys Los Angeles and Redondo Railway and Redondo Improvement Co.

1906 LARY Eagle Rock line completed
      Cummings Street line built southeast to Indiana Street
      PE line reaches Balboa
      Line extended to Sierra Madre
      Line built to Oak Knoll
      Huntington syndicate buys Oak Knoll property

1907 LARY Ninth Street line built on Tenth Street to Grammercy
      PE tracks reach Covina and Glendora
      Huntington and Harriman discuss possible sale of PE to SP

1908 LARY Seventh Street line built to Los Angeles River
      Temple Street line built up Hoover to Monroe Street
      PE line reaches La Habra
      Huntington sells interurbans in Fresno and Santa Clara County to SP
      PL&P Redondo steam plant completed
      Domestic Gas, a PL&P subsidiary, buys City Gas Co.

1909 LARY PAYE cars introduced
      PE line from Covina to San Dimas completed

1910 LARY Seventh Street line built to Indiana Street
      Santa Fe line extended to Randolph Street
      Los Angeles Railway Corporation formed
      City Railway of Los Angeles, a subsidiary of LARY, incorporated
      PE/SP deal—Huntington and SP agree to trade stock: former now owns
          all LARY stock; latter owns all stock of PE
      Los Angeles and Redondo Railway transferred to PE
      PL&P reincorporated
      Southern California Gas Company incorporated

1911 PL&P sells Warner ranch and riparian rights of San Luis Rey River

1912 Los Angeles City Council talks to Huntington about purchasing LARY
      Huntington sells Childs property
      Sells interest in Porter ranch
      Purchases Hotel Wentworth

1913 PL&P Big Creek hydroelectric facility opens
      Huntington trades his interest in SoCal Gas to Kerckhoff and Balch for
          their interest in PL&P

1914 LARY Vermont line extended from Vernon to First Street
Jitney competition begins
PL&P buys distribution systems in San Fernando, Compton, Huntington Beach, and Glendora
Acquires controlling interest in Ventura County Power Company
Huntington Hotel, formerly the Wentworth, opens

1915 PL&P opens Huntington Lodge at Big Creek
Huntington closes deal with SoCal Edison, merging PL&P and SoCal Edison

1916 LARY Brooklyn Avenue line completed to Boyle Heights
PL&P acquires controlling interest in Mt. Whitney Power and Electric

1917 LARY no longer competes with jitneys in major downtown area; new ordinance forbids jitneys from operating in main commercial zone of downtown Los Angeles
PL&P merger with SoCal Edison approved by California Railroad Commission

1918 LARY no longer competes with jitneys; autos no longer allowed to operate next to trolley tracks

1919 Huntington creates trust to establish Henry E. Huntington Library and Art Gallery in San Marino

Acknowledgments

This project began serendipitously six years ago when I was a graduate student looking for a dissertation topic. My mentor, Ed Perkins, suggested I speak with Martin Ridge of the Huntington Library about research possibilities available at that institution. Martin mentioned several collections but then made me aware of an unexcavated treasure—the Henry Huntington Papers had recently been opened, and a full-scale study of Huntington as a businessman had not been undertaken. Because I was born and raised in southern California, I was well aware of the Huntington name, and I jumped at the chance to examine this entrepreneur.

During the writing of this book I have accrued many debts, and I would like to thank several people and institutions. Ed Perkins, my teacher and good friend, provided constant encouragement and valuable criticism of early versions of the manuscript, and he taught me the ins and outs of the historical profession. Frank Mitchell, another member of my dissertation committee, challenged me to rethink several parts of the study. Mark Desmond, a good friend who happened to be an accountant, assisted me in deciphering some of Huntington's financial records.

I was lucky to do most of my research at the Huntington Library, which made the task easier by granting me two summer fellowships. Many people at this institution were extremely helpful. After suggesting my topic, Martin Ridge checked up on my progress from time to time and offered several important insights. Other

167

people at the library provided invaluable assistance. These included Edwin Carpenter, Bill Frank, Alan Jutzi, Brita Mack, Susan Naulty, Fred Perez, and Mary Wright. Besides a fine staff, the Huntington Library boasts an outstanding atmosphere for research; and the lunchtime discussions with scholars, especially John Reid, Donald Dickinson, and Jim Thorpe, provided me with a wealth of information.

Gathering and preparing photographs and maps for publication can be difficult. However, I was fortunate to have the help of Bill Myers and Southern California Edison, the Los Angeles City Archives, the California Department of Transportation, the Huntington Hotel and Cottages, and Michael Adams.

Several of my colleagues at Simpson College were helpful, and I wish to thank them. Jerry Israel, our academic dean, was very supportive of my research efforts. Owen Duncan, another member of the history department, took the time to read over portions of the study. And the Simpson College Library staff, especially Pat Mayhew and Mike Wright, worked hard and without complaint to keep up with my many interlibrary loan requests.

I am also grateful for the hard work of several people at the Ohio State University Press. My series editors, Mansel G. Blackford and K. Austin Kerr, were patient with me and offered constructive criticism of an earlier version of the manuscript. Alex Holzman and Lynne Bonenberger assisted me in many ways throughout the entire publication process, and the anonymous reader's critique helped sharpen the study. I'm sure the book is better because of their efforts.

A very special thanks go to my family and especially my parents, to whom this book is dedicated. Mom and Dad not only provided me with a fine education, but they also showed genuine interest in this project and offered continuous encouragement along the way.

Novelist John Irving once wrote: "You've got to get obsessed and stay obsessed." Now having completed this book, I think I understand what he meant. Fortunately, my wife, Jacqueline Crawford-Friedricks, put up with my obsession, read countless revisions, and mastered the difficult role of being both my strongest critic, on the one hand, and my closest friend, on the other. An educator in her own right, Jackie put aside her work many times to look over the book as it took shape. I therefore want to thank her for her efforts and constant support.

Notes

1 Henry E. Huntington (hereafter cited as HEH), quoted in Spencer Crump, *Ride the Big Red Cars: How the Trolleys Helped Build Southern California* (Los Angeles: Trans-Anglo Books, 1962), 10.

2 See, for example, John N. Ingham, *The Iron Barons: A Social Analysis of an American Urban Elite, 1874–1964* (Westport, Conn.: Greenwood Press, 1978); Frederic C. Jaher, *The Urban Establishment: Upper Strata in Boston, New York, Charleston, Chicago, and Los Angeles* (Urbana: University of Illinois Press, 1982); and Edward J. Davies II, *The Anthracite Aristocracy: Leadership and Social Change in the Hard Coal Regions of Northeastern Pennsylvania, 1800–1930* (DeKalb: Northern Illinois University Press, 1985). See also Burton W. Folsom, Jr., *Urban Capitalists: Entrepreneurs and City Growth in Pennsylvania's Lackawanna and Lehigh Regions, 1800–1920* (Baltimore: Johns Hopkins University Press, 1981).

3 Recent works on Los Angeles concentrating on the post-1920 period include Scott L. Bottles, *Los Angeles and the Automobile: The Making of the Modern City* (Berkeley, Los Angeles, and London: University of California Press, 1987); Marc A. Weiss, *The Rise of the Community Builders: The American Real Estate Industry and Urban Land Planning* (New York: Columbia University Press, 1987); and Bernard Marchand, *The Emergence of Los Angeles: Population and Housing in the City of Dreams, 1940–1970* (London: Pion, 1986).

4 Robert M. Fogelson, *The Fragmented Metropolis: Los Angeles, 1850–1930* (Cambridge: Harvard University Press, 1967), 108; and Marchand, 62–66. As Fogelson points out, before 1920, the Los Angeles work force was largely involved in trades and professions, and the region's principal industries—which included flour mills, foundries, slaughterhouses, and carpentry shops—were

small in scale and oriented toward the local market. Large-scale industry did not really appear in southern California until the 1920s. Rather than establishing branch factories in southern California, national corporations continued shipping their products west, until after World War I, when rapid population growth and rising transit costs made it advantageous to build plants in the Los Angeles basin. See Fogelson, 121–30.

5 Although the discovery of oil in the 1890s certainly played a role in the region's development, its real impact was felt after 1910, when demand for petroleum rapidly rose with increased automobile sales, and especially after 1920, when large oil fields were found. Fred W. Viehe, "Black Gold Suburbs: The Influence of the Extractive Industry on the Suburbanization of Los Angeles, 1890–1930," *Journal of Urban History* 8 (November 1981): 3–26, argues that although trolley lines—largely Huntington's—were responsible for the suburban development of the north, northeast, and western portions of the Los Angeles basin, as well as Long Beach, Redondo Beach, Santa Monica, and Hollywood, the southern part of Los Angeles and northern Orange County were primarily developed because of the location of oil fields. Viehe's article is provocative, but, as he says, "this [his article] is not meant to depreciate the influence of interurban transportation, but rather to place its role in proper perspective." Thus, although oil appears to have been significant in the growth of some cities in southern parts of metropolitan Los Angeles, the interurban remained the essential component in laying out and developing southern California.

6 Earl Pomeroy, *The Pacific Slope: A History of California, Oregon, Washington, Idaho, Utah, and Nevada* (Seattle: University of Washington Press, 1965), 139–42. For more background on the promotion of Los Angeles, see Judith W. Elias, "The Selling of a Myth: Los Angeles Promotional Literature, 1885–1915" (M.A. thesis, California State University, Northridge, 1979).

7 Carey McWilliams, *Southern California: An Island on the Land*, 2nd ed. (Santa Barbara, Calif.: Peregrine Smith, 1973), 13.

8 See Lawrence H. Larsen, *The Urban West at the End of the Frontier* (Lawrence, Kansas: Regents Press of Kansas, 1978), 45. For a social and cultural sketch of the Los Angeles urban elite, see Jaher, 577–685.

9 For more information on Thomas Burke and the development of Seattle, see Robert C. Nesbit, *"He Built Seattle": A Biography of Judge Thomas Burke* (Seattle: University of Washington Press, 1961); John R. Finger, "The Seattle Spirit, 1851–1893," *Journal of the West* 13 (Summer 1974): 28–45; and Mansel G. Blackford, "Civic Groups, Political Action, and City Planning in Seattle, 1892–1915," *Pacific Historical Review* 49 (November 1980): 557–80.

10 For the story of William Ralston, see David Lavender, *Nothing Seemed Impossible: William C. Ralston and Early San Francisco* (Palo Alto, Calif.: American West Publishing, 1975); and William Issel and Robert Cherny, *San Francisco, 1865–1932: Politics, Power, and Urban Development* (Berkeley, Los Angeles, and London: University of California Press, 1986).

11 More on James Phelan is available in Issel and Cherny.

12 For a discussion of Smith's involvement with trolleys and land development in the Oakland area, see George H. Hildebrand, *Borax Pioneer: Francis Marion Smith* (San Diego: Howell-North Books, 1982); and Kenneth T. Jackson, *Crabgrass Frontier: The Suburbanization of the United States* (New York: Oxford University Press, 1985).

13 For a discussion of boosterism in southern California, see, for example, Jaher, 628–29.

14 See Collis Potter Huntington Estate Material, Huntington Vault Material, box 3, Last Will and Testament of Collis Potter Huntington, Henry Edwards Huntington Collection (hereafter cited as HEH), 24/5.

15 The idea that Henry Huntington wished to emulate Collis Huntington has been noted in several sources. See, for example, Crump, *Ride the Big Red Cars*; and Isaac F. Marcosson, *A Little Known Master of Millions: The Story of Henry E. Huntington—Constructive Capitalist* (Boston: E. H. Rollins and Sons, 1914). Marcosson (1877–1961) was a respected newspaperman, biographer, and editor. He served on the staffs of the *Louisville Times*, *World's Work*, and the *Saturday Evening Post*, and he was the editor of Doubleday publishing. An ardent advocate of free enterprise, he wrote many works on business, history, and economics.

16 Moses Shermin, quoted in Fogelson, 314.

17 HEH, quoted in *Los Angeles Examiner*, 12 Dec. 1904.

18 For an explanation of relationship between the SP and the AT&SF, see Nelson Trottman, *History of the Union Pacific: A Financial and Economic Survey* (New York: Ronald Press, 1923), 319–32; and Don L. Hofsommer, *The Southern Pacific, 1901–1985* (College Station, Tex.: Texas A&M University Press, 1986), 58–59.

19 Glenn S. Dumke, "Growth of the Pacific Electric and Its Influence upon the development of Southern California to 1911," (M.A. thesis, Occidental College, 1939), 119; Jaher, 612–13; Grace H. Stimson, *Rise of the Labor Movement in Los Angeles* (Berkeley: University of California Press, 1955), 200–201; Louis B. Perry and Richard S. Perry, *A History of the Los Angeles Labor Movement, 1911–1941* (Berkeley: University of California Press, 1963), 4–6; Kelker, De Leuw and Company, *Report and Recommendations on a Comprehensive Rapid Transit Plan for the City and County of Los Angeles* (Chicago: Kelker, De Leuw and Company, 1925), 17–34; and U.S. Bureau of the Census, *Thirteenth Census of the United States: 1910: Abstract of Census and Supplement for California* (Washington, D.C.: Government Printing Office, 1913), 568–69, 684. For a comparison of Los Angeles's population growth with other U.S. cities, see Fogelson, 78–79.

20 See, for example, the *Los Angeles Times*, 9–10 July 1905.

21 John B. Miller, quoted in Southern California Edison pamphlet, *The Greater Edison* (1917), 5 (pamphlet is located in scrapbook of George Ward Collection at the Huntington Library).

22 Derived from HEH's personal balance sheets, 1900–27, HEH 11/2/1–4.

23 In 1910, the Los Angeles basin's streetcar network was divided up be-

tween HEH and the Southern Pacific. By this time, HEH was willing to get out
of the unprofitable Pacific Electric because he believed it had largely served
its purpose of providing transit lines to many of his subdivisions. In a complex deal that involved trading of stock, HEH ended up the sole owner of the
profitable, intraurban, downtown-oriented Los Angeles Railway, and the SP
secured outright ownership of the interurban Pacific Electric.

24 Reyner Banham, *Los Angeles: The Architecture of Four Ecologies* (New
York: Penguin Press, 1971), 34.

25 For more information on the layout of the Los Angeles basin and the
impact of the automobile, see Mark Foster, "The Model-T, the Hard Sell,
and Los Angeles's Urban Growth: The Decentralization of Los Angeles during the 1920s," *Pacific Historical Review* 44 (November 1976): 459–84; Bottles;
and Eric H. Monkkonen, *America Becomes Urban: The Development of U.S. Cities
and Towns, 1780–1980* (Berkeley, Los Angeles, and London: University of
California Press, 1988).

26 See Banham.

27 Neal Peterson, quoted in *Los Angeles Times*, 18 July 1989.

28 Quoted from Dumke, "Growth of the Pacific Electric," 114.

29 See *Los Angeles Times*, 12 Apr. 1903.

30 Foster, "Model-T, the Hard Sell, and Los Angeles's Urban Growth,"
476–77.

31 *Santa Ana Blade*, 1 June 1906, quoted in Crump, *Ride the Big Red
Cars*, 77.

32 Ibid., 114.

33 Foster, "Model-T, the Hard Sell, and Los Angeles's Urban Growth,"
473. Furthermore, Foster noted the importance of streetcars to pre-1920 Los
Angeles by examining the relationship between trolley lines and street location. Using Los Angeles city maps drawn between 1902 and 1919, he found
only a few streets located more than six blocks from a trolley line (p. 476).

34 Jaher, 612–19.

35 For the best account of the subdivider's role in city development and
the rise of urban planning, see Weiss, especially 9–13, 79–140; and Fogelson,
106–07.

36 Weiss, 3.

37 HEH's real estate holdings were largely in the northeastern portions
of Los Angeles County, an area of more than four thousand square miles.
He owned about 35 percent of present-day Alhambra and shared ownership
of the central business district of Glendale. In Pasadena, he held a majority
interest in the Oak Knoll area, as well as property west of Annandale Country Club, land on North Lake Avenue, and one thousand acres in the city's
Rosemead section. HEH owned about 25 percent of the land in San Gabriel,
about 25 percent of South Pasadena, and approximately 75 percent of San
Marino. Furthermore, he owned business properties in downtown Los Angeles and held a substantial interest in Huntington Park and Vernon. He retained
90 percent of Redondo Beach, a minority interest in Huntington Beach and

Beverly Hills, real estate in Long Beach, and land in Newport Beach. All of these areas became densely settled over the course of the twentieth century. Information on HEH's landholdings comes from transcript of interview with A. G. Walker, 1 Mar. 1960, HEH 19/1.

38 For more information on the use of deed restrictions to determine the makeup of subdivisions, see Weiss.

39 Kevin Starr, *Inventing the Dream: California through the Progressive Era* (New York: Oxford University Press, 1985), 86.

40 See, for example, HEH to George Patton, 6 July 1904, HEH 7862.

41 Quoted from Donald D. Decker and Mary L. Decker, *Reflections on Elegance: Pasadena's Huntington Hotel since 1906* (Laguna Niguel, Calif.: Royal Literary Publications, 1985), 57–58.

42 HEH, quoted in *The Biblio: A Journal for Booklovers* 1 (February 1922): 158.

43 Marcosson, 23–34.

44 Huntington Land and Improvement Company Board of Directors Minutes, 5 Aug. 1927, HEH 1/F41/C.

CHAPTER 2

1 HEH to Mary Leonora (Huntington) Foster, 8 June 1862, HEH 645.

2 David Lavender, *The Great Persuader* (Garden City, N.Y.: Doubleday and Co., 1970), 5. This is the best biography of Collis Huntington. Other works include Cerinda W. Evans, *Collis Potter Huntington* (Newport News, Va.: Mariners' Museum, 1954); Oscar Lewis, *The Big Four* (New York: Alfred Knopf, 1938); and Stuart Daggett, *Chapters in the History of the Southern Pacific* (New York: Ronald Press, 1922). For additional biographical material on Collis, see the autobiographical letter from Collis Huntington to James Speyer, 26 Dec. 1899, and autobiographical notes edited with biographical notes by Charles Nordhoff, Collis Potter Huntington Papers (hereafter cited as CPH), microfilm, series 4, reel 1. The collection, on microfilm and labeled MS. 739, is held at the Huntington Library. The Collis Huntington Papers are held by Syracuse University.

3 HEH's old-stock, middle-class background placed him in a group from which the majority of the nation's business elite between the years 1870 and 1910 emerged. See essays by Francis Gregory and Irene Neu and by William Miller in William Miller, ed., *Men in Business* (New York: Harper Torchbooks, 1962).

4 For a glimpse of Solon Huntington's conservative nature, see Lavender, *Great Persuader*, 1–5, 32, 45. Solon's business sense, or lack of it, was the underlying theme of this letter from Collis to Solon, 17 May 1883, HEH 11114: "I am satisfied however that you are making nothing out of your farms, but that you are, on the contrary, losing every year, and I would advise you to sell out everything in the way of farming property at the best price you can obtain

and let me invest it in something that will be sure to pay interest always. That, with what the rental you will get, will give you all the money you will need to spend."

5 Lavender, *Great Persuader*, 17, 47.

6 Norman E. Tutorow, *Leland Stanford: Man of Many Careers* (Menlo Park, Calif.: Pacific Coast Publishers, 1971), 69–70.

7 Ibid., 72. See also Lavender, *Great Persuader*, 113.

8 Tutorow, 74.

9 Lavender, *Great Persuader*, 122–23, 143–45, 182.

10 Ibid., 245.

11 Ibid., 251–53, 271. See also Julius Grodinsky, *Transcontinental Railroad Strategy, 1869–1893: A Study of Businessmen* (Philadelphia: University of Pennsylvania Press, 1962), 28–29.

12 Lavender, *Great Persuader*, 412 n. 3. See also Joseph Doherty, "Smooth is the Road," *Tracks* 3 (June 1953): 45. (*Tracks* was an in-house publication of the Chesapeake and Ohio Railroad.)

13 HEH to Harriet Saunders Huntington, 16 May 1870, HEH 686.

14 Ibid., 13 June 1870, HEH 687. See also, for example, HEH to Harriet Huntington, 15 Aug. 1870, HEH 693; ibid., 5 Oct. 1870, HEH 694; or ibid., 22 Aug. 1871, HEH 700; or ibid., 30 Oct. 1871, HEH 704. HEH remained very close to his mother, and although she continued to live the rest of her life in Oneonta, once HEH and his sister, Caroline, moved to California in the 1890s, Harriet spent several months every year visiting her children on the West Coast. Following his father's death in 1890, HEH took over managing his mother's finances.

In his late teens and early twenties, HEH apparently attended church regularly, took communion, and told his mother that she could "rest assured I never close my eyes without praying" (22 Aug. 1871, HEH 700). Although he remained a member of the Presbyterian church, the religiosity of his letters all but disappears by about 1874.

15 HEH to Harriet Huntington, 5 July 1870, HEH 688.

16 Ibid., 16 May 1870, HEH 686; 24 July 1870, HEH 690; 31 July 1870, HEH 691.

17 See HEH Papers, box 19/3. This is part of the Robert O. Schad Collection of biographical material on HEH. File 3 is a chronological outline of HEH's life (hereafter cited as ROS chronological file).

18 This story varies depending on the source. For comparison, see Marcosson, 11–12; and Doherty, "Smooth is the Road," *Tracks* 2 (February 1952): 49. My account is based on HEH's correspondence. See HEH to Harriet Huntington, 13 Apr. 1871, HEH 697, and April 1871, HEH 696; HEH to Harriet and Solon Huntington, 20 May 1871, HEH 734. See also ROS chronology, HEH 19/3.

19 HEH to Harriet and Solon Huntington, 20 May 1871, HEH 734.

20 Marcosson, 12. The sawmill became so efficient that the price of an individual railroad tie dipped from one dollar to twenty-eight cents.

21 HEH to Harriet Huntington, 18 Apr. 1872, HEH 708; ROS chronological file, HEH 19/3. Mary Alice Prentice was the sister of Clara Prentice Huntington, the young girl Collis Huntington and his wife adopted. The father of the Prentice girls, a grocer, was drowned in a flash flood in Sacramento in 1862.

22 HEH to Harriet Huntington, 31 Jan. 1872, HEH 706. As if a portent of the future, this letter makes no mention of religious matters, and business appears to be the driving force in HEH's life. HEH to Harriet Huntington, 1 July 1872, HEH 710.

23 Collis Huntington to HEH, 23 Apr. 1873, CPH Papers, microfilm, series 1, reel 5.

24 See, for example, Richard Franchot to I. E. Gates, 12 Dec. 1873, CPH Papers, microfilm, series 1, reel 6; S. P. Franchot to Richard Franchot, 25 June 1874; and Richard Franchot to Collis Huntington, 12 July 1874, CPH Papers, microfilm, series 1, reel 7.

25 See HEH to Collis Huntington, 1 Feb. 1875, CPH Papers, microfilm, series 1, reel 7; and ibid., 2 June 1875 and 26 Sept. 1875, CPH Papers, microfilm, series 1, reel 8.

26 See HEH to Collis Huntington, 26 Sept. 1875, CPH Papers, microfilm, series 1, reel 8; and ibid., 6 Dec. 1875, CPH Papers, microfilm, series 1, reel 9.

27 The Southern Pacific Railroad was organized by San Francisco businessmen in 1865 and chartered to run from San Francisco to San Diego and then turn east to the California / Arizona border. In 1868 the SP, remaining a paper railroad, came under the control of the Central Pacific. Two years later, the SP was merged with the San Francisco and San Jose Railroad, the Santa Clara and Pajaro Valley Railroad, and the California Southern, to form the Southern Pacific of California. Construction of the SP began slowly; only eighty miles of track between San Francisco and Gilroy were opened by the end of 1870. By 1877, the SP had built more than seven hundred miles of track and had reached the California / Arizona border. Then the SP of Arizona and the SP of New Mexico rapidly laid rails across the deserts, and in 1881 the SP met the Texas and Pacific Railroad in the small town of Sierra Blanca, ninety miles southeast of El Paso. San Francisco was then connected with New Orleans, but Collis was determined to have a solely owned SP road to New Orleans. To accomplish this, the SP took a controlling interest in the Galveston, Harrisburg, and San Antonio Railroad in July 1881. Using the right-of-way granted to the GH&SA, the SP completed its own railroad to New Orleans in 1884. The line ran down from San Francisco through California to Yuma, Arizona; it then moved east through Tucson, El Paso, Sierra Blanca, Del Rio, San Antonio, Houston, Galveston, and finally to New Orleans.

To fulfill his dream of traveling from the Pacific to the Atlantic over tracks he either wholly owned or largely controlled, Collis convinced Crocker and Stanford (Hopkins had died in 1878) to join with him and other associates to build a rail connection between New Orleans and Memphis. The job required rehabilitating several roads Collis already owned, plus additional construction. Under the name of the Louisville, New Orleans and Texas Railroad, the 450-mile project was completed in October 1884. The Chesapeake and Ohio system was thereby connected with the SP.

28 Grodinsky, 163–65. For information of HEH's appointment, see Collis Huntington to Willard V. Huntington, 8 Apr., 9 July, and 22 Oct. 1881, CPH Papers, microfilm, series 2, reel 34, vol. 256.

29 HEH to Collis Huntington, 28 Feb. 1872, CPH Papers, microfilm, series 1, reel 27.

30 Marcosson, 15. Although obviously biased in favor of HEH, this source provides the most detailed description of HEH's activities on the eastern railroads from 1881 to 1892.

31 Robert O. Schad, *Henry E. Huntington: Founder of the Library* (San Marino, Calif.: Huntington Library, 1937), 8.

32 HEH to Harriet Huntington, 20 Oct. 1882, HEH 11126.

33 ROS chronology, HEH 19/3.

34 See Collis Huntington to HEH, 26 Mar. 1885, CPH Papers, microfilm, series 2, reel 24, vol. 157; and Collis Huntington to HEH, 1 Feb. 1886, HEH 3120.

35 For information on the Kentucky Central, see Maury Klein, *History of the Louisville and Nashville Railroad* (New York: Macmillan Co., 1972), 296–97; and Grodinsky, 163, 298. For specifics on the KC, such as rolling stock, trackage, and earnings, see *Poor's Manual of Railroads* (New York: Poor's Railroad Manual Company). This was an annual publication; see the years 1882–91.

36 The story was remembered by Los Angeles journalist, Otheman Stevens. Although it does not specify the exact location of the incident or the specific railroads involved, Stevens's account stressed that the episode took place in a "southern city where a railroad he [HEH] headed faced strong competition." Although it could have taken place when HEH headed the Elizabeth, Lexington and Big Sandy Railroad, it most likely occurred while on Kentucky Central where HEH faced stiff competition from Louisville and Nashville and the Illinois Central. See Otheman Stevens to Robert Schad, 11 July 1929, HEH 19/3.

37 See Marcosson, 16; and *Poor's Manual of Railroads*, 1888–90.

38 Evans, 582–83.

39 Neill C. Wilson and Frank J. Taylor, *Southern Pacific: The Roaring Story of a Fighting Railroad* (New York: McGraw-Hill Book Co., 1952), 102–03, 240; and Tutorow, p. 108.

40 Tutorow, 269.

41 Ibid., 263.

42 The Sargent Affair referred to an incident in which Huntington and Stanford, then the governor of California, supposedly agreed to back Aaron A. Sargent for U.S. senator in 1885. The election was to be decided by the California legislature, which was dominated by Republicans. All that was required was an indication from Stanford that he supported Sargent, and he would be elected. Stanford balked, and he himself was elected to the senate. Huntington and Sargent believed they had been double-crossed, and it was thought

that the release of this information might damage Stanford's political career. See Lavender, *Great Persuader*, 344–46; and Tutorow, 263–70.

43 Tutorow, 264–65.

CHAPTER 3

1 Collis Huntington to Joseph Willcutt, 13 Feb. 1893, HEH 3269.

2 HEH to Collis Huntington, 7 June 1892, HEH 5795. Slowly, HEH's job and powers expanded. The *San Francisco Chronicle*, 1 Jan. 1894, recorded: "When H. E. Huntington came here his position was a nominal one as representative of his uncle, but the power and duties of the Assistant to the President expanded. He gradually superceded Mr. Towne [SP second vice-president] in the management of affairs which hitherto had been exclusively under the charge of Vice President Crocker. . . . H. E. Huntington is an able man."

3 Edgar M. Kahn, *Cable Car Days in San Francisco* (Stanford: Stanford University Press, 1944), 40. See also Tutorow, 210; and George W. Hilton, *The Cable Car in America* (Berkeley: Howell-North Books, 1971), 23, 193.

4 Hilton, 25, 201; Kahn, 42; and Bion J. Arnold, *Report on the Improvement and Development of the Transportation Facilities of San Francisco* (San Francisco: The Hicks-Judd Co., 1913), 417.

5 Arnold, 412, 415. The seven other companies, all chartered in the 1860s, were Omnibus Railroad; North Beach and Mission Railway; Central Railroad; City Railroad; San Francisco and San Jose Railroad; Front, Mission and Ocean Railroad (in 1887 this became the Sutter Street Railway); and the Potrero and Bay View Railroad.

6 Ibid., 55, 120–23.

7 Kahn, 123.

8 Ibid., 122–23. Arnold, unnumbered pages; inside of front cover, plate 5, table 1. The population of San Francisco from 1880 to 1910 in ten-year increments was as follows:

1880	233,959
1890	298,997
1900	342,782
1910	416,912

9 Hilton, 31, 207.

10 *Poor's Directory of Railway Officials and Manual of American Street Railways, 1892* (New York: Poor's Railroad Manual Co., 1892), 251.

11 HEH to Collis Huntington, 3 Feb. 1893, HEH 5871; and HEH to Collis Huntington, 9 Feb. 1893, HEH 3265.

12 Ibid., 3 Feb. 1893, HEH 5872; and Collis Huntington to HEH, 9 Feb. 1893, HEH 3264.

13 HEH to Collis Huntington, 31 Dec. 1892, HEH 5838; and Collis Huntington to HEH, 5 Jan. 1893, HEH 3245.

14 HEH to Collis Huntington, 25 Jan. 1893, HEH 5860.

15 J. L. Willcutt to Fred Crocker, 13 Jan. 1893, HEH 8780.

16 Hilton, 229. See also Kahn, 124–26.

17 HEH to Collis Huntington, 13 Mar. 1893, HEH 5898. The Ferries and Cliff House Railway did $50,000 more in business than in the preceding year. HEH and his uncle were not alone in believing that the Omnibus line was too expensive to purchase; Fred Crocker and Thomas Hubbard, a member of the SP board of directors, did not think it was the proper time to purchase the railway. See HEH to Collis Huntington, 15 Apr. 1893, HEH 5926.

18 HEH to Collis Huntington, 12 July 1893, HEH 5987.

19 Collis Huntington to HEH, 10 Aug. 1893, HEH 3379.

20 HEH to Collis Huntington, 22 Sept. 1893, HEH 6059. To join into the merger, the larger companies received stock in the new company. The Market Street Cable Railway Company received 74.27 percent of the shares in the new company, Omnibus was given 18.50 percent, Ferries and Cliff House got 7.14 percent, and North Beach and Mission Railway received 0.09 percent interest in the Market Street Railway.

21 ROS chronology, HEH 19/3.

22 The California Street Cable Company operated only 16.5 miles of track, Geary Street Park and Ocean—owned by the SP—held 8 miles of track, Metropolitan owned 11 miles, Presidio and Ferries had 11.5 miles, the San Francisco and San Mateo employed 21 miles, and the Sutter Street Cable Railway held 13 miles of track. See *Poor's Manual of Railroads, 1894*, 1042.

23 Collis Huntington to HEH, 23 Oct. 1893, HEH 3430.

24 On HEH's economizing and expense reduction, see HEH to Collis Huntington, 5 Aug. 1893, HEH 6026; HEH to Collis Huntington, 25 Aug. 1893, HEH 6043; and Collis Huntington to HEH, 30 Aug. 1893, HEH 3391.

25 HEH to Collis Huntington, 15 Nov. 1893, HEH 6102.

26 The Market Street Railway Annual Report of 1894, 1–3, HEH 8866. Horse car lines were rapidly becoming losing properties. E. P. Vining, general manager of the Market Street system, wrote to HEH on 22 June 1895, HEH 8805: "It is hardly necessary to say that the day of the horse car has passed. People will not pay to ride in horse cars if they can help it and to a great extent, they do manage to help it by walking instead of riding. . . . Horses work efficiently for two years. Our horses have been in service four to six years and are twelve to sixteen years old. We cannot continue present service without purchasing more horses and it would be unwise to do so." Market Street moved quickly to convert its horse lines to electricity and to sell their aging animals. The company was disposing of their horses at a rate of three to four a day. Management decreased the number of horses from 1,076 in September 1894 to 388 in June 1895. See HEH 8798, and HEH 8804.

27 HEH to E. P. Vining, 6 May 1897, HEH 8127; E. P. Vining to HEH, 7 May 1897, HEH 8853; and E. P. Vining to HEH, 8 Oct. 1897, HEH 8821.

28 Collis Huntington to HEH, 9 Apr. 1896, HEH 3868.

29 Quoted from Monkkonen, 161.

30 HEH to Collis Huntington, 15 June 1893, HEH 5962; and Collis Huntington to HEH, 20 June 1893, HEH 3331.

31 See the *San Francisco Chronicle*, 3 Apr. 1896; and the *San Francisco Examiner*, 24 Sept. 1895, and 6 Jan. 1896. For his planned expansions, HEH apparently did obtain loans totaling approximately $500,000 from Isaias W. Hellman and the Nevada Bank. Hellman and his associates, Antoine Borel and Christian DeGuigne, eventually accepted Market Street Railway bonds in repayment of the loan. See the *San Francisco Examiner*, 8 Feb. 1896.

32 See the *San Francisco Call*, 21 Oct. 1895; and the *San Francisco Examiner*, 24 Sept. 1895, and 8 Jan. 1896. According to HEH's letter of 23 Dec. 1895 to Collis Huntington (HEH 6580), Market Street expected to pay its first dividend of sixty cents per share in the last quarter of 1895 ending 31 December.

33 Track mileage was taken from the annually published *Poor's Manual of Railroads* for the years 1895–1900. Earnings were found in Market Street Financial Reports, HEH 8880. Operating expenses came from letter from HEH to Collis Huntington, 15 Mar. 1899, HEH 7149.

34 HEH to Collis Huntington, 1 Nov. 1897, HEH 6922.

35 Alfred D. Chandler, Jr., *The Visible Hand: The Managerial Revolution in American Business* (Cambridge: Harvard University Press, 1977), 147. For more on railroad competition from the 1870s to the 1890s and the changing strategies from cooperation to system building, see 122–87.

36 Franklin Hoyt, "Railroad Development in Southern California, 1868–1900" (Ph.D. diss., University of Southern California, 1951), 232–35.

37 HEH to Collis Huntington, 1 Nov. 1897, HEH 6922; and HEH to Collis Huntington, 26 Aug. 1897, HEH 6854.

38 Ibid., 1 Nov. 1897, HEH 6922.

39 Periods for comparison are the forty months prior to HEH's arrival in San Francisco, 1 Jan. 1889 to 30 Apr. 1892, and the forty months after HEH took the job with the Southern Pacific, 1 Apr. 1892 to 31 July 1895. See HEH to Collis Huntington, 7 Nov. 1895, HEH 6563.

40 *Los Angeles Evening Express*, 6 Nov. 1897.

41 See newspaper clipping scrapbook, unmarked clipping, HEH 7/6, vol. 1, p. 268, and ROS chronology, HEH 19/3.

42 *San Francisco Chronicle*, 21 Mar. 1895; and *San Francisco Examiner*, 1 and 22 Mar. 1896.

43 Marcosson, 16.

44 R. Hal Williams, *The Democratic Party and California Politics, 1880–1896* (Stanford: Stanford University Press, 1973), 194. More information on the strike's ramifications in California may be found in Ira B. Cross, *A History of the Labor Movement in California* (Berkeley: University of California Press, 1935), 218–21; and Robert Knight, *Industrial Relations in the San Francisco Bay Area, 1900–1918* (Berkeley: University of California Press, 1960), 33–34. For coverage of the Pullman Strike in general, see Almont Lindsey, *The Pullman Strike* (Chicago: University of Chicago Press, 1942).

45 HEH to Collis Huntington, 27 June 1894, HEH 6198; and HEH to Collis Huntington, 2 July 1894, HEH 6205.

46 *Los Angeles Times*, 4 July 1894; Williams, 195.

47 HEH to David Parry, 14 Sept. 1903, HEH 7861.

48 HEH to Collis Huntington, 7 Aug. 1894, HEH 6241.

49 Ibid., 6 Feb. 1895, HEH 6435.

50 HEH to Lovell White, 1 and 10 Sept. 1898, HEH 8155; *Los Angeles Times*, 15 Sept. 1898; *Los Angeles Herald*, 16 Sept. and 27 Dec. 1898.

51 Henry and Mary Huntington had four children:

Howard Edwards	b. 1876, d. 1922
Clara Leonora	b. 1878, d. 1965
Elizabeth Vincent	b. 1880, d. 1965
Marian Prentice	b. 1883, d. 1970

When the Huntingtons were living in San Francisco, Howard began working for the engineering department on the Coast Division of the SP in 1894 and often was not home. The daughters often traveled with their mother. In addition to the trip to Europe in 1897, all three girls went to Banff, Alberta, with Mary in 1899; in 1901, Mary, Clara, and Elizabeth took a year-long trip to Europe. For information on the family, see journals of Edmund Burke Holladay 1894–1902, HEH 53/2.

52 Ibid., see 17 Oct. 1897, and 5 Apr. 1898.

53 See, for example, ibid., 7 July 1897.

54 See Collis Holladay to Robert Schad, 7 Dec. 1938, HEH 19/3; and the *Oneonta (N.Y.) Star*, 29 Mar. 1901.

55 See the journals of Edmund Burke Holladay, 1917–18, HEH 10968.

56 Over the years, Philip Speyer and Company, the American representative of L. Speyer-Ellisen and Company of Frankfurt, Germany, sold millions of dollars of SP bonds. Although the Speyers were not very friendly with the Huntingtons, Collis enjoyed the confidence of James Speyer. With the banker's help, Collis worked out a plan to acquire the Hopkins / Searles and Crocker shares in the SP and at the same time laid out a schedule to pay the federal government the Central Pacific's debt. According to an unmarked clipping in a newspaper clipping scrapbook, HEH 7/6, vol. 2, p. 69, Speyer and Company, in association with Kuhn, Loeb and Company, provided Collis with $28 million to buy out his partners. These firms apparently received a majority on the SP's board of directors.

57 *San Francisco Chronicle*, 9 Apr. and 22 Oct. 1899; *San Francisco Examiner*, 15 June 1900. See also newspaper clipping scrapbook, unmarked clipping, HEH 7/6, vol. 2, p. 69.

58 HEH to Herman Shainwald, 20 Aug. 1900, HEH 7956.

59 HEH to William Crocker, 30 Aug. 1900, HEH 5283.

60 HEH to I. W. Hellman, 4 Sept. 1900, HEH 5572.

61 *New York Times*, 6 Sept. 1900. According to Daggett, 426, by 1900, Collis held 37.5 percent of the SP stock. The Speyers controlled a larger percentage of stock than the Huntingtons; when Collis died, the bankers no longer wished the Huntington family to run the SP, and they were able to gather enough support to name their chosen successor to the SP presidency.

62 HEH to Thomas Hubbard, 8 Nov. 1901, HEH 5726.

63 HEH to Moses H. Sherman, 21 Aug. 1900, HEH 8201.

CHAPTER 4

1 HEH, quoted from Crump, *Ride the Big Red Cars*, 52.

2 See David Jones, *Urban Transit Policy: An Economic and Political History* (Englewood Cliffs, N.J.: Prentice-Hall, 1985), 32, 37; and Charles W. Cheape, *Moving the Masses: Urban Transit Policy in New York, Boston, and Philadelphia, 1880–1912* (Cambridge: Harvard University Press, 1980), 172, 215.

3 *Poor's Manual of Railroads, 1898*, 940. *Poor's* lists the LARY's mileage at 73.66. See also Howard J. Nelson, *The Los Angeles Metropolis* (Dubuque, Iowa: Kendall / Hunt Co., 1983), 266; and Kelker, De Leuw and Company, *Report and Recommendations*, 45. Both these sources claim LARY held 72 miles of track. Ira Swett, "Los Angeles Railway," *Interurbans*, Special No. 11 (1951): 37. According to Swett, the Los Angeles Railway held 104 miles of track by 1897.

4 Hilton, 175, 331.

5 See Swett, "Los Angeles Railway," 17; and Nelson, 158.

6 Swett, "Los Angeles Railway," 37.

7 Collis Huntington to HEH, 23 Nov. 1898, HEH 4293.

8 Swett, "Los Angeles Railway," 21; and Dumke, "Growth of the Pacific Electric," 40–41.

9 HEH to Lovell White, 1 Sept. 1898, HEH 8155.

10 *Los Angeles Times*, 15 Sept. 1898.

11 Swett, "Los Angeles Railway," 20, 37.

12 Ibid., 20; for Huntington's acquisition of the Los Angeles and Pasadena, see the *Los Angeles Times*, 27 Dec. 1898; and the *Los Angeles Herald*, 27 Dec. 1898; see also *Poor's Manual of Railroads, 1899*, 926–27.

13 *Los Angeles Times*, 1 Jan. 1900.

14 The firm was most likely based in Arizona because of that state's lax incorporation laws. See Crump, *Ride the Big Red Cars*, 44. Crump states that once HEH was restored to the SP, the PE of Arizona incorporation was dropped. However, when the PE of California was incorporated in November 1901, it consisted of several railroads, one of which was the PE of Arizona. See HEH to William B. Dana, 16 Dec. 1901, HEH 5287. See also Swett, "Los Angeles Railway," 20; and Laurence R. Veysey, "The Pacific Electric Railway, 1910–1953: A Study in the Operations of Economic, Social, and Political Forces upon American Local Transportation" (1953), 19. This typescript is available at Occidental College Library.

15 *Los Angeles Express*, 2 May 1901.

16 *San Francisco Bulletin*, 21 July 1901; see also ibid., 4 July 1901.

17 The quotation is from *PE Topics* 1 (July 1906): 8. Randolph's retirement from the PE is noted in the *Los Angeles Herald*, 12 Apr. 1904. For more on Randolph, see Dumke, "Growth of the Pacific Electric," 72–75.

18 According to Collis Huntington's will, Arabella Huntington received two-thirds of her deceased husband's SP stock, real estate in New York, and one-half of the entire estate. After granting his other relatives specific items, Collis bequeathed one-third of his SP stock and the remainder of his estate to HEH. Because of the will, Arabella and HEH came to share a joint interest

in many businesses. Their shared business interests included stockholdings in such firms as

    Newport News Shipbuilding and Dry Dock Company
    Newport News Light and Power Company
    Old Dominion Land Company
    Chesapeake and Ohio Railroad
    Chesapeake and Nashville Railroad
    Astoria and Columbia River Railroad
    Galveston, Harrisburg and San Antonio Railway
    Raquette Lake Railroad
    Rocky Mountain Coal and Iron Company
    Occidental and Oriental Steamship Company
    Hammond Lumber Company

See Last Will and Testament of Collis Potter Huntington, HEH 24/5, and Collis Potter Huntington Estate Material, Huntington Vault Material, box 3.

19 *San Francisco Bulletin*, 29 June 1901.

20 Edwin L. Lewis, "Street Railway Development in Los Angeles and Environs" 2 vols. (1938), 2: 39. A copy of this unpublished typescript is available at the Huntington Library.

21 *Los Angeles Herald*, 23 June 1901; *Los Angeles Express*, 26 June 1901; and *Pomona Times*, 10 July 1901.

22 Swett, "Los Angeles Railway," 38. Shorb was a station on the SP line located southwest of Alhambra. According to Franklin Hoyt, "Railroad Development in Southern California, 1868–1900" (Ph.D. diss., University of Southern California, 1951), 203, it stood near present-day Atlantic Avenue and Mission Road in Alhambra.

23 John Bicknell to HEH, 23 Oct. 1901, HEH 1327.

24 Joseph McBride to William Herrin, 14 Sept. 1908, HEH 9532.

25 For a copy of the Pacific Electric's 1901 Articles of Incorporation, see Crump, *Ride the Big Red Cars*, 235–36.

26 HEH to William B. Dana, 16 Dec. 1901, HEH 5287.

27 Crump, *Ride the Big Red Cars*, 235–36; and Dumke, "Growth of the Pacific Electric," 58. See also George W. Hilton and John F. Due, *The Electric Interurban Railways in America* (Stanford: Stanford University Press, 1960), 406–12.

28 Dumke, "Growth of the Pacific Electric," 74; and Crump, *Ride the Big Red Cars*, 45, 53, 58.

29 See David Brodsly, *LA Freeway: An Appreciative Essay* (Berkeley: University of California Press, 1981), 67. Brodsly continues: "Settlements, for example, paralleled the Santa Fe road at intervals of a mile and a half. More than half of these boomtowns failed, but more than thirty survived to provide a nuclei for subsequent growth of the county. They were Alhambra, Altadena, Arcadia, Azusa, Belvedere, Burbank, Claremont, Covina, Eagle Rock, Gardena, Glendale, Glendora, Hawthorne, Hollywood, Inglewood, La Verne, Lynwood, Monrovia, Puente, Redondo Beach, Rivera, San Dimas, Sawtelle,

Sierra Madre, South Pasadena, Sunland, Tropico, Tujunga, Verdugo Hills, Vernon, Watts, and Whittier."

30 HEH to A.C. Howe, 16 April, 1902, HEH 5663. HEH kept close watch on the city's population growth; his figures were nearly accurate. The Los Angeles population according to Kelker, De Leuw and Company, *Report and Recommendations*, 21, was as follows:

	City	County
1880	11,093	20,000
1890	50,395	101,454
1900	102,479	170,298

31 *Los Angeles Times*, 17 Apr. 1903. Patton, a prominent lawyer, large land-holder, and one-time Los Angeles district attorney, arrived in southern California in 1866. He married one of the daughters of Benjamin D. Wilson, a wealthy early settler of the area. This link to the Wilson family brought Patton into contact with J. de Barth Shorb who had also married a Wilson daughter. It is likely that through this relationship, Patton met HEH. After it was announced that Patton was to head HEH's land office, the 30 Apr. 1903 *Los Angeles Herald*, reported that HEH had purchased a controlling interest in the San Gabriel Wine Company. For information on Patton, see *History of Los Angeles: City and County of California*, 2 vols. (Los Angeles: J.R. Finnelly and Son Publishing Co. 1931), 2: 203–04. For information on Wilson and Shorb, see Glenn S. Dumke, *The Boom of the Eighties in Southern California* (San Marino, Calif.: Huntington Library, 1944); and Midge Sherwood, *Days of Vintage, Years of Vision* (San Marino, Calif.: Orizaba Publications, 1982).

32 See transcript of interview with HEH employee, A.G. Walker, 23 Mar. 1960, HEH 19/1.

33 Crump, *Ride the Big Red Cars*, 60.

34 HEH to Antoine Borel, 2 Jan. 1903, HEH 12498; and Los Angeles Land Company, Minutes of Directors Meetings, 23 May 1903, 13–15, HEH 1/I9.

35 Howard Huntington to Harriet Huntington, 21 Mar. 1903, HEH 11155.

36 HEH to John Boyd, 1 May 1902, HEH 5182.

37 The purchase of the property is described in the *Los Angeles Times*, 5 Mar. 1902; for information on the building, see the *Los Angeles Examiner*, 8 Sept. 1904; and Swett, "Los Angeles Railway," 40.

38 See Collis Potter Huntington Estate Material, Huntington Vault Material, box 3. The executors of Collis's estate were Charles Tweed and Isaac Gates.

39 *Los Angeles Times*, 1 Sept. 1907.

40 ROS chronology file, summary of bound clippings, 10 July 1903, HEH 19/3.

41 I.W. Hellman to HEH, 17 July 1901, HEH 2542.

42 See *History of Los Angeles*, 2: 7–10; and Hank Johnson, *The Railroad*

That Lighted Southern California (Los Angeles: Trans-Anglo Books, 1966), 10–11. See also William Myers, *Iron Men and Copper Wires: A Centennial History of the Southern California Edison Company* (Glendale, Cal.: Trans-Anglo Books, 1983); William C. Jones, "The Corporate Evolution of the Southern California Edison Company and Its Financial History from 1909 to 1928" (M.B.A. thesis, University of Southern California, 1929), 31–32; and William W. Clary, *History of the Law Firm of O'Melveny and Myers, 1885–1965*, 2 vols (Los Angeles: O'Melveny and Myers, 1966), 1: 266–82. See also Henry W. O'Melveny, *William G. Kerckhoff: A Memorial* (Los Angeles: Adcraft Press, 1935). This book was privately printed, and only 100 copies were made. The Huntington Library holds a copy in the rare book stacks.

43 William G. Kerckhoff to HEH, 24 July 1901, HEH 8440.

44 Ibid., 13 March 1902, HEH 9582; Pacific Light and Power's Articles of Incorporation, HEH 11/7/2. Although the Kerckhoff group took 49 percent of the new PL&P stock, some of their shares were turned over to stockholders of the San Gabriel Electric Company.

45 Jones, "Corporate Evolution of Southern California Edison," 31; and Dumke, "Growth of the Pacific Electric," 44–45.

46 Kerckhoff to *Commercial and Financial Chronicle*, 13 Nov. 1902, HEH 9580.

47 See Kerckhoff to HEH, 27 May 1903, HEH 9585; and Dumke, "Growth of the Pacific Electric," 45.

48 See transcript of interview with A. G. Walker, 23 March 1960, HEH 19/1; see also ROS chronology file, summary of bound clippings, 24 July 1903, HEH 19/3.

49 Bion J. Arnold, "The Transportation Problem of Los Angeles," *California Outlook*, 4 Nov. 1911, 3; and Nelson, *Los Angeles Metropolis*, 158.

50 Swett, "Los Angeles Railway," 37–38, 18–19; and Moses H. Sherman to HEH, 5 Sept. 1901, HEH 9887. For more information on Dunn, see Lewis, "Street Railway Development," 2: 39.

51 HEH to Hervey Lindley, 19 Oct. 1901, HEH 7680; and Hervey Lindley to HEH, 21 Oct. 1901, HEH 8544.

52 Swett, "Los Angeles Railway," 37–38.

53 Steven L. Easlon, *The Los Angeles Railway through the Ages* (Anaheim, Calif.: Easlon Publications, 1973), 16–17.

54 HEH to *Railroad Gazette*, 20 Feb. 1902, HEH 7917.

55 *Los Angeles Times*, 22 June 1902.

56 Crump, *Ride the Big Red Cars*, 58–59; and Hilton and Due, *Electric Interurban Railways in America*, 410.

57 See Nelson, *Los Angeles Metropolis*, 267; and Crump, *Ride the Big Red Cars*, 110.

58 Dumke, "Growth of the Pacific Electric," 110.

59 Ibid., 67. Although mainly providing interurban service, the PE also operated approximately twenty-five local streetcar lines primarily in the cities of Los Angeles, Long Beach, and Pasadena (see Crump, *Ride the Big Red Cars*, 75).

60 E. A. Adams to C. E. Graham, 24 1903, HEH 11300.

61 Dumke, "Growth of the Pacific Electric," 59–61.

62 For outstanding PE bonds, see *Commercial and Financial Chronicle, Street Railway Supplement*, 28 Feb. 1903. Information on HEH's holdings of PE bonds is taken from his personal balance sheets, December 1902 and 1903, HEH 11/2/1.

63 Christian DeGuigne to Isaias W. Hellman, 28 January 1903, HEH 1361; and breakdown of outstanding Pacific Electric stock, Pacific Electric auditor to HEH, 4 Feb. 1903, HEH 9534.

64 Figures for the Pacific Electric are taken from HEH's personal account book, HEH 7687; Los Angeles Railway's earnings come from the company's annual reports, 1900–03, HEH 2/2.

65 Crump, *Ride the Big Red Cars*, 61.

CHAPTER 5

1 *Los Angeles Times*, 5 May 1908.

2 Sam W. Wall, "Huntington: What He has Done and What He Failed to Do," *Los Angeles Financier*, 5 Nov. 1910, 300.

3 *Los Angeles Examiner*, 29 May 1908.

4 *Los Angeles Times*, 1 Sept. 1907.

5 HEH to Harriet Huntington, 21 October 1904, HEH 729.

6 *Los Angeles Times*, 2 Apr. 1903.

7 Marcosson, 8–9, 29–30.

8 See journals of Edmund Burke Holladay, HEH 53/2.

9 The brevity of the divorce hearing is noted in Crump, *Ride the Big Red Cars*, 87; see also journals of Edmund Burke Holladay, 22 Mar. 1906, HEH 53/2. Contemporary accounts of the divorce of HEH and Mary Huntington may be found in *Los Angeles Examiner*, *San Francisco Call*, and the *San Francisco Examiner*, all for 22 Mar. 1906.

10 Clara Huntington to Robert Schad, 19 Apr. 1929, HEH 19/3.

11 Riverside and Arlington Railway Company, Minutes of Directors Meeting, 7 Apr. 1903, HEH 9065; see also "Lines of the Pacific Electric: Northern and Eastern Division," *Interurbans* Special No. 61 (1976): 90. Huntington gained a controlling share in the San Bernardino Valley Traction Company by June 1907; see *Los Angeles Examiner*, 20 June 1907.

12 *Los Angeles Express*, 28 Apr. 1903, and *Los Angeles Times*, 24 Apr. 1903; William Kerckhoff to HEH, 28 Apr. 1903, HEH 8447. Crump, *Ride the Big Red Cars*, 64, states that HEH also acquired an interurban system in Santa Clara County. Long-distance trolley lines as well as extensive statewide interurban systems were becoming common in Ohio, Indiana, and Michigan (see Hilton and Due, 255–90).

13 Hilton and Due, 14–15, 197–207.

14 HEH to E. H. Harriman, 20 Jan. 1903, HEH 5559.

15 William Andrews Clark (1839–1925) was a Montana mine operator,

banker, entrepreneur, and politician. For biographical sketch on Clark, see John Ingham, ed., *Biographical Dictionary of American Business Leaders* (Westport, Conn.: Greenwood Press, 1983), 3: 166–67. For information on the agreement between Clark and Harriman, see George Kennan, *E. H. Harriman: A Biography*, 2 vols. (Boston: Houghton Mifflin Co., 1922), 1: 344–46; and Trottman, 319–24.

16 For information on the three-cent franchise, see the *Los Angeles Times*, 28 Mar., 4 and 8 Apr. 1903; *Los Angeles Express*, 1 and 9 Apr. 1903, *Los Angeles Herald*, 1 and 8 Apr. 1903; and Crump, *Ride the Big Red Cars*, 62.

17 *Los Angeles Times*, 16 June 1903.

18 Bound newspaper clipping scrapbook, unmarked clipping, 16 June 1903, HEH 7/2/1, 3.

19 William Hook, T. J. Hook, and Mary Hook to W. A. Clark, Agreement for sale and purchase of Los Angeles Traction Company, 14 Apr. 1903, HEH 2773.

20 *Los Angeles Times*, 18 Apr. 1903.

21 Crump, *Ride the Big Red Cars*, 68.

22 *Los Angeles Record*, 5 May 1903.

23 Agreement between HEH, Hellman, Borel, DeGuigne, and Harriman, 7 May 1903, HEH 5605. Prior to the deal, Bicknell, Randolph, and Slauson had apparently sold their interest in the Pacific Electric to Huntington. Then in March 1903, the remaining 95,480 shares of PE stock were subscribed to at one dollar per share as follows:

HEH	37,567.20
Hellman	9,103.63
Borel	9,103.63
DeGuigne	3,034.54
LA Land Co.	36,671.00

All the PE stock owned by the Los Angeles Land Company, a holding company in which HEH held the largest percentage of stock—with the minority interest held by Hellman, Borel, and DeGuigne—went to Harriman. So that Harriman would be an equal partner with HEH in the PE, Harriman received 3,655.66 shares of stock from Hellman, Borel, and DeGuigne. See also Joseph McBride to William Herrin, 14 Sept. 1908, HEH 9532. Following the May deal, the PE stock breakdown was as follows:

HEH	40,326.66
Harriman	40,326.66
Hellman	8,291.76
Borel	8,291.76
DeGuigne	2,763.16

For additional information on the payment made to the Hooks and to the SP, see HEH to Isaias Hellman, 30 June 1903, HEH 5600, and Isaias Hellman to Epes Randolph, 10 July 1903, HEH 2574.

24 See certificate for issuance of Pacific Electric bonds, 7 Nov. 1903, HEH 34/A/3; *Commercial and Financial Chronicle, Street Railway Supplements*, 28 Feb. 1903, and 27 Feb. 1904. The PE had $3,555,000 bonds outstanding in February 1903 and $8,494,000 outstanding in February 1904. No more PE bonds were sold while HEH held stock in the railroad.

25 HEH to Isaias Hellman, 3 June 1903, HEH 5596.

26 Although HEH owned all the stock and initially advanced $10 for each $100 in shares subscribed, directors' shares (5 shares each) were held under the names of John Muir; Epes Randolph; George Patton; Howard Huntington; S. C. Baxter, the PE auditor; and George Pillsbury, the PE chief engineer. Incorporated at the same time was the Pacific Electric Land Company, also wholly owned by HEH. Its purpose was to purchase land and acquire right-of-way for the LAIU. See Los Angeles Inter-Urban list of stockholders, 4 June 1903, HEH 8572; the *Los Angeles Express*, 6 June 1903; and Dumke, "Growth of the Pacific Electric," 36–37. By November 1904, the LAIU directorate included SP men William Herrin, William Hood, and H. I. Bettis (see HEH 34/A/4).

27 For information on cash advances and issuance of a similar amount of LAIU bonds, see A. D. McDonald to Isaias Hellman, 6 Apr. 1909, and receipts issued to the SP, HEH 34/A/4. By April 1905, the officers of both the PE and the LAIU were

HEH	president
William Herrin	vice-president
George Mulks	secretary
Isaias Hellman	treasurer

See the corrected final proof for the *American Street Railway Journal*, April 1905, HEH 7819; and George Mulks to C. B. Seger, 27 Mar. 1907, HEH 34/A/4.

28 *Los Angeles Express*, 12 Oct. 1903; *Los Angeles Times*, 26 Mar. 1904; *Los Angeles Herald*, 30 June 1904; HEH to *Commercial and Financial Chronicle*, 5 July 1904, HEH 1663. See also, Crump, *Ride the Big Red Cars*, 75.

29 HEH to George Patton, 25 Apr. 1904, HEH 12904.

30 Isaias Hellman to HEH, 25 Nov. 1904, HEH 2576.

31 HEH agreed to pay $598,374.91 for one-half of Hellman, Borel, and DeGuigne's holdings of PE stock and LAIU bonds. His initial payment of $163,592 was in various stocks, but no Los Angeles Railway stock was given in payment. HEH paid the remainder in three installments due in six, twelve, and eighteen months. See Isaias Hellman, Antoine Borel, and Christian DeGuigne to HEH, 7 Dec. 1904, HEH 2576.

32 *Los Angeles Examiner*, 21 Mar. 1906.

33 Ibid., 29 May 1908.

34 Dumke, "Growth of the Pacific Electric," 70–72; *Commercial and Financial Chronicle, Street Railway Supplement*, 13 Oct. 1906, 57, and 29 Feb. 1908, 56.

35 See Ed Fletcher, *Memoirs of Ed Fletcher* (San Diego: Pioneer Printers,

1952), 101–31; Elizabeth W. Richards, *Del Mar Decades* (Del Mar, Cal.: Santa Fe Federal Savings and Loan Association, 1974), 30–34; Joseph J. Hill, *The History of Warner's Ranch and Its Environs* (Los Angeles: Young and McCallister, 1927), 173; Clary, 276–78; and the *Los Angeles Express*, 18 July 1907.

36 *Los Angeles Express*, 24 July 1907.

37 Keith L. Bryant, Jr., *History of the Atchison, Topeka and Santa Fe Railway* (New York: Macmillan Publishing Co., 1974), 205–6.

38 See Trottman, 327–32; and Richard Pourade, *The History of San Diego: Gold in the Sun* (San Diego: Union Tribune Publishing Co. 1965), 45–47, 86, 92, 118, 166. See also Hofsommer, 58–59.

39 *Los Angeles Examiner*, 1 Feb. 1907; *Los Angeles Evening News*, 8 Mar. 1907; and Pourade, 15, 45–46.

40 Clary, 278; and Hill, 173.

41 Crump, *Ride the Big Red Cars*, 100, 248–49. The new cities incorporated between 1900 and 1910 in Los Angeles County were Covina (1901); Alhambra, Arcadia, Azusa, and Hollywood (1903); Venice and Wilmington (1904); Vernon (1905); Glendale, Huntington Park, La Verne, and Sawtelle (1906); Hermosa Beach, Sierra Madre, and Watts (1907); Belmont Heights and Inglewood (1908).

42 *Los Angeles Herald*, 23 July 1904.

43 The Pacific Electric and Los Angeles Inter-Urban net earnings were as follows:

Year	PE	LAIU
1904	−$71,891	
1905	$90,711	−$108,495
1906	$49,726	−$ 93,032
1907*	$27,932	−$127,799

*1907 figures are for January through October 1907.

See HEH's personal account book, HEH 7687. Huntington Land and Improvement Company figures are taken from HL&I Auditor's Reports, HEH 1/AA/A.

44 Los Angeles Railway's Annual Reports, 1904–06, HEH 2/2. LARY's return on investment follows:

1904	11.0 percent
1905	7.3 percent
1906	8.0 percent
1907	4.9 percent

45 Howard Huntington to Harriet Huntington, 15 Jan. 1904, HEH 11156.

46 Lewis, "Street Railway Development," 2: 51, 167; *Los Angeles Examiner*, 28 Mar. 1922; Howard Huntington to HEH, 20 Feb. 1907, HEH 8593; and HEH to Howard Huntington, 25 Feb. 1907, HEH 8593.

47 Swett, "Los Angeles Railway," 40.

48 HEH to Isaias Hellman, 20 May 1904, HEH 5603.

49 Swett, "Los Angeles Railway," 40–41; G.J. Kuhrts, chief engineer, LARY, to HEH, 4 Dec. 1909, HEH 8517.

50 *Pasadena Star News*, and the *Los Angeles Evening News*, for 28 Jan. 1907; George Patton to HEH, 4 Feb. 1907, HEH 8330. HEH's personal account book, HEH 7687, lists the stockholders of the LARY, as of 8 March 1905:

HEH	27,370 shares
Howard Huntington	100
C. A. Henderson	10
E. B. Holladay	10
J. D. Bicknell	5
G. S. Patton	5
W. S. Dunn	5
A. Borel	5,000*
C. DeGuigne	2,500*
I. Hellman	5,005*
I. Hellman, Jr.	2,495*
J. Meyer	2,500*
A. Parrott	5,000*

Harriman purchased the Hellman group's 45 percent interest of the LARY (Hellman group members designated by asterisks) in 1907. I. W. Hellman, Jr., was probably placed on the directorate to maintain a close connection with this powerful banking family.

51 See the *Los Angeles Times*, 12 July 1905; Dumke, "Growth of the Pacific Electric," 20; and Register of HEH Companies, November 1907, HEH 8231.

52 See the *Los Angeles Examiner*, 23 Mar. 1906; and William A. Myers and Ira L. Swett, *Trolleys to the Surf: The Story of the Los Angeles Pacific Railway* (Glendale, Calif.: Interurbans Publications, 1976), 198–204.

53 Weiss, 79–140. The city of Los Angeles did not have any zoning regulations until 1908 when it passed the country's first land-use zoning law. Beginning in 1921, the city moved toward zoning areas strictly for single-family residences. Effective regulation over metropolitan subdivision began in 1922 when the Los Angeles Board of Supervisors established the Los Angeles County Regional Planning Commission, empowered to "plan for and regulate the use of land in all unincorporated areas of the huge county. The Commission, the first of its kind in the U.S., was also charged with coordinating its county land-use planning activities with the city planning commissions of Los Angeles, Pasadena, Long Beach, and the county's other incorporated cities" (Weiss, 13).

54 For subdividers' use of deed restrictions, see ibid., 10–12, 45–47, 68–72.

55 *Los Angeles Examiner*, 3 Dec. 1905; Carol Green Wilson, *California Yan-*

kee: William R. Staats—Business Pioneer (Claremont, Calif.: Saunders Press, 1946), 94–95.

56 See William R. Staats Co., Oak Knoll pamphlet (1906); Oak Knoll Tract Map (1912), HEH 9977; and Wilson, 94–95.

57 *Pasadena Star News*, 27 Nov. 1909; Huntington Land and Improvement Company, Minutes of Directors Meeting, 29 Nov. 1909, 33, HEH 1/F41/B; and Oak Knoll Tract Map (1912), HEH 9977.

58 See the *Los Angeles Herald*, 13 Sept. 1912; and the *Los Angeles Examiner*, 25 Sept. 1912. The Huntington name had emerged as a valuable commodity in southern California, denoting quality and prestige, and Allen P. Nichols, a Pomona developer, wanted to use it. He wrote the streetcar magnate requesting the right to use his name on a subdivision in the east San Gabriel Valley. In December 1906, HEH granted Nichols permission to use the Huntington name on the tract: "Naturally, I would not like my name put at the head of anything which is not or is not likely to be a success; but the character of yourself and friends seems to me to be a pretty good guarantee that what you are doing will prove a decided success." See HEH to Allen P. Nichols, 6 Dec. 1906, HEH 7835.

59 Fogelson, 154.

60 See *Los Angeles Herald*, 10 and 14 June, 5 Oct. 1903, and 14 Sept. 1907. See also prospectus for Alfred Dolge Manufacturing Company, 8 May 1903; and the articles of incorporation for the Dolgeville Land Company, 9 May 1903, HEH 11/5/3; *PE Topics* 2 (December 1906): 56–57. Other manufacturers that set up in Dolgeville included Electric Heating and Manufacturing Plant and Tallyrand Manufacturing (makers of metal pipe). See advertisement for Dolgeville in November 1906 *PE Topics*.

61 Myers and Swett, 50; see also Dennis Shanahan, *Old Redondo: A Pictorial History of Redondo Beach, California* (Redondo Beach: Legends Press, 1982); and Redondo Improvement Company, Minutes of Directors Meetings, 15 and 20 July 1905, 108–09, HEH 1/R/11.

62 *Los Angeles Times*, 20 July 1905.

63 Myers and Swett, 51; Crump, *Ride the Big Red Cars*, 80–81. See also the *Los Angeles Record*, 10 and 13 July 1905; and Charles N. Glaab and A. Theodore Brown, *History of Urban America* (New York: Macmillan Publishing Co., 1967), 282.

64 Edmund Burke Holladay to Harriet Huntington, 13 July 1905, HEH 2679. By the end of July, HEH had incorporated a new land company, the Huntington-Redondo Company, through which he and his associates, the Martin family of San Francisco and J. D. Harvey, obtained 1,020 acres south of Redondo. The company's first subdivision in this area was known as Clifton-by-the-Sea; HEH and architect Myron Hunt built homes here (see transcript of A. G. Walker tape on HEH's real estate holdings, HEH 19/1).

65 Shanahan, 55–58; and Myers and Swett, 51.

66 William L. Kahrl, *Water and Power: The Conflict over Los Angeles' Water Supply in the Owens Valley* (Berkeley: University of California Press, 1982), 96–

98; and William W. Robinson, *The Story of the San Fernando Valley* (Los Angeles: Title Insurance and Trust Co., 1961), 35–40.

67 The phrase "quietly and alone" comes from Marcosson, 30. For quotation, see *Los Angeles Examiner*, 25 Aug. 1905.

68 Kahrl, 97–99, 138, 198; and Fred W. Viche, Letter to the Editor, *Southern California Quarterly* 70 (Fall 1988): 370.

69 Kahrl, 185–88; and Crump, *Ride the Big Red Cars*, 116–19.

70 HEH to William Kerckhoff, 20 July 1904, HEH 7658.

71 Clary, 272–75. See also Henry O'Melveny to HEH, 31 May 1904, HEH 9273; A. C. Balch to HEH, 13 June 1904, HEH 5134; and Henry O'Melveny to HEH, 16 June 1904, HEH 7841.

72 HEH to Henry O'Melveny, 21 June 1904, HEH 7841.

73 William Kerckhoff to HEH, 23 July 1903, HEH 9587; and William Kerckhoff to HEH, 24 July 1903, HEH 9588.

74 HEH to William Kerckhoff, 18 July 1904, HEH 7657; HEH to A. C. Balch, 19 July 1904, HEH 5135; and William Kerckhoff to HEH, 23 July 1904, HEH 9596. On the start-up of the Kern power plant, see, ROS chronology file, summary of bound clippings, 29 Dec. 1904, HEH 19/3; and Swett, "Los Angeles Railway," 40, which places the opening of the Kern facility in January 1905.

75 O'Melveny, 55–56, and Nelson Van Valen, "A Neglected Aspect of the Owens River Aqueduct Story: The Inception of the Los Angeles Municipal Electric System," in *A Southern California Historical Anthology*, ed. Doyce Nunis, Jr. (Los Angeles: Historical Society of Southern California, 1984), 307.

76 Dumke, "Growth of the Pacific Electric," p. 45; Swett, "Los Angeles Railway," 41; *Los Angeles Times*, 29 Dec. 1906; and the *Commercial and Financial Chronicle, Railroad Supplement*, Sept. 1908, 61.

77 See Register of HEH Companies, HEH 8231; *Los Angeles Evening News*, 3 Sept. 1907; Huntington Land and Improvement Company, Minutes of Directors Meetings, 4 Sept. 1907, 236, and 8 Feb. 1908, 255, HEH 1/F41/A; and San Gabriel Valley Water Company. See also Minutes of Directors Meetings, 29 Aug. 1904, 37; 26 May 1906, 74; 5 Nov. 1907, 100; and 18 Feb. 1908, 108, HEH 1/U.

78 See HEH to George Ward, 27 Dec. 1904, 18 Jan. 1905, and biographical papers in the George C. Ward Collection, box 2; transcripts of interviews with A. G. Walker, 23 Mar. and 8 Apr. 1960 (in the latter interview, Walker said that Patton resigned as head of HL&I in either 1910 or 1911), HEH 19/1; and Wilson, 139.

CHAPTER 6

1 *Los Angeles Herald*, 1 Jan. 1908.

2 *Los Angeles Times*, 26 Apr. 1910.

3 Samuel T. Clover, *Constructive Californians—Men of Outstanding Ability*

Who Have Added Greatly to the Golden State's Prestige (Los Angeles: Saturday Night Publishing Co., 1926), 1.

4 See, for example, the *Los Angeles Examiner*, 8 Sept. 1908, which reported that Huntington and Harriman agreed to spend $2 million on PE expansions.

5 Huntington Land and Improvement Company Trial Balance Sheets, 1908–13, HEH 1/DD/1–5.

6 HEH to William Herrin, 24 Jan. 1905, HEH 5633.

7 *Los Angeles Express*, 25 May 1907.

8 *Los Angeles Times*, 30 June 1908; and Crump, *Ride the Big Red Cars*, 91.

9 Dumke, "Growth of the Pacific Electric," 76; and Hilton and Due, 406–13.

10 *Los Angeles Times*, 18 Aug. 1909, *Los Angeles Express*, 19 Apr. 1910. See also Los Angeles Railway pamphlet, May 1910; and Los Angeles Railway scrapbook of newspaper clippings, vol. 2 (located in the Huntington Library rare book stacks).

11 Swett, "Los Angeles Railway," 41; G. J. Kuhrts to HEH, 4 Dec. 1909, HEH 8517; Los Angeles Railway Annual Report, 1908, HEH 2/2; and C. A. Henderson to Howard Huntington, 25 May 1911, HEH 8634.

12 William Herrin to HEH, 28 July 1910, HEH 12290; and HEH to William Herrin, 29 July 1910, HEH 12721. The PE's net earnings come from California Railroad Commission, *Annual Report*, 1912 / 1913, 988–89.

13 See LAIU list of stockholders, 20 June 1908, HEH 8572.

14 See Huntington Vault Material, box 1; and HEH 34/A/4.

15 Hilton and Due, 114.

16 Dumke, "Growth of the Pacific Electric," 78; and California Railroad Commission, *Annual Report*, 1912 / 1913, 988–99, 1207.

17 Hilton and Due, 142.

18 California Railroad Commission, *Case No. 4002: Report on the Local Transportation Requirements of Los Angeles* (Los Angeles, 1935), 72.

19 *Los Angeles Times*, 12 Nov. 1910.

20 Lewis, "Street Railway Development," 2: 68; and Swett, "Los Angeles Railway," 41.

21 C. A. Henderson to HEH, 12 June 1911, HEH 2590.

22 California Railroad Commission, *Annual Report*, 1914 / 1915, 585; and California Railroad Commission, *Opinions and Orders*, 1 January to 29 May 1915, 274. Net return on investment is calculated by using the stated capitalization of the company. However, because it was common in this period for street railways to overstate the invested capital and the corresponding value of the road and equipment, the net return should be considered a low estimate (see Hilton and Due, 183–91).

23 Los Angeles Railway Annual Reports, 1912–14, HEH 2/2. Up to 1911, this company's fiscal year ended 31 Dec.; beginning with the annual report of 1912, the fiscal year ended 30 June.

24 See promissory note, Los Angeles Railway Corporation to Los Angeles Railway Company, 1 Dec. 1910, HEH 8621; and *Los Angeles Examiner*, 12 Oct. 1912.

25 See HEH's personal balance sheet, December 1911, HEH 11/2/1.

26 Epes Randolph to HEH, 2 May 1911, HEH 14120; and HEH to Epes Randolph, 8 May 1911, HEH 14120.

27 California Railroad Commission, *Opinions and Orders*, 1 Jan. to 29 May 1915, 276.

28 California Railroad Commission, *Annual Report*, 1911 / 1912, 1–17; and Board of Public Utilities, City of Los Angeles, *Annual Report*, 1909 / 1910. See also Spencer C. Olin, Jr., *California's Prodigal Sons: Hiram Johnson and the Progressives, 1911–1917* (Berkeley: University of California Press, 1968), 37–40.

29 HEH to Howard Huntington, 3 June 1911, HEH 7629.

30 *Los Angeles Herald*, 26 Oct., 23 Nov. 1911, and 2 Feb. 1912; *Los Angeles Examiner*, 13 Dec. 1911; and *Los Angeles Express*, 2 Mar. 1912.

31 *Los Angeles Herald*, 5 Mar., 27 May 1912; *Los Angeles Times*, 25 May 1912; *Los Angeles Express*, 25 July 1912; and *Los Angeles Municipal News*, 12 July 1912.

32 Lewis, "Street Railway Development," 2: 151–54; *Los Angeles Tribune*, 9 Jan. 1914; and *Los Angeles Examiner*, 8 Jan. 1914.

33 Lewis, "Street Railway Development," 2: 86.

34 Huntington Land and Improvement Company Trial Balance Sheets, 1908–13, HEH 1/DD/1–5; and HL&I Auditor's Reports, HEH 1/AA/A–D.

35 Huntington Land and Improvement Company uncatalogued Ledger, 1902–03, 3; and Pacific Light and Power Company Index, HEH 8/8. See also *Los Angeles Times*, 6 Mar. 1913. On 12 Mar. 1913, six days after the sale, HEH purchased three lots at the corner of Eleventh and Broadway with the proceeds from the property. On this land, he planned to construct the eleven-story Los Angeles Railway Building. The project was not begun until April 1920, and the Los Angeles Railway Corporation moved its offices from the PE Building to its own facility in May 1922.

36 See Fogelson, 231–32; O'Melveny, 58–61; George Wallace, *Joseph Francis Sartori: 1858–1946* (Los Angeles: Ward Richie Press, 1948), 78–79; and *Los Angeles Examiner*, 26 Aug. 1908, 17 Dec. 1910. For information on Lowe, see Charles Seims, *Mount Lowe: The Railway in the Clouds* (San Marino, Calif.: Golden West Books, 1976), 25–28.

37 Board of Public Utilities, City of Los Angeles, *Annual Report*, 1909 / 1910, 58. Two other firms, Southern California Edison and Economic Gas, distributed approximately 2 to 3 percent of the city's gas.

38 *Los Angeles Examiner*, 17 Dec. 1910. For the story of Southern California Gas Company, see Douglas R. Littlefield and Tanis C. Thorne, *The Spirit of Enterprise: The History of Pacific Enterprises from 1886 to 1989* (Los Angeles: Pacific Enterprises, 1990).

39 California Railroad Commission, *Annual Report*, 1911 / 1912, 447; and *Walker's Manual of California Securities: 1920 Edition* (San Francisco: H. D. Walker, 1920), 307. Of the $6.4 million SoCal Gas bonds sold, PL&P purchased $4 million in November 1910.

40 *Los Angeles Examiner*, 6 Aug. 1911; *Los Angeles Herald*, 15 Jan. 1912; O'Melveny, 61; and *Moody's Manual of Investments: Public Utility Securities, 1926* (New York: Moody's Investment Service, 1926), 108–09.

41 Board of Public Utilities, City of Los Angeles, *Annual Report*, 1913 / 1914, 31.

42 *Walker's Manual of California Securities: 1908*, 28; and statement of PL&P earnings and expenses, HEH 11/7/2.

43 Myers, 60–61; and Johnson, 11.

44 Ibid., pp. 102–03; and David Redinger, *The Story of Big Creek* (Los Angeles: Eureka Press, 1949), 1–33. See also John Eastwood's 1905 report on hydroelectric power development of Big Creek, HEH 11/7/2.

45 Dumke, "Growth of the Pacific Electric," 45; Johnson, 12–14; *Los Angeles Examiner*, 19 Feb. 1910; and *Los Angeles Times*, 1 Mar. 1910.

46 Robert Hereford, *A Whole Man, Henry Mauris Robinson, and Half a Century, 1890–1940* (Pacific Grove, Cal.: Boxwood Press, 1985), 55–67; Big Creek cost sheet, 24 Jan. 1914, HEH 11/7/2; William Salomon and Company to HEH, 26 Oct. 1911, HEH 9780; HEH's personal balance sheet, December 1911, HEH 11/2/1; and HL&I Minutes of Directors Meetings, 1 and 2 Sept. 1910, 75. HEH 1/F41/B.

47 See Redinger, 10–18; Johnson, 13–15; and *Los Angeles Examiner*, 31 Jan. 1912.

48 Redinger, 31–32; PL&P and William Salomon and Company, Bond Agreement, 1 May 1913, Huntington Vault Material, box 4; and Big Creek cost sheet, 24 Jan. 1914, HEH 11/7/2.

49 William Dunn to C. E. Graham, 14 July 1913, Huntington Vault Material, box 4.

50 C. E. Graham to HEH, 29 July and 14 Aug. 1913, Huntington Vault Material, box 4; and HL&I Minutes of Directors Meeting, 14 Aug. 1913, 189, HEH 1/F41/B.

51 *Los Angeles Times*, 9 Nov. 1913; Big Creek cost sheet, 24 Jan. 1914, HEH 11/7/2; Redinger, 10–11, 31–32; and Myers, 109.

52 California Railroad Commission, *Annual Report*, 1912 /1913, 1405, 1459; and HL&I Minutes of Directors Meeting, 15 June 1915, 270, HEH 1/ F41/B.

53 HEH / Kerckhoff-Balch gas and power deal, 14 Apr. 1913, Huntington Vault Material, box 4. As of 24 Feb. 1914, HEH's ownership of PL&P stock was as follows:

PL&P Stock	Total Outstanding	HEH–Owned
First-preferred stock	30,570	29,322
Second-preferred stock	99,750	96,602
Common stock	105,595	104,685

See list of PL&P stockholders, 24 Feb. 1914, HEH 11/7/2.

54 For newspaper accounts, see *New York Times* and *New York Morning Herald*, of 17 July 1913; HEH to E. B. Holladay, 16 July 1913, HEH 678. In HEH's letter to his sister, Caroline Holladay, on 13 July 1913, HEH 656, HEH

expressed joy regarding his upcoming marriage: "I cannot tell you how happy I am my dear sister, and I hope to make up for all I have lost and again have a home and a home such as I have never had. Bell [Arabella, his bride] is so good and kind to me, and I know she will make my life very happy."

CHAPTER 7

1 Transcript of interview with Leslie Bliss, Huntington librarian, 3 Jan. 1968; and transcript of interview with Alfonso Gomez, HEH's valet, 11 Apr. 1959, HEH 19/1. For information on Chateau Beauregard, see HEH to Caroline Holladay, Sept. 1913, HEH 659; and Chateau Beauregard financial records, HEH 12/1, 12/3, and 12/7. The Huntingtons' location is best tracked by the journals of Edmund Burke Holladay, HEH 53/2 and HEH 10968. According to Holladay, HEH and Arabella were in Europe in 1913, 1914, 1920, and 1921.

2 See Hilton and Due, 211–12; and Jones, *Urban Transit Policy*, 37–40.

3 *Los Angeles Examiner*, 17 Sept. 1916.

4 HEH to William Dunn, 6 Sept. 1923, HEH 12614.

5 For information on the relationship between Dunn and HEH, see the transcript of interview with A. G. Walker, 23 Mar. 1960, HEH 19/1; Lewis, "Street Railway Development," 2: 39; and transcript of interview with Emma Quigley, 21 Apr. 1960, HEH 19/1. The continued closeness between the two men is recorded in the Quigley transcript, where she recounts how HEH and Dunn shared the same office after the Los Angeles Railway Corporation left the PE Building for the new Los Angeles Railway Building in 1922.

6 Swett, "Los Angeles Railway," 43; for information on the Los Angeles Railway's reorganization, see *Los Angeles Examiner*, 6 Dec. 1913; *Los Angeles Express*, 10 Dec. 1913; *Los Angeles Times*, 7 Jan. 1914; and California Railroad Commission, *Opinions and Orders*, 1 Jan. to 29 May 1915, 272–85.

7 *Los Angeles Tribune*, 3 Dec. 1913; *Los Angeles Herald*, 31 Dec. 1913; and *Walker's Manual of California Securities, 1920*, 186–87. See also William Dunn to HEH, 27 Apr. 1914, Huntington Vault Material, box 1.

8 Edgerton, quoted in California Railroad Commission, *Opinions and Orders*, 1 Jan. to 29 May 1915, 284.

9 John Miller, *Fares, Please! A Popular History of Trolleys, Horsecars, Streetcars, Buses, Elevateds, and Subways* (New York: Dover Publications, 1960), 147–49; and Lewis, "Street Railway Development," 2: 114–17. For an examination of jitneys' impact on the West Coast, see Carlos Schwantes, "The West Adopts the Automobile: Technology, Unemployment, and the Jitney Phenomenon of 1914–1917," *Western Historical Quarterly* 16 (July 1985): 307–26.

10 Dunn, quoted in *Los Angeles Examiner*, 13 Nov. 1914.

11 Schwantes, 308–9.

12 See *Los Angeles Times*, 8 Jan. 1915; Lewis, "Street Railway Development," 2: 126; and Los Angeles Railway Annual Reports, 1914–18, HEH 2/2.

13 Fogelson, 167; and Los Angeles Railway Annual Reports, 1914–18, HEH 2/2. The railroad's operations for this period in terms of earnings and expenses per car mile follow:

Year	Gross Revenues per car mile	Expenses per car mile	Net Earnings per car mile
1914	23.26 cents	16.02 cents	7.24 cents
1915	21.60 "	14.94 "	6.66 "
1916	20.72 "	14.04 "	6.68 "
1917	20.26 "	14.95 "	5.31 "
1918	20.86 "	17.44 "	3.42 "

14 HEH to William Dunn, 11 Oct. 1915, HEH 12574; 14 Oct. 1915, HEH 12575.

15 California Railroad Commission, *Opinions and Orders*, 1 Jan. to 30 Apr. 1916, 194–96. See also Swett, "Los Angeles Railway," 43.

16 Railroad Commission of the State of California Engineering Department, *Application 4238: Report on the Service, Operating, and Financial Conditions of the Los Angeles Railway Corporation* (Los Angeles, 1919), 10, 29–30; Miller, *Fares, Please!*, 115–22; and Lewis, "Street Railway Development," 2: 115–22.

17 *Los Angeles Tribune*, 3 and 13 Apr. 1915.

18 William Dunn to HEH, 3 Aug. 1915, HEH 11717.

19 Los Angeles Railway Annual Reports, 1914–18, HEH 2/2.

20 See William Dunn to Charles Graham, 22 June 1917, HEH 11677; and Charles Graham to William Dunn, 16 Jan. 1915, HEH 11900.

21 Lewis, "Street Railway Development," 2: 123–24; *Los Angeles Herald*, 4 May 1917; and Swett, "Los Angeles Railway," 43–44. Following the successful election in June 1917 banning jitneys from the business district, the LARY granted the second pay raise. Together, the two wage hikes added approximately $240,000 to the Los Angeles Railway's payroll.

22 Los Angeles Railway Annual Reports, 1913–18, HEH 2/2; and Swett, "Los Angeles Railway," 43–44.

23 Mark S. Foster, "The Decentralization of Los Angeles during the 1920s" (Ph.D. diss., University of Southern California, 1971), 182; and Board of Public Utilities, City of Los Angeles, *Annual Report*, 1916 / 1917, 25.

24 See, for example, agreement between HL&I and Baker and Burbank, Huntington Land and Improvement Company, Board of Directors Minutes, 8 Jan. 1906, HEH 1/F41/A; agreement between Huntington-Redondo Company and Henry S. Judson, Huntington-Redondo Company, Board of Directors Minutes, 6 Feb. 1914, HEH 1/H/20; and Oak Knoll Marino Sales Pamphlet, HEH 194420.

25 See the Huntington Land and Improvement Company's monthly balance sheets, 1/DD/1–5.

26 The HL&I balance sheet of December 1923, HEH 1/DD/5, records more than $1 million in unrealized real estate profits prior to 1913. Statement of lot sales in California, Huntington Vault Material, box 4.

27 Quoted from letter from Charles Graham to HEH, 2 Aug. 1915, HEH 11966.

28 California Railroad Commission, *Opinions and Orders*, 1 Jan. to 30 June 1914, 350–54, 380–84, 778–79, 1307–08.

29 Myers, 64–66.

30 George Ward to Charles Graham, 26 Mar. 1914, George Ward to HEH, 16 May 1914, HEH 11/7/2; and *Los Angeles Times*, 1 Apr. 1914. The distribution of Ventura County Power Company's stock was as follows:

	common stock	preferred stock
prior to deal		
outstanding	8,101	3,817
unissued	6,899	6,183
total	15,000	10,000
following deal		
HEH owned	6,980.6	3,371.8
owned by outsiders	1,120.4	445.2

For information on HEH's acquisition of Mt. Whitney Power and Electric Company, see *Los Angeles Tribune*, 6 Sept. 1916; and Myers, 98–99.

31 See Huntington Vault Material, box 3.

32 *Los Angeles Examiner*, 4 July 1915; and Redinger, 46–47.

33 John B. Miller, quoted in *Los Angeles Times*, 2 Dec. 1916.

34 See William Kerckhoff to HEH, 20 Jan. 1902, HEH 13237; and William Kerckhoff to HEH, 24 Mar. 1902, HEH 8441.

35 William Kerckhoff to HEH, 25 June 1903, HEH 8452.

36 Ibid., 24 Oct. 1908, HEH 8456.

37 HEH to William Kerckhoff, 19 Feb. 1909, HEH 8219; and printed prospectus of proposed new corporation, HEH 8220. For information on Pacific Lighting and C. O. G. Miller, see Charles M. Coleman, *P. G. and E. of California: The Centennial Story of Pacific Gas and Electric Company, 1852–1952* (New York: McGraw-Hill Book Co., 1952), 46–49.

38 Van Valen, "Owens River Aqueduct Story," 290–311.

39 Fogelson, 233–35, and Myers, 148.

40 Board of Public Utilities, City of Los Angeles, *Annual Report*, 1913/1914, 17; see also Fogelson, 234–36; and Myers, 147–48.

41 Charles Graham to George C. Luebbers, regarding proposed sale of HEH's Safety Insulated Wire and Cable Company, 17 May 1910, Huntington Vault Material, box 3.

42 Huntington was hampered with an enlarged prostate in October 1915,

but he recovered in early 1916, and the expected surgery was not required (see William Dunn to Charles Graham, 14 and 18 Oct. 1915; and Charles Graham to William Dunn, 15 Oct. 1915, HEH 11906). For information on Miller's proposal of creating a new issue of SoCal Edison second-preferred stock, see Charles Graham to HEH, 14 and 15 Dec. 1915; and Charles Graham to A. N. Kemp, 16 Dec. 1915, Huntington Vault Material, box 2.

43 See memorandum between HEH and John B. Miller, 30 Dec. 1915, HEH 7773; and California Railroad Commission, *Opinions and Orders*, 1 Apr. to 1 Aug. 1917, 262–71. When HEH sold his shares in the PL&P to SoCal Edison, only a small percentage of PL&P stock was held by outsiders.

PL&P Stock	Total Outstanding	HEH–Owned
First-preferred	50,000	46,175
Second-preferred	99,750	96,602
Common	105,595	104,685

44 See *Los Angeles Examiner*, 4 Dec. 1916; *Los Angeles Times*, 24 Mar. 1917; California Railroad Commission, *Opinions and Orders*, 1 Apr. to 1 Aug. 1917, 401–14; and Myers, 150–51.

45 John B. Miller, quoted in Southern California Edison pamphlet, *The Greater Edison* (1917), 4.

46 This library, which consisted of works by such authors as John Ruskin, William Thackeray, Charles Dickens, Walter Scott, and George Bancroft, was mentioned by relatives of S. P. Franchot, HEH's partner in the St. Albans sawmill, in letters to the Huntington Library in the 1920s and 1930s. The library came into Franchot's possession as part of the dissolution of the sawmill partnership. See N. V. V. Franchot to Robert Schad, 4 May 1929; Mrs. N. V. V. Franchot to Robert Schad, 17 June 1937; and Robert Schad to Caroline Holladay, 31 Oct. 1938, HEH 19/3.

47 James Thorpe, "The Founder and His Library," *Huntington Library Quarterly* 32 (August 1969): 299.

48 See Donald C. Dickinson, "Mr. Huntington and Mr. Smith," *The Book Collector* 37 (Autumn 1988): 366–93; and John E. Pomfret, *The Henry E. Huntington Library and Art Gallery from Its Beginnings to 1969* (San Marino, Calif.: Huntington Library, 1969), 7–20.

49 HEH, quoted in Thorpe, 301, 303.

50 See Robert R. Wark, "Arabella Huntington and the Beginnings of the Art Collection," *Huntington Library Quarterly* 32 (August 1969): 309–31. For more on Arabella's influence on HEH, see notes of Collis Holladay's talk to Junior League Docents, October 1968, HEH 19/3.

51 For information on the creation of the Huntington gardens, see William Hertrich, *The Huntington Botanical Gardens* (San Marino, Calif.: Huntington Library, 1949).

CHAPTER 8

1 Louise Ward Watkins, *Henry Edwards Huntington: A Character Sketch of a Great Man* (Gardena, Calif.: Spanish American Institute Press, 1928), 12. A copy of this work is available at the Huntington Library.

2 Over the past twenty years, historical studies of California labor have proliferated, but most emphasize workers' responses to industrialism. Relatively few have focused on the labor policies of large employers, as well as the workers' efforts to unionize, thereby integrating business and labor history. See, for example, Luis L. Arroyo, "Industrial Unionism and the Los Angeles Furniture Industry, 1918–1954" (Ph.D. diss., University of California, Los Angeles, 1979); Joel Franks, "Bootmakers and Shoemakers in Nineteenth-Century San Francisco: A Study in Class, Culture, Ethnicity, an ¬pular Protest in an Industrializing Community" (Ph.D. diss., University of California, Irvine, 1983); Michael Kazin, *Barons of Labor: The San Francisco Building Trades and Urban Power in the Progressive Era* (Urbana: University of Illinois Press, 1987); John A. Lawrence, "Behind the Palaces: The Working Class and the Labor Movement in San Francisco, 1877–1901" (Ph.D. diss., University of California, Berkeley, 1979).

3 The low density and dispersed nature of metropolitan Los Angeles compared with other areas across the nation is discussed in Fogelson, 143. In 1930, the San Francisco / Oakland metropolitan district, which was approximately one-half the size of the Los Angeles metropolis, had a central city-to-outlying suburb population ratio of thirty to one; the Los Angeles ratio was only three to one.

4 Lewis, "Street Railway Development," 2: 222; and Stimson, 237.

5 For discussions on the various methods employers used to block workers from a unified movement, see David Gordon, Richard Edwards, and Michael Reich, *Segmented Workers, Divided Workers: The Historical Transformation of Labor in the United States* (New York: Cambridge University Press, 1982), 138–44. See also Sanford M. Jacoby, *Employing Bureaucracy: Managers, Unions, and the Transformation of American Industry, 1900–1945* (New York: Columbia University Press, 1985).

6 Lewis, "Street Railway Development," 2: 184–85; and Stimson, 237.

7 HEH to Los Angeles Railway Committee of Trainmen, 11 Dec. 1902, HEH 7686.

8 Robert Gottlieb and Irene Wolt, *Thinking Big: The Story of the Los Angeles Times, Its Publishers, and Their Influence on Southern California* (New York: G. P. Putnam's Sons, 1977), 50. For additional information on Harrison Gray Otis, see David Halberstam, *The Powers That Be* (New York: Alfred A. Knopf, 1979), 94–122; and Richard C. Miller, "Otis and His *Times*" (Ph.D. diss., University of California, Berkeley, 1961).

9 Halberstam, 109.

10 *Los Angeles Times*, 21 June 1904. For an example of Otis's editorials, see *Los Angeles Times*, 29 Mar. 1903.

11 See HEH to David Parry, 14 Sept. 1903, HEH 7861; David Parry to HEH, 5 Oct. 1903, HEH 9614.

12 Stimson, 255–56; and Charles Wollenberg, "Working on El Traque: The Pacific Electric Strike of 1903," *Pacific Historical Review* 42 (August 1973): 360.

13 Philip Taft, *Organized Labor in American History* (New York: Harper and Row, 1964), 222.

14 See Stimson, 258; and David Montgomery, *Workers' Control in America: Studies in the History of Work, Technology, and Labor Struggles* (New York: Cambridge University Press, 1979), 61.

15 Stimson, 258.

16 See *Los Angeles Times*, 12 and 20 Feb. 1903; and Lewis, "Street Railway Development," 2: 185.

17 *Los Angeles Times*, 26, 29 Mar., 29, 30 Apr., 8 May, and 7 Oct. 1903; Lewis, "Street Railway Development," 2: 184–86; Stimson, 267; and Perry and Perry, 71. For more on the practice of using labor spies, see Charles K. Hyde, "Undercover and Underground: Labor Spies and Mine Management in the Early Twentieth Century," *Business History Review* 60 (Spring 1986): 1–27.

18 Pacific Electric Railway Company Trainmen to HEH and Epes Randolph, 2 May 1903, HEH 9572.

19 HEH to Andrew B. Hammond, 25 Jan. 1904, HEH 5534; Wollenberg, 358–62; and Crump, *Ride the Big Red Cars*, 142–43.

20 *Los Angeles Record*, 24 and 25 Apr. 1903; and *Los Angeles Times*, 25 Apr. 1903.

21 Wollenberg, 365–67; and Stimson, 267.

22 *Los Angeles Record*, 2, 5–8 May 1903; *Los Angeles Times*, 6–9 May 1903; Stimson, 262; and Cross, *Labor Movement in California*, 280.

23 See Michael Kazin, "The Great Exception Revisited: Organized Labor and Politics in San Francisco and Los Angeles, 1870–1940," *Pacific Historical Review* 55 (August 1986): 381; and James R. Green, *World of the Worker: Labor in Twentieth-Century America* (New York: Hill and Wang, 1980), 11.

24 *Los Angeles Record*, 11 May 1903; and *Los Angeles Times*, 12, 13, 19, 24 May 1903.

25 HEH to George Miles, 1 Mar. 1904, HEH 12835.

26 Central Labor Council of Los Angeles, *Los Angeles—A Model Open Shop City* (Los Angeles, 1 Nov. 1907), 3. A copy of this pamphlet is in the Huntington Library.

27 See Stuart D. Brandes, *American Welfare Capitalism: 1880–1940* (Chicago: University of Chicago Press, 1976), 12–14.

28 Transcript of interview with Myron Hunt, 1 Feb. 1930, HEH 19/3; see also Marcosson, 20.

29 For background on welfare capitalism, see Irving Bernstein, *The Lean Years: A History of the American Worker, 1920–1933* (Boston: Houghton Mifflin Co., 1960), 157–89; Brandes; David Brody, *Workers in Industrial America: Essays on the Twentieth-Century Struggle* (New York: Oxford University Press,

1980); Charles W. Cheape, *Family Firm to Modern Multinational: The Norton Company, a New England Enterprise* (Cambridge: Harvard University Press, 1985); Elizabeth Fones-Wolf, "Industrial Recreation, the Second World War, and the Revival of Welfare Capitalism, 1934–1960," *Business History Review* 60 (Summer 1986): 232–57; Morrell Heald, *The Social Responsibilities of Business: Company and Community, 1900–1960* (Cleveland: The Press of Case Western Reserve University, 1970); Daniel Nelson, "The Company Union Movement, 1900–1937: A Reexamination," *Business History Review* 56 (Autumn 1982): 335–57; and Gerald Zahavi, "Negotiated Loyalty: Welfare Capitalism and the Shoemakers of Endicott Johnson: 1920–1940," *Journal of American History* 71 (December 1983): 602–20.

30 For a sketch of sundry programs of welfare capitalism on various steam railroads, see Walter Licht, *Working for the Railroad: The Organization of Work in the Nineteenth Century* (Princeton: Princeton University Press, 1983), 28–29, 137–47, 201–12.

31 *Los Angeles Railway Company Regulations of Medical Department, Effective October 1, 1902* (N.p., n.d.). A copy of this document is available in the Huntington Library. See also Brandes, 100-101. For more on forms of company social control and attempts to Americanize the work force, see Stephen Meyer III, *The Five Dollar Day: Labor Management and Social Control in the Ford Motor Company, 1908–1921* (Albany: State University of New York Press, 1981); and Herbert G. Gutman, *Work, Culture and Society in Industrializing America* (New York: Vintage Books, 1977), 5–9.

32 Similar thinking of other businessmen is described by Brandes, 75–77.

33 *Los Angeles Herald*, 8 Jan. 1908.

34 *Los Angeles Examiner*, 6 and 17 Sept. 1911; *Los Angeles Express*, 11 Sept. 1911; *Los Angeles Times*, 10 and 19 Sept. 1911, 14 Dec. 1915; and *Los Angeles Herald*, 9 Dec. 1915. See also Swett, "Los Angeles Railway," 42.

35 See the weekly issues of the Los Angeles Railway's employee newspaper, *Two Bells*, June through October 1920. Publication of this newspaper began in June 1920. For a satire on management's use of interdivisional competition to build company pride and improve work performance, see Kurt Vonnegut, Jr., *Player Piano* (New York: Delacorte Press, 1952).

36 Stimson, 340–41.

37 Ibid. The metal trades strike ended in 1912. Although the metal workers did not achieve their goal of the eight-hour day, they did make small wage gains, but their pay continued to lag behind workers in San Francisco.

38 *Los Angeles Herald*, 17 Sept. 1911, 17 Aug. 1914; and *Los Angeles Tribune*, 24 Aug. 1913. Although the company picnic brought together employees from all the firm's divisions, the event took place only once a year and did not provide a forum for the airing of worker dissatisfactions. Huntington's employees appear to have approved of these fringe benefits, yet the various aspects of welfare capitalism did not seem to permanently reduce labor resistance. Organized labor largely opposed such programs. Although Huntington desired to improve working conditions through paternalism, he also wished to extend

his domination over his laborers. According to Daniel Nelson, welfare capitalism can be viewed as a move by management—akin to its earlier steps to increase its control over production—to gain further control over the worker. See his *Managers and Workers: Origins of the New Factory System in the United States, 1880–1920* (Madison: University of Wisconsin Press, 1975), 120–21.

39 Perry and Perry, 71–72; *Los Angeles Examiner, Los Angeles Times,* and *Los Angeles Tribune,* all for 13 Sept. 1914.

40 Perry and Perry, 73; and Lewis, "Street Railway Development," 2: 228. Compared with union scale for various trades in Los Angeles, the LARY's wage rate for platform men of twenty-five to thirty cents per hour (with a sixty- to seventy-hour work week) was low. See chart below taken from Perry and Perry, 246.

UNION WAGE RATES AND HOURS IN LOS ANGELES, 1913

Occupation	Rate per Hour in Cents	Hours Worked per Week
Bricklayers	75	44
Building laborers	34.4	44
Carpenters	50	48
Cement finishers	62.5	48
Compositors		
Book and job	46.9	48
Newspaper-day work	62.5	45
Electrotypers		
Molders	50	48
Finishers	50	48
Granite Cutters	62.5	48
Inside wiremen	50	48
Painters	43.8	48
Plasterers	75	44
Plumbers	56.3	48
Sheet metal workers	56.3	44
Structural ironworkers	50	48
Typesetting		
Book and job	58.3	48
Newspaper	62.2	45

41 Nelson, "Company Union Movement," 340–47; and John R. Commons, Don Lescohier, and Elizabeth Brandeis, *History of Labor in the United States, 1896–1932* (New York: Macmillan Co., 1935), 337–41.

42 Lewis, "Street Railway Development," 2: 185–88.

43 Perry and Perry, 75.

44 Ibid., 76; and William Dunn to HEH, 2 Dec. 1918, HEH 11728.

45 HEH to William Dunn, 5 Dec. 1918, HEH 10964.

46 *Los Angeles Times,* 4 and 8 July 1919, and *Los Angeles Record,* 17 and 23 July 1919.

47 In addition to involving the intracity LARY, the strike included employees of the interurban Pacific Electric as well as those of the steam railroads entering Los Angeles. See Perry and Perry, 78, 86; and *Los Angeles Times*, 15 and 16 Aug. 1919.

48 *Los Angeles Times*, 26–30 Aug., 24–26 Sept., 26 Oct. 1919; *Los Angeles Examiner*, 28–30 Aug. and 26 Sept. 1919.

49 HEH to New York Chamber of Commerce, 27 Nov. 1922, HEH 12855.

CHAPTER 9

1 Quoted from transcript of interview with HEH's valet, Alfonzo Gomez, tape F, 7 Feb. 1959, HEH 19/1.

2 For information on Hale, see Helen Wright, *Explorer of the Universe: A Biography of George Ellery Hale* (New York: E. P. Dutton and Co., 1...).

3 Ibid., 372–73.

4 George Hale to Arabella Huntington, 14 Feb. 1914, C. M. Campbell (secretary of Arabella Huntington) to George Hale, 15 Apr. 1915; and George Hale to HEH, 17 Apr. 1915, George E. Hale Collection (hereafter cited as GEH), box 22, California Institute of Technology Archives.

5 George Hale to HEH, 17 Apr. 1914; and HEH to George Hale, 20 Apr. 1914, GEH Collection, box 22.

6 George Hale to HEH, 11 May 1914; and HEH to George Hale, 5 Oct. 1914, GEH Collection, box 22.

7 George Hale to HEH, 28 Mar. 1916, HEH 2370.

8 HEH to George Hale, 22 Apr. 1916, GEH Collection, box 22.

9 Wright, 380; and Pomfret, 43.

10 See the Trust Indenture establishing the Henry E. Huntington Library and Art Gallery, 30 Aug. 1919, HEH 27/4, and HEH Institutional Archives 12.5.4.

11 Pomfret, 46–51.

12 Ibid., 51–52, 64–65.

13 William Dunn to Charles Graham, 3 Apr. 1922, HEH 11668. Howard Huntington died of stomach cancer; see journals of Edmund Burke Holladay, 1922, HEH 10968.

14 George Hapgood to Joseph Duveen, 29 Oct. 1924, HEH 10834. Arabella Huntington had been in poor health from about 1916. According to Burke Holladay, Arabella had rheumatism and sciatica. See journals of Edmund Burke Holladay, 1914–24, HEH 10968.

15 See journals of Edmund Burke Holladay, 1925–26, HEH 10968.

16 HEH to Mrs. J. E. Brown, 15 Feb. 1926, HEH 12507.

17 HEH to Mrs. Lasalle Pickett, 4 May 1927, HEH 7900.

18 See journals of Edmund Burke Holladay, 1927, HEH 10968.

19 *Los Angeles Examiner*, 27 Nov. 1908.

20 Transcript of interview with Alfonzo Gomez, tape J, 11 Apr. 1959, HEH 19/1.

21 Otheman Stevens to Robert Schad, 11 July 1929, HEH 19/3.

22 Few photographs were hung on the walls of HEH's office in the Los Angeles Railway Building. One was a shadowbox frame of Collis Huntington, and another was the picture of Collis, HEH, and a newsboy on a New York City street in 1895. See transcript of interview with Emma Quigley, 21 Apr. 1967, HEH 19/1.

23 HEH to Rev. Dr. Jacob Voorsanger, 30 Aug. 1900, HEH 8130.

24 HEH left $2 million to build the hospital. See the Last Will and Testament of Henry Edwards Huntington, 1 Aug. 1925, HEH 27/3.

25 John B. Miller, quoted in *The Greater Edison*, 5–6.

26 Board of Public Utilities, City of Los Angeles, *Annual Report*, 1912 / 1913, and 1913 / 1914.

27 Theodore Dreiser, *The Titan* (1914; reprint ed., New York: New American Library, 1965), 428.

28 The descriptive phrase "appetite for risk" comes from Connie Bruck's article about businessman William Farley. See Connie Bruck, "The World of Business: The Billion-Dollar Mind," *New Yorker*, 7 Aug. 1989, 78.

29 See Pomfret; HEH Institutional Archives 12.7.6; and HEH personal balance sheets, HEH 11/2/1–4.

Bibliography

MANUSCRIPT COLLECTIONS

Graves, Jackson A. Papers. Huntington Library, San Marino, California.

Hale, George E. Papers. Archives, California Institute of Technology, Pasadena, California.

Huntington, Collis P. Papers. Microfilm, Huntington Library, San Marino, California.

Huntington, Henry E. Papers. Huntington Library, San Marino, California.

This collection was my major primary source and includes Huntington's personal and business papers. It contains family and business correspondence, as well as papers related to steam and electric railroads, real estate, electric power development, the Huntington Library and Art Gallery, and Newport News Shipbuilding and Dry Dock Company. The collection is divided into a catalogued and an uncatalogued section.

The catalogued portion consists of 22,490 items arranged chronologically from 1840 to 1970 in two hundred boxes. Largely personal and business correspondence, these papers are identified by call numbers preceded by the abbreviation of the collection's name. The Henry E. Huntington Collection is thus referred to as the HEH Collection.

The larger uncatalogued section of this archive includes

1. The official financial reports of the various Huntington companies. This encompasses annual reports, ledgers and journals, cash books, and minutes of directors' meetings.
2. Huntington's personal financial records.
3. The papers of Robert O. Schad, librarian at the Huntington Library,

pertaining to the life of Henry Huntington. Labeled the Huntington Biographical Project, these papers were gathered mainly between 1929 and 1933. Interviews with people who knew Huntington were conducted as recently as the 1970s and are included here. Unlike the catalogued half of the HEH Collection, which is listed in the manuscript card catalog, the uncatalogued portion is listed and explained in a Summary Report and Inventory Sheet for the HEH Collection.
4. Four uncatalogued boxes of material known as the Huntington Vault Material.
5. Three uncatalogued ledgers and journals of the Huntington Land and Improvement Company.

Huntington, Henry E. Institutional Papers. Huntington Library, San Marino, California.
Hutchings, Jean. Papers. Riverside Municipal Museum, Riverside, California.
Los Angeles Board of Public Utilities Files, Los Angeles City Archives, Los Angeles.
Los Angeles Railway Corporation Collection, Huntington Library, San Marino, California.
Ward, George C. Papers. Huntington Library, San Marino, California.
Watkins, Louise Ward. Papers. Huntington Library, San Marino, California.
Willard, Charles D. Papers. Huntington Library, San Marino, California.

INTERVIEW

Interview with Harriet Doerr, Pasadena, California. 14 July 1989.

U.S. GOVERNMENT DOCUMENTS

U.S. Census Office. *Thirteenth Census of the United States: 1910: Abstract of Census and Supplement for California.* Washington, D.C.: Government Printing Office, 1913.
————. *Fourteenth Census of the United States. 1920.* Vol. 2: *Population.* Washington, D.C.: Government Printing Office, 1922.

STATE OF CALIFORNIA DOCUMENTS

California Railroad Commission. *Annual Reports,* 1911–25.
————. *Case No. 4002: Report on the Local Public Transportation Requirements of Los Angeles.* Los Angeles, 1935, Huntington Library.
————. *Case No. 4461: Report on Urban Mass Passenger Transportation Facilities and Requirements of Los Angeles.* Los Angeles, 1940, Huntington Library.
————. *Orders and Opinions,* 1911–25.

California Railroad Commission Engineering Department. *Application 4238: Report on Service, Operating, and Financial Conditions of the Los Angeles Railway Corporation.* Los Angeles, 1919, Los Angeles City Archives.

Ready, Lester S., J. O. Marsh, and Richard Sachse. *Joint Report on Street Railway Survey, City of Los Angeles to Railroad Commission of the State of California.* Los Angeles, 1925, Los Angeles City Archives.

CITY OF LOS ANGELES DOCUMENTS

Board of Public Utilities, City of Los Angeles. *Annual Reports,* 1909–25.
——— . *Minutes,* 1909–25.

NEWSPAPERS AND PERIODICALS

California Outlook
Commercial and Financial Chronicle
Electric Railway Journal
Journal of Electricity, Power, and Gas
Los Angeles Evening News
Los Angeles Examiner
Los Angeles Express
Los Angeles Financier
Los Angeles Herald
Los Angeles Realtor
Los Angeles Record
Los Angeles Times
Los Angeles Tribune
New York Morning Herald
New York Times
New Yorker
Oneonta (N.Y.) Star
The P. E. Magazine
Pasadena Star News
Pomona Times
San Francisco Bulletin
San Francisco Call
San Francisco Chronicle
San Francisco Examiner
Southern California Business
Sunset
Tracks
Two Bells

BOOKS AND ARTICLES

Abott, Carl. *The New Urban America: Growth and Politics in Sunbelt Cities.* Chapel Hill, N.C.: University of North Carolina, 1981.

Aitken, Hugh G. J. "The Entrepreneurial Approach to Economic History." In *Approaches to American Economic History.* Edited by George Rogers Taylor and Lucius F. Ellsworth. Charlottesville, Va.: University of Virginia, 1971. Pp. 1–16.

Akin, Edward N. *Flagler: Rockefeller Partner and Florida Baron.* Kent, Ohio, and London: Kent State University Press, 1988.

Angel, William D., Jr. "To Make a City: Entrepreneurship on the Sunbelt Frontier." In *The Rise of the Sunbelt Cities.* Edited by David C. Perry and Alfred J. Watkins. Beverly Hills: Sage Publications, 1977. Pp. 109–28.

Armstrong, Christopher, and H. V. Nelles. *Monopoly's Moment: The Organization and Regulation of Canadian Utilities, 1830–1930.* Philadelphia: Temple University Press, 1986.

Arnold, Bion J. *Report on the Improvement and Development of the Transportation Facilities of San Francisco.* San Francisco: The Hicks-Judd Co., 1913.

———. "The Transportation Problem of Los Angeles." *California Outlook,* 4 Nov. 1911: 2–20.

Athern, Robert G. *Union Pacific Country.* Chicago: Rand McNally and Co., 1971.

Banham, Reyner. *Los Angeles: The Architecture of Four Ecologies.* New York: Penguin Press, 1971.

Barrett, Paul. *The Automobile and Urban Transit: The Formation of Public Policy in Chicago, 1900–1930.* Philadelphia: Temple University Press, 1983.

Baur, John E. *Health Seekers of Southern California, 1870–1900.* San Marino, Calif.: Huntington Library, 1959.

Bernstein, Irving. *The Lean Years: A History of the American Worker, 1920–1933.* Boston: Houghton Mifflin Co., 1960.

Blackford, Mansel G. "Civic Groups, Political Action, and City Planning in Seattle, 1892–1915." *Pacific Historical Review* 49 (November 1980): 557–80.

———. *The Politics of Business in California, 1890–1920.* Columbus: Ohio State University Press, 1977.

Bottles, Scott L. *Los Angeles and the Automobile: The Making of the Modern City.* Berkeley, Los Angeles, and London: University of California Press, 1987.

Brandes, Stuart D. *American Welfare Capitalism: 1880–1940.* Chicago: University of Chicago Press, 1976.

Brodsly, David. *LA Freeway: An Appreciative Essay.* Berkeley: University of California Press, 1981.

Brody, David. *Workers in Industrial America: Essays on the Twentieth-Century Struggle.* New York: Oxford University Press, 1980.

Bruchey, Stuart, ed. *The Colonial Merchant: Sources and Readings.* New York: Harcourt, Brace and World, 1966.

———. *Small Business in American Life.* New York: Columbia University Press, 1980.

Bryant, Keith L., Jr. *History of the Atchison, Topeka and Santa Fe Railway.* New York: Macmillan Publishing Co., 1974.

Buder, Stanley. *Pullman: An Experiment in Industrial Order and Community Planning, 1880–1930.* New York: Oxford University Press, 1967.

Burton, George Ward. *Men of Achievement: Los Angeles.* Los Angeles: Los Angeles Times Publishing, 1904.

Burton, Katherine. *Henry E. Huntington.* Norton, Mass.: Periwinkle Press, 1939.

Caughey, John, and Laree Caughey. *Los Angeles: Biography of a City.* Berkeley: University of California Press, 1976.

Central Labor Council of Los Angeles. *Los Angeles—A Model Open Shop City.* Los Angeles. 1 Nov. 1907.

Chandler, Alfred D., Jr. *The Visible Hand: The Managerial Revolution in American Business.* Cambridge: Harvard University Press, 1977.

Cheape, Charles W. *From Family Firm to Modern Multinational: The Norton Company, a New England Enterprise.* Cambridge: Harvard University Press, 1985.

———. *Moving the Masses: Urban Public Transit in New York, Boston, and Philadelphia, 1880–1912.* Cambridge: Harvard University Press, 1980.

The City of Beverly Hills: From Bean Field to Beautiful City. Beverly Hills: Gibraltar Savings, 1970.

Clary, William W. *History of the Law Firm of O'Melveny and Myers.* Los Angeles: O'Melveny and Myers, 1965.

Cleland, Robert G. *Cattle on a Thousand Hills: Southern California, 1850–1880.* San Marino, Calif.: Huntington Library, 1951.

Cleland, Robert G., and Frank B. Putnam. *Isaias W. Hellman and the Farmers and Merchants Bank.* San Marino, Cal.: Huntington Library, 1965.

Clover, Samuel T. *Constructive Californians: Men of Outstanding Ability Who Have Added Greatly to the Golden State's Prestige.* Los Angeles: Saturday Night Publishing, 1926.

Cochran, Thomas C. "The Entrepreneur in American Capital Formation." In *Capital Formation and Economic Growth.* Princeton: Princeton University Press, 1955.

———. *Railroad Leaders, 1845–1890: The Business Mind in Action.* New York: Russell and Russell, 1965.

Cochran, Thomas C., and William Miller. *The Age of Enterprise.* New York: Macmillan Company, 1942.

Coleman, Charles M. *P. G. and E. of California: The Centennial Story of Pacific Gas and Electric Company, 1852–1952.* New York: McGraw-Hill Book Co., 1952.

Collier, Peter, and David Horowitz. *The Rockefellers: An American Dynasty.* New York: New American Library, 1976.

Commons, John R., Don Lescohier, and Elizabeth Brandeis. *History of Labor in the United States, 1896–1932.* New York: Macmillan Co., 1935.

Craemer, Ester R. *La Habra: The Pass through the Hills.* Fullerton, Calif.: Sultana Press, 1969.

Cross, Ira. *A History of the Labor Movement in California.* Berkeley: University of California Press, 1935.

Crump, Spencer. *Henry Huntington and the Pacific Electric*. Los Angeles: Trans-Anglo Books, 1970.

————. *Ride the Big Red Cars: How the Trolleys Helped Build Southern California*. Los Angeles: Trans-Anglo Books, 1962.

Daggett, Stuart. *Chapters on the History of the Southern Pacific*. New York: Ronald Press Co., 1922.

Davies, Edward J., II. *The Anthracite Aristocracy: Leadership and Social Change in the Hard Coal Regions of Northeastern Pennsylvania, 1800–1930*. DeKalb, Ill.: Northern Illinois University Press, 1985.

Decker, Donald D., and Mary L. Decker. *Reflections on Elegance: Pasadena's Huntington Hotel since 1906*. Laguna Niguel, Calif.: Royal Literary Publications, 1985.

Decker, Peter. *Fortunes and Failures: White Collar Mobility in Nineteenth-Century San Francisco*. Cambridge: Harvard University Press, 1978.

Dickinson, Donald C. "Mr. Huntington and Mr. Smith." *The Book Collector* 37 (Autumn 1988): 366–93.

Dreiser, Theodore. *The Titan*. 1914; reprint ed., New York: New American Library, 1965.

Dulles, Foster R. *Labor in America: A History*. Arlington Heights, Ill.: Harlan Davidson, 1966.

Dumke, Glenn. *The Boom of the Eighties in Southern California*. San Marino, Cal.: Huntington Library, 1944.

Easlon, Steven L. *The Los Angeles Railway through the Years*. Anaheim, Cal.: Easlon Publications, 1973.

Evans, Cerinda W. *Collis Potter Huntington*. 2 vols. Newport News, Va.: Mariners' Museum, 1954.

Fairchild, Charles B. *Street Railways: Their Construction, Operations, and Maintenance*. New York: Street Railway Publishing Co., 1892.

Finger, John R. "The Seattle Spirit, 1851–1893." *Journal of the West* 13 (Summer 1974): 28–45.

Fletcher, Ed. *Memoirs of Ed Fletcher*. San Diego: Pioneer Printers, 1952.

Fogelson, Robert M. *The Fragmented Metropolis: Los Angeles, 1850–1930*. Cambridge: Harvard University Press, 1967.

Folsom, Burton W., Jr. *Urban Capitalists: Entrepreneurs and City Growth in Pennsylvania's Lackawanna and Lehigh Regions, 1880–1920*. Baltimore: Johns Hopkins University Press, 1981.

Foner, Philip S. *History of the Labor Movement in the United States: The Policies and Practices of the American Federation of Labor, 1900–1909*. New York: International Publishers, 1964.

Fones-Wolf, Elizabeth. "Industrial Recreation, the Second World War, and the Revival of Welfare Capitalism, 1934–1960." *Business History Review* 60 (Summer 1986): 232–57.

Foster, Mark S. *From Streetcar to Superhighway: American City Planners and Urban Transportation*. Philadelphia: Temple University Press, 1981.

————. "The Model-T, the Hard Sell, and Los Angeles's Urban Growth: The

Decentralization of Los Angeles during the 1920s." *Pacific Historical Review* 44 (November 1975): 459–84.

Friedricks, William B. "Capital and Labor in Los Angeles: Henry E. Huntington vs. Organized Labor, 1900–1920." *Pacific Historical Review* 59 (August 1990): 375–95.

———. "Henry E. Huntington and Real Estate Development in Southern California, 1898–1917." *Southern California Quarterly* 71 (Winter 1989): 327–40.

———. "A Metropolitan Entrepreneur Par Excellence: Henry E. Huntington and the Growth of Southern California, 1898–1927." *Business History Review* 63 (Summer 1989): 329–55.

Fulton, William. "'Those Were Her Best Days': The Streetcar and the Development of Hollywood Before 1910." *Southern California Quarterly* 66 (Fall 1984): 235–56.

Gale, Zona. *Frank Miller of the Mission Inn*. New York: D. Appleton-Century Co., 1938.

Glaab, Charles N. *Kansas City and the Railroads: Community Policy in the Growth of a Regional Metropolis*. Madison, Wis.: State Historical Society of Wisconsin, 1962.

Glaab, Charles, and A. Theodore Brown. *A History of Urban America*. New York: Macmillan Publishing Co., 1967.

Goldfield, David R. *Urban Growth in the Age of Sectionalism: Virginia, 1847–1861*. Baton Rouge, La.: Louisiana State University Press, 1977.

Gordon, David, Richard Edwards, and Michael Reich. *Segmented Workers, Divided Workers: The Historical Transformation of Labor in the United States*. New York: Cambridge University Press, 1982.

Gordon, Dudley. *Charles F. Lummis: Crusader in Corduroy*. Los Angeles: Cultural Assets Press, 1972.

Gottleib, Robert, and Irene Wolt. *Thinking Big: The Story of the Los Angeles Times, Its Publishers, and Their Influence on Southern California*. New York: G. P. Putnam's Sons, 1977.

Graves, Jackson. *My Seventy Years in California, 1857–1927*. Los Angeles: Times-Mirror Press, 1927.

Green, James R. *World of the Worker: Labor in Twentieth-Century America*. New York: Hill and Wang, 1980.

Greenberg, Dolores. *Financiers and Railroads, 1869–1889: A Study of Morton, Bliss, and Company*. Newark: University of Delaware Press, 1980.

Grodinsky, Julius. *Transcontinental Railroad Strategy, 1869–1893: A Study of Businessmen*. Philadelphia: University of Pennsylvania Press, 1962.

Gutman, Herbert G. *Work, Culture, and Society in Industrializing America*. New York: Vintage Books, 1977.

Haber, Samuel. *Efficiency and Uplift: Scientific Management in the Progressive Era, 1890–1920*. Chicago: University of Chicago Press, 1964.

Haeger, John D. *The Investment Frontier: New York Businessmen and the Economic Development of the Old Northwest*. Albany: State University of New York Press, 1981.

Halberstam, David. *The Powers That Be*. New York: Alfred A. Knopf, 1979.

Hays, Samuel P. *The Response to Industrialism, 1885–1914*. Chicago: University of Chicago Press, 1957.

Heald, Morrell. *The Social Responsibility of Business: Company and Community, 1900–1960*. Cleveland: The Press of Case Western Reserve University, 1970.

Heilbroner, Robert L. *The Making of Economic Society*. Englewood Cliffs, N.J.: Prentice-Hall, 1962.

Hereford, Rockwell. *A Whole Man, Henry Mauris Robinson, and a Half Century, 1890–1940*. Pacific Grove, Calif.: Boxwood Press, 1985.

Hertrich, William. *The Huntington Botanical Gardens*. San Marino, Calif.: Huntington Library, 1949.

Higgs, Robert. *The Transformation of the American Economy*. New York: John Wiley and Sons, 1971.

Hildebrand, George H. *Borax Pioneer: Francis Marion Smith*. San Diego: Howell-North Books, 1982.

Hill, Joseph J. *The History of Warner's Ranch and Its Environs*. Los Angeles: Young and McCallister, 1927.

Hilton, George W. *The Cable Car in America*. Berkeley: Howell-North Books, 1971.

Hilton, George W., and John F. Due. *The Electric Interurban Railways in America*. Stanford: Stanford University Press, 1960.

History of Los Angeles: City and County of California. 2 vols. Los Angeles: J. R. Finnelly and Son Publishing Co., 1931.

Hodas, Daniel. *The Business Career of Moses Taylor: Merchant, Finance Capitalist, and Industrialist*. New York: New York University Press, 1976.

Hofsommer, Don L. *The Southern Pacific, 1901–1985*. College Station, Tex.: Texas A&M University Press, 1986.

Howard, Daniel L. *Southern California and the Pacific Electric*. Los Angeles: Daniel L. Howard, 1980.

Hoyt, Franklin. "The Los Angeles and San Gabriel Valley Railroad." *Pacific Historical Review* 20 (August 1951): 227–40.

Hughes, Jonathan. *The Vital Few: American Economic Progress and Its Protagonists*. Boston: Houghton Mifflin Co., 1965.

Hughes, Thomas P. *Networks of Power: Electrification in Western Society, 1880–1930*. Baltimore: Johns Hopkins University Press, 1983.

The Huntington Family in America. Hartford, Conn.: Huntington Family Association, 1915.

Hyde, Charles K. "Undercover and Underground: Labor Spies and Mine Management in the Early Twentieth Century." *Business History Review* 60 (Spring 1986): 1–27.

Ingham, John N., ed. *Biographical Dictionary of American Business Leaders*. 4 vols. Westport, Conn.: Greenwood Press, 1983.

———. *The Iron Barons: A Social Analysis of an American Urban Elite, 1874–1965*. Westport, Conn.: Greenwood Press, 1978.

Issel, William. "'Citizens Outside the Government': Business and Urban Policy in San Francisco and Los Angeles." *Pacific Historical Review* 57 (May 1987): 117–45.

Issel, William, and Robert Cherny. *San Francisco, 1865–1932: Power, Politics, and Urban Development.* Berkeley: University of California Press, 1986.

Jackson, Kenneth T. *Crabgrass Frontier: The Suburbanization of the United States.* New York: Oxford University Press, 1985.

Jacoby, Sanford M. *Employing Bureaucracy: Managers, Unions, and the Transformation of Work in American Industry, 1900–1945.* New York: Columbia University Press, 1985.

Jaher, Frederic C. *The Urban Establishment: Upper Strata in Boston, New York, Charleston, Chicago, and Los Angeles.* Urbana: University of Illinois Press, 1982.

Johnson, Hank. *The Railroad That Lighted Southern California.* Los Angeles: Trans-Anglo Books, 1965.

Jones, David W., Jr. *Urban Transit Policy: An Economic and Political History.* Englewood Cliffs, N.J.: Prentice-Hall, 1985.

Kahn, Edgar M. *Cable Car Days in San Francisco.* Stanford: Stanford University Press, 1944.

Kahn, Judd. *Imperial San Francisco: Politics and Planning in an American City, 1897–1906.* Lincoln and London: University of Nebraska Press, 1979.

Kahrl, William L. *Water and Power: The Conflict over Los Angeles' Water Supply in the Owens Valley.* Berkeley: University of California Press, 1982.

Kazin, Michael. *Barons of Labor: The San Francisco Building Trades and Urban Power in the Progressive Era.* Urbana: University of Illinois Press, 1987.

———. "The Great Exception Revisited: Organized Labor in San Francisco and Los Angeles, 1870–1940." *Pacific Historical Review* 55 (August 1986): 371–402.

Kelker, De Leuw and Company. *Report and Recommendations on a Comprehensive Rapid Transit Plan for the City and County of Los Angeles.* Chicago: Kelker, De Leuw and Co., 1925.

Kennan, George. *E. H. Harriman: A Biography.* 2 vols. Boston: Houghton Mifflin Co., 1922.

Kirkland, Edward. *Dream and Thought in the Business Community, 1860–1900.* Ithaca, N.Y.: Cornell University Press, 1956.

Klein, Maury. *History of the Louisville and Nashville Railroad.* New York: Macmillan Publishing Co., 1972.

———. *The Life and Legend of Jay Gould.* Baltimore: Johns Hopkins University Press, 1986.

Klotz, Ester. *The Mission Inn: Its History and Artifacts.* Riverside, Calif.: Rubidoux Printing, 1981.

Knight, Robert. *Industrial Relations in the San Francisco Bay Area, 1900–1918.* Berkeley: University of California Press, 1960.

Kolko, Gabriel. *The Triumph of Conservatism: A Reinterpretation of American History, 1900–1916.* New York: Macmillan Co., 1963.

Larsen, Lawrence H. *The Urban West at the End of the Frontier.* Lawrence, Kan.: Regents Press of Kansas, 1978.

Larson, John L. *Bonds of Enterprise: John Murray Forbes and Western Development in America's Railway Age.* Cambridge: Harvard University Press, 1984.

Lavender, David. *The Great Persuader.* Garden City, N.Y.: Doubleday and Co., 1970.

———. *Nothing Seemed Impossible: William Ralston and Early San Francisco.* Palo Alto, Calif.: American West Publishing Co., 1975.

Lewis, Oscar. *The Big Four.* New York: Alfred A. Knopf, 1938.

Licht, Walter. *Working for the Railroad: The Organization of Work in the Nineteenth Century.* Princeton: Princeton University Press, 1983.

Lindsey, Almont. *The Pullman Strike.* Chicago: University of Chicago Press, 1942.

"Lines of the Pacific Electric: Northern and Eastern Division." *Interurbans,* Special no. 61 (1976).

Link, Arthur S., and Richard L. McCormick. *Progressivism.* Arlington Heights, Ill.: Harlan Davidson, 1983.

Littlefield, Douglas R., and Tanis C. Thorne. *The Spirit of Enterprise: The History of Pacific Enterprises from 1886 to 1989.* Los Angeles: Pacific Enterprises, 1990.

Livesay, Harold C. *American Made: Men Who Shaped the American Economy.* Boston: Little, Brown and Co., 1979.

———. "Entrepreneurial Persistence through the Bureaucratic Age." *Business History Review* 51 (Winter 1977): 415–43.

———. "Entrepreneurial Dominance in Businesses Large and Small, Past and Present." *Business History Review* 63 (Spring 1989): 1–21.

McAfee, Ward. *California Railway Era, 1850–1911.* San Marino, Calif.: Golden West Books, 1973.

McKelvey, Blake. *The Emergence of Metropolitan America, 1915–1966.* New Brunswick, N.J.: Rutgers University Press, 1966.

McShane, Clay. *Technology and Reform: Street Railways and the Growth of Milwaukee, 1887–1900.* Madison: State Historical Society of Wisconsin, 1974.

McWilliams, Carey. *Southern California: An Island on the Land.* 2nd ed. Santa Barbara, Calif.: Peregrine Smith, 1978.

Marchand, Bernard. *The Emergence of Los Angeles: Population and Housing in the City of Dreams, 1940–1970.* London: Pion, 1986.

Marcosson, Isaac F. *A Little Known Master of Millions: The Story of Henry E. Huntington—Constructive Capitalist.* Boston: E. H. Rollins and Sons, 1914.

Marshall, James. *The Railroad That Built an Empire.* New York: Random House, 1945.

Martin, Albro. *James J. Hill and the Opening of the Northwest.* New York: Oxford University Press, 1976.

Mercer, Lloyd M. *E. H. Harriman: Master Railroader.* Boston: Twayne Publishers, 1985.

Meyer, Stephen, III. *The Five Dollar Day: Labor Management and Social Control in the Ford Motor Company, 1908–1921.* Albany: State University of New York Press, 1981.

Miller, John. *Fares Please! A Popular History of Trolleys, Horsecars, Streetcars, Buses, Elevateds, and Subways.* New York: Dover Publications, 1960.

Miller, William, ed. *Men in Business: Essays on the Role of the Entrepreneur.* New York: Harper and Row, 1962.

Miller, Zane L. *The Urbanization of Modern America: A Brief History.* New York: Harcourt Brace Jovanovich, 1973.

Monkkonen, Eric H. *America Becomes Urban: The Development of U.S. Cities and Towns, 1780–1980.* Berkeley, Los Angeles, and London: University of California Press, 1988.

Montgomery, David. *Workers' Control in America: Studies in the History of Work, Technology, and Labor Struggles.* New York: Cambridge University Press, 1979.

Moody's Manual of Investments: Public Utility Securities, 1926. New York: Moody's Investment Service, 1926.

Mowry, George E. *The California Progressives.* Berkeley: University of California Press, 1951.

Myers, William A. *Iron Men and Copper Wires: A Centennial History of the Southern California Edison Company.* Glendale, Calif.: Trans-Anglo Books, 1983.

Myers, William A., and Ira L. Swett. *Trolleys to the Surf: The Story of the Los Angeles Pacific Railway.* Glendale, Calif.: Interurban Publications, 1976.

Nadeau, Remi. *City-Makers: The Story of Southern California's First Boom, 1868–1876.* Los Angeles: Trans-Anglo Books, 1965.

———. *Los Angeles: From Mission to Modern City.* New York: Longmans, Green and Co., 1960.

Nash, Gerald D. *The American West in the Twentieth Century: A Short History of an Urban Oasis.* Englewood Cliffs, N.J.: Prentice-Hall, 1973.

———. "The California Railroad Commission, 1876–1911." *Southern California Quarterly* 44 (December 1962): 287–306.

———. *State Government and Economic Development: A History of the Administrative Policies in California, 1849–1933.* Berkeley: Institute of Governmental Studies, 1964.

———. "Urban Development in the Southwest: A Review Essay." *Journal of Urban History* 11 (August 1985): 471–80.

Nelson, Daniel. "The Company Union Movement, 1900–1937: A Reexamination." *Business History Review* 56 (Autumn 1982): 335–57.

———. *Managers and Workers: Origins of the New Factory System in the United States, 1880–1920.* Madison: University of Wisconsin Press, 1975.

Nelson, Howard J. *The Los Angeles Metropolis.* Dubuque, Iowa: Kendall/Hunt Co., 1983.

Nesbit, Robert C. *"He Built Seattle": A Biography of Judge Thomas Burke.* Seattle: University of Washington Press, 1961.

Newmark, Harrison. *Sixty Years in Southern California, 1853–1913.* New York: Knickerbocker Press, 1916.

O'Flaherty, Joseph S. *An End and a Beginning: The South Coast and Los Angeles, 1850–1887.* New York: Exposition Press, 1972.

————. *Those Powerful Years: The South Coast and Los Angeles, 1887–1917.* New York: Exposition Press, 1978.

Olin, Spencer C., Jr. *California's Prodigal Sons: Hiram Johnson and the Progressives, 1911–1917.* Berkeley: University of California Press, 1968.

O'Melveny, Henry. *William G. Kerckhoff: A Memorial.* Los Angeles: Adcraft Press, 1935.

Ozanne, Robert. *A Century of Labor-Management Relations at McCormick and International Harvester.* Madison: University of Wisconsin Press, 1967.

Perkins, Edwin J., and Steven Ross. "Integrating Business History and Labor History." *Business and Economic History* 15 (1986): 43–52.

Perry, Louis B., and Richard S. Perry. *A History of the Los Angeles Labor Movement, 1911–1941.* Berkeley: University of California Press, 1963.

Pomeroy, Earl. *The Pacific Slope: A History of California, Oregon, Washington, Idaho, Utah, and Nevada.* Seattle: University of Washington Press, 1965.

Pomfret, John E. *The Henry E. Huntington Library and Art Gallery from Its Beginnings to 1969.* San Marino, Calif.: Huntington Library, 1969.

Poor's Directory of Railway Officials and Manual of American Street Railways, 1892. New York: Poor's Railroad Manual Co., 1892.

Poor's Manual of Railroads. New York: Poor's Railroad Manual Co., 1884–1902.

Post, Robert C. "American Electric Railway Beginnings: Trolleys and Draft Dummies in Los Angeles." *Southern California Quarterly* 69 (Fall 1988): 203–21.

Pourade, Richard. *The History of San Diego: Gold in the Sun.* San Diego: Union Tribune Publishing Co., 1965.

Quiett, Glenn C. *They Built the West: An Epic of Rails and Cities.* New York: D. Appleton-Century Co., 1934.

The Ranch of the Gathering Waters (Rancho Rodeo de las Aguas). Los Angeles: Security First National Bank, 1934.

Redinger, David. *The Story of Big Creek.* Los Angeles: Eureka Press, 1949.

Richards, Elizabeth W. *Del Mar Decades.* Del Mar, Cal.: Santa Fe Federal Savings and Loan Assoc., 1974.

Robinson, William W. *Land in California: The Story of Mission Lands, Ranchos, Squatters, Mining Camps, Railroad Grants, Land Script, Homesteads.* Berkeley: University of California Press, 1948.

————. *Ranchos Become Cities.* Pasadena, Calif.: San Pasqual Press, 1939.

————. *The Story of the San Fernando Valley.* Los Angeles: Title Insurance and Trust Co., 1961.

Rolle, Andrew. *Los Angeles: From Pueblo to City of the Future.* San Francisco: Boyd and Fraser, 1981.

Rose, Mark H., and John G. Clark. "Light, Heat, and Power: Energy Choices in Kansas City, Wichita, and Denver, 1900–1935." *Journal of Urban History* 5 (May 1979): 340–64.

Schad, Robert. *Henry Edwards Huntington: Founder of the Library.* San Marino, Calif.: Huntington Library, 1937.

Schiesl, Martin J. *The Politics of Efficiency: Municipal Administration and Reform in America, 1800–1920.* Berkeley: University of California Press, 1977.

Schlesinger, Arthur M. *The Rise of the American City: 1878–1898*. New York: Macmillan, 1933.

Schnore, Leo F., ed. *The New Urban History: Quantitative Explorations by American Historians*. Princeton: Princeton University Press, 1972.

Schwantes, Carlos A. "The West Adopts the Automobile: Technology, Unemployment, and the Jitney Phenomenon of 1914–1917." *Western Historical Quarterly* 16 (July 1985): 307–26.

Seims, Charles. *Mount Lowe: Railroad to the Clouds*. San Marino, Calif.: Golden West Books, 1976.

Seligman, Ben B. *The Potentates*. New York: Dial Press, 1971.

Selvin, David. *A Place in the Sun: A History of California Labor*. San Francisco: Boyd and Fraser, 1981.

Shanahan, Dennis. *Old Redondo: A Pictorial History of Redondo Beach, California*. Redondo Beach: Legends Press, 1982.

Sherwood, Midge. *Days of Vintage, Years of Vision*. San Marino, Calif.: Orizaba Publications, 1982.

Smallwood, Charles. *The White Front Cars of San Francisco*. Glendale, Calif.: Interurban Press, 1978.

Sobel, Robert. *The Entrepreneurs: Explorations within the American Business Tradition*. New York: Weybright and Talley, 1974.

Spalding, William A. *History and Reminiscences: Los Angeles, City, County, and California*. 3 vols. Los Angeles: Finnell and Sons Publishing Co., 1931.

Starr, Kevin. *Inventing the Dream: California through the Progressive Era*. New York: Oxford University Press, 1985.

Stein, Lou. *San Diego County Place-Names*. San Diego: Tofua Press, 1975.

Steiner, Rodney. *Los Angeles: The Centrifugal City*. Dubuque, Iowa: Kendall / Hunt Publishing Co., 1981.

Stimson, Grace H. *Rise of the Labor Movement in Los Angeles*. Berkeley: University of California Press, 1955.

Swett, Ira L. "Los Angeles and Redondo." *Interurbans*, Special no. 20 (1957).

———. "Los Angeles Railway." *Interurbans*, Special no. 11 (1951).

Taft, Philip. *Organized Labor in American History*. New York: Harper and Row, 1964.

Tarr, Joel A. *Transportation Innovation and Changing Spatial Patterns in Pittsburgh, 1850–1934*. Pittsburgh: Public Works Historical Society, 1978.

Taylor, George R. "The Beginnings of Mass Transportation in Urban America." *Smithsonian Journal of History*. Pts. 1 and 2. (Summer and Autumn 1966): 35–50, 31–54.

Tazewell, William L. *Newport News Shipbuilding: The First Century*. Newport News, Va.: Mariners' Museum, 1986.

Teaford, Jon C. *The Twentieth-Century American City: Problems, Promise and Reality*. Baltimore: Johns Hopkins University Press, 1986.

———. *The Unheralded Triumph: City Government in America*. Baltimore: Johns Hopkins University Press, 1984.

Thorpe, James. "The Creation of the Gardens." *Huntington Library Quarterly* 32 (August 1969): 333–50.

———. "The Founder and His Library." *Huntington Library Quarterly* 32 (August 1969): 291–308.

Trottman, Nelson. *History of the Union Pacific: A Financial and Economic Survey.* New York: Ronald Press Co., 1923.

Tutorow, Norman. *Leland Stanford: Man of Many Careers.* Menlo Park, Calif.: Pacific Coast Publishers, 1978.

Vance, James E. *Geography and Urban Evolution in the San Francisco Bay Area.* Berkeley: Institute of Government Studies, 1964.

Van Valen, Nelson. "A Neglected Aspect of the Los Angeles Municipal Electric System." In *A Southern California Historical Anthology.* Edited by Doyce B. Nunis, Jr., Los Angeles: Historical Society of Southern California, 1984. Pp. 289–311.

Viehe, Fred W. "Black Gold Suburbs: The Influence of the Extractive Industry on the Suburbanization of Los Angeles, 1890–1930." *Journal of Urban History* 8 (November 1981): 3–26.

Vonnegut, Kurt, Jr. *Player Piano.* New York: Delacorte Press, 1952.

Wade, Richard C. "An Agenda for Urban History." In *American History: Retrospect and Prospect.* Edited by George A. Billias and Gerald N. Grob. New York: Free Press, 1971. Pp. 367–98.

———. *The Urban Frontier: The Rise of Western Cities, 1790–1830.* Cambridge: Harvard University Press, 1959.

Walker's Manual of Securities. San Francisco: H. D. Walker, 1908, 1920, 1922.

Wallace, George. *Joseph Francis Sartori.* Los Angeles: Ward Richie Press, 1948.

Wark, Robert R. "Arabella Huntington and the Beginnings of the Art Gallery." *Huntington Library Quarterly* 32 (August 1969): 309–31.

Warner, Sam B., Jr. *Streetcar Suburbs: The Process of Growth in Boston, 1870–1900.* Cambridge: Harvard University Press, 1962.

———. *The Urban Wilderness: A History of the American City.* New York: Harper and Row, 1972.

Watkins, Louise W. *Henry Edwards Huntington: A Character Sketch of a Great Man.* Gardena, Calif.: Spanish American Institute Press, 1928.

Weiss, Marc A. *The Rise of the Community Builders: The American Real Estate Industry and Urban Land Planning.* New York: Columbia University Press, 1987.

Wheeler, Kenneth W. *To Wear a City's Crown: The Beginnings of Urban Growth in Texas.* Cambridge: Harvard University Press, 1968.

Wiebe, Robert H. *Businessmen and Reform: A Study of the Progressive Movement.* Cambridge: Harvard University Press, 1962.

———. *The Search for Order, 1877–1920.* New York: Hill and Wang, 1967.

Wilcox, Delos F. *Preliminary Report on Local Transportation Policy Submitted to the City Council of the City of Los Angeles.* Los Angeles, 28 Apr. 1927.

Willard, Charles D. *A History of the Chamber of Commerce of Los Angeles.* Los Angeles: Kingsley-Barnes and Neurer, 1899.

Williams, R. Hal. *The Democratic Party and California Politics, 1880–1896.* Stanford: Stanford University Press, 1973.

Wilson, Carol Green. *California Yankee: William R. Staats—Business Pioneer.* Claremont, Calif.: Saunders Press, 1946.

Wilson, Neill, and Frank J. Taylor. *Southern Pacific: The Roaring Story of a Fighting Railroad*. New York: McGraw-Hill, 1952.

Winther, Oscar O. "The Rise of Metropolitan Los Angeles, 1870–1910." *Huntington Library Quarterly* 10 (1947): 391–405.

Wollenberg, Charles. "Working on El Traque: The Pacific Electric Strike of 1903." *Pacific Historical Review* 42 (August 1973): 358–69.

Workman, Boyle. *The City That Grew*. Los Angeles: Southland Publishing Co., 1936.

Wright, Helen. *Explorer of the Universe: A Biography of George Ellery Hale*. New York: E. P. Dutton and Co., 1966.

Yago, Glenn. *The Decline of Transit: Urban Transportation in German and U. S. Cities*. New York: Cambridge University Press, 1984.

Zahavi, Gerald. "Negotiated Loyalty: Welfare Capitalism and the Shoemakers of Endicott Johnson: 1920–1940." *Journal of American History* 71 (December 1983): 602–20.

DISSERTATIONS, THESES, AND UNPUBLISHED MATERIAL

Arroyo, Luis L. "Industrial Unionism and the Los Angeles Furniture Industry, 1918–1954." Ph.D. diss., University of California, Los Angeles, 1979.

Culton, Donald R. "Charles Dwight Willard, Los Angeles City Booster and Professional Reformer, 1880–1914." Ph.D. diss., University of Southern California, 1971.

Dumke, Glenn S. "The Growth of the Pacific Electric and Its Influence upon the Development of Southern California to 1911." M.A. thesis, Occidental College, 1939.

Elias, Judith W. "The Selling of a Myth: Los Angeles Promotional Literature, 1885–1915." M.A. thesis, California State University, Northridge, 1979.

Foster, Mark S. "The Decentralization of Los Angeles during the 1920s." Ph.D. diss., University of Southern California, 1971.

Franks, Joel. "Bootmakers and Shoemakers in Nineteenth-Century San Francisco: A Study in Class, Culture, Ethnicity, and Popular Protest in an Industrializing Community." Ph.D. diss., University of California, Irvine, 1983.

Haeger, John D. "From Merchant to Urban Developer: John Jacob Astor and the Business Revolution in America." Paper presented at the Organization of American Historians' Meeting, March, 1985.

Hoyt, Franklin. "Railroad Development in Southern California, 1868–1900." Ph.D. diss., University of Southern California, 1951.

Jones, William C. "The Corporate Evolution of the Southern California Edison Company and Its Financial History from 1909 to 1928." M.B.A. thesis, University of Southern California, 1929.

Lawrence, John A. "Behind the Palaces: The Working Class and the Labor Movement in San Francisco, 1877–1901." Ph.D. diss., University of California, Berkeley, 1979.

Lewis, Edwin L. "Street Railway Development in Los Angeles and Environs,

1878–1938." 2 vols. 1938. This typescript is available at the Huntington Library.

Miller, Richard C. "Otis and His *Times*." Doctoral diss., University of California, Berkeley, 1961.

Post, Robert C. "Street Railways in Los Angeles: Robert Widney to Henry Huntington." M.A. thesis, University of California, Los Angeles, 1967.

Van Valen, Nelson S. "Power Politics: The Struggle for Municipal Ownership of Electric Utilities in Los Angeles, 1905–1937." Ph.D. diss., Claremont Graduate School, 1964.

Veysey, Laurence R. "The Pacific Electric Railway, 1910–1953: A Study in the Operations of Economic, Social, and Political Forces upon American Local Transportation." Available at Occidental College Library.

Weber, Robert D. "Rationalizers and Reformers: Chicago Local Transportation in the Nineteenth Century." Ph.D. diss., University of Wisconsin, 1971.

Wright, Mabel. "History of the Pacific Electric Railway." M.A. thesis, University of Southern California, 1930.

Index

Mammoth Power Company, 112
Marcosson Isaac F., 16, 71, 171n15
Market Street and Fairmount Railway, 34–35
Market Street Cable Railway, 31–35
Market Street Railroad, 31–32
Market Street Railway, 35–37, 46, 48, 50, 54, 55; earnings, 40; and electrifying lines, 37–39; expansion of, 39–40
Marshall, Torrance, 119
Mateo Street and Santa Fe Avenue Streetcar Company, 54, 57
Mellon, Andrew, 147
Memphis, 23, 26, 28
Mendoza, Isaac, 133
Mentone Power Company, 94
Merchants' and Manufacturers' Association, 138, 143
Metropolitan Club, 61
Mexican Federal Union, 140
Midway Gas Company, 110–11
Miller, C. O. G., 17, 129
Miller, Frank, 13
Miller, Henry, 92
Miller, John B., 131, 132; on Henry Huntington's impact in southern California, 8, 153; and Southern California Edison, 17, 128–29, 131, 132–33
Miller and Lux Land and Cattle Company, 92–93
Millikan, Robert A., 151
Millspaugh, W. S., 42
Milwaukee, 39
Minneapolis, 144
Mission Inn, 13
Monrovia, 41, 56, 57, 65, 71, 80
Morgan, J. P., 15, 147
Morgan Library, 147
Morse, S. F., 42
Mt. Lowe Railway, 57, 109
Mt. Whitney Power and Electric Company, 127
Muir, John A., 56, 83

National Association of Manufacturers, 137–38
National Cash Register, 141
National Street Railway Association, 138
National War Labor Board, 145–46
New Orleans, 25, 28

Newport Beach, 9, 76, 77, 78
Newport News, Va., 23, 25
Newport News Shipbuilding and Dry Dock Company, 56, 150
New York Chamber of Commerce, 146
New York City, 19, 21, 22, 23, 24, 45, 60–61, 101, 117, 151
Nickerson, H. M., 128
North Beach and Mission Railway, 34–35

Oak Knoll, 13–14, 79, 88–89
Oak Knoll Company, 88
Oakland, 4, 144
Occidental College, 14
Ocean Beach Railway, 35
Oceanside, 80
O'Melveny, Henry W., 62, 93
Omnibus Cable Company, 34–35
Oneonta, N.Y., 19, 45, 158
Oneonta Park, 45, 88, 89
Ontario and San Antonio Heights Railway, 62
Ontario Electric Company, 62
Orange, 9
"Orange Empire," 72
Otis, Harrison G., 11, 137
Owens Valley Aqueduct, 91, 128, 130
Oxnard, 127

Pacific Electric Building, 15, 60, 71
Pacific Electric Railway, 6–7, 48, 50, 58, 74, 150, 154, 184n59; expansion of, 64–65, 71–72, 76, 77, 78–80, 101; impact on southern California, 9–11, 65, 82; incorporated, 6, 56–57, 181n14; and labor relations, 139–41; net earnings, 66, 83, 101, 104, 188n43; planned interurban routes, 57–58; and Southern Pacific, 69, 72–76, 78, 95–96, 102–4, 116, 186n23
Pacific Electric Railway of Arizona, 54–55, 57
Pacific Improvement Company, 39, 56
Pacific Light and Power Company, 7, 39, 115, 140, 154–55; and Big Creek hydroelectric power facility, 109, 111–15, 118, 126–27; expansion of, 62, 92–94, 127–28; and Huntington Lodge, 128; incorporated, 7, 62; incorporates Southern California Gas, 110–11; and jitneys, 122; and Kern River hydroelectric power